OKANAGAN COLLEGE LIBRARY

04402269

P9-DTY-325

OKANAGAN COLLEGE
LIBRARY
BRITISH COLUMBIA

Prismatic Publics
Innovative Canadian Women's
Poetry and Poetics

Edited by Kate Eichhorn
and Heather Milne

Coach House Books | Toronto

copyright © the contributors, 2009
interviews © Kate Eichhorn and Heather Milne, 2009

first edition

Published with the generous assistance of the Canada Council for the Arts and the
Ontario Arts Council. Coach House Books also acknowledges the financial support
of the Government of Canada through the Book Publishing Industry Development
Program.

LIBRARY AND ARCHIVES CANADA CATALOGUING IN PUBLICATION

Prismatic publics : innovative Canadian women's poetry and poetics / edited by Kate
Eichhorn and Heather Milne.

ISBN 978-1-55245-221-9

     1. Canadian poetry (English)--Women authors. 2. Canadian poetry
(English)--21st century. I. Eichhorn, Kate II. Milne, Heather, 1973-

PS8283.W6P75 2009   C811'.60809287   C2009-904240-1

Contents

Contents

Introduction

Questioned at the border, the writers in this anthology would all check out as Canadian and female. However, nation and gender are politically saturated concepts, and when adopted as selection criteria or frameworks for analysis, linguistic innovation is often eclipsed. For the purposes of this anthology, we chose to define 'innovative' poetry and poetics as writing that, at the very least, approaches language as an inherent problematic and subject of inquiry rather than mere vehicle for representation. While many of our dialogues explore how poetics are structured by the publics in which they take shape, this book privileges the aesthetic over the identitary. Staying attuned to linguistic innovation and experimentation, we believe this anthology does the work it set out to do by staging encounters with some of the best writers working in and in response to feminist, Language, conceptual, investigative and other poetic traditions.

But if, as we claim, our concern is with innovative poetry and poetics, why edit an anthology that remains bound by the constraints of gender and nation at all? Although this question dogged us from the outset, we had no way of anticipating that we would find ourselves editing this book in the midst of the most significant debate on feminist poetics in the past decade. What would come to be known as the 'numbers trouble' started with the presentation and eventual publication of Jennifer Ashton's article 'Our Bodies, Our Poems' and Jennifer Scappettone's response. The subsequent publication of Juliana Spahr and Stephanie Young's 'Numbers Trouble' and Ashton's retort in the *Chicago Review* ignited months of online debate on questions of gender, poetics and the so-called 'separatist anthology' in early 2008. Ashton claimed that anthologies of innovative writing by women are inherently contradictory because much of this writing works to destabilize fixed notions of the gendered body. Structuring an anthology around the category of 'women's writing' maintains a 'logic of essentialism ... despite all claims to the contrary' (221). Ashton concedes that historically there may have been reasons to risk such essentialism, but now that women have achieved parity with men in terms of publishing and related venues, this risk can no longer be justified. Spahr and Young, and many of the writers and critics who eventually weighed in online, countered that there is little basis upon which to substantiate Ashton's claims of 'parity' in innovative writing communities where women often continue to find themselves underrepresented, misread and read for the wrong reasons.

In the end, the 'numbers trouble' resolved few quantitative questions about the presence of women in the contemporary literary avant-garde, but the debate would reify rather than shake our commitment to this project. As Scappettone observes, 'Until *Moving Borders* was printed in 1998, and the Where Lyric Meets Language conference and anthology followed, women were consistently slighted in representations of the avant-garde because a corrective focus on gender threatened to undercut the critique of identity or to trump aesthetic standards and because women had not yet assumed sufficient sway over poetic discourse or the means of production' (179–80). She further argues that Ashton fails to recognize that the aforementioned anthologies helped to the lay the groundwork for many of the new and emerging critical, curatorial, editorial and publishing venues where women writers are now investigating how 'Intermittent poetic acts may summon without reifying the lyric I as a socially moored body' (180). Significantly, Scappettone emphasizes that there are important generational differences that mark these recent interventions: 'emerging from a climate repoliticized by right-wing ascendancy, these acts necessarily deploy tactics deviating from those of the eighties or the nineties' (180). But in this climate, old tactics also take on new roles. If the so-called 'separatist anthology' was once valued as an important vehicle because it was believed to hold the potential to represent what was absent, the value of such collections may now lie precisely in their ability to generate dialogue, incite debate and demarcate differences. So, for us, the 'numbers trouble' confirmed what we already suspected – the presence of and desire to expand a public dialogue on gender and poetics that is both attuned to the realities and discourses of a new generation of writers and critics and attentive to histories of innovative women's writing.

That the 'numbers trouble' debate was staged primarily in the United States seemed to make little difference. As publishing, reviewing and dialogues between writers increasingly occur online, the nation is no longer as relevant to the circulation of writing and ideas as it once was, nor does it limit these conversations to the extent that it once did. However, it would be premature to conclude that the nation no longer matters. There are no existing Canadian anthologies of innovative women's writing; this will be the first. Although several Canadian writers appear in Maggie O'Sullivan's *Out of Everywhere* (a British publication), no Canadian writers appear in Claudia Rankine and Juliana Spahr's *American Women Poets in the 21st Century: Where Lyric Meets Language* or Cynthia Hogue and Elizabeth Frost's *Innovative Women Poets: An Anthology of Contemporary*

Poetry and Interviews. Notably, the editors of these American anthologies felt compelled neither to justify nor even to acknowledge their reasons for adopting the nation as a selection criteria, reminding us that, south of the border, the nation still does not readily present itself as a problematic. There are, of course, other important historical differences that cannot be ignored. Canadian women writers have always shaped the nation's literary avant-garde, often playing central roles in defining the contours of new movements and schools of writing both as aesthetic innovators and cultural activists. Considering the contributions of modernist writers, such as Dorothy Livesay and Phyllis Webb, Daphne Marlatt's role as a founding editor of *Tish* and Nicole Brossard's role as a founding editor of *La barre du jour* in the 1960s, the groundbreaking work of Marlatt and Gail Scott on the feminist collective Tessera in the 1980s, and Lisa Robertson and Catriona Strang's involvement in the Kootenay School of Writing collective in the 1990s, our lineage is clearly different from the one that led Scappettone to conclude that, until recently, women writers had 'not yet assumed sufficient sway over poetic discourse or the means of production.' As Sina Queyras observes, 'In many ways Canadian feminist poetics has been a model for feminist poets in the U.S.'

Without losing sight of these important historical and contemporary differences, this project ultimately exists in tension with the nation. Almost half of the writers included in this anthology have spent time living and working outside of Canada, primarily in the United States, and most of the writers have strong ties to literary communities that transcend the nation's borders. Although geographic specificity is still a focus of some of the writing in this anthology, much of it is preoccupied with the emergence of global spaces, movement, exile and travel. Many writers move between national and international contexts, exploring past and present acts of nation making. The selections from M. NourbeSe Philip's *Zong!* might be read as residual shards of a language placed violently under erasure in the name of nation building. Rachel Zolf's most recent work explores the conflict between Israel and Palestine, questioning what it means for a nation to speak in one's name as it commits violent acts against a neighbour. Other writers, including Margaret Christakos, investigate home in and through the deterritorialized domain of the Internet, destabilizing conventional understandings of the domestic on many fronts.

While few of the writers in this anthology have an uncomplicated relationship to nation, and most, for a range of reasons, maintain a complex relationship to gender and its implied identitary and political bonds, they are all engaged in work that is informed by or seeks to engage in the construction and interrogation of publics. Throughout the 1990s and into the new millennium, the concept of publics has, as Michael Warner observes, 'gone traveling' (10). We have come to accept the fact that 'public' means many things to many people and that these meanings are culturally and historically contingent. But this concept has proven stubbornly persistent even as it has drifted away from its original context. Perhaps this is because under modernity the concept of 'public' has always recognized that the circulation of texts, be they literary, journalistic or judicial, is important not because texts hold the potential to mirror the world but rather because they are actively engaged in making social worlds by fostering dialogues, bridging, assimilating and reifying differences, and authorizing and delegitimizing ways of speaking, knowing and being.

The 'prismatic publics' referenced in our title evoke publics that are even further fractured. They are marked by the surprising and often ephemeral forms that appear through the bending, turning and breakage of properties. Appropriately, our title is also a somewhat 'bent' form of found material – an ekphrasis culled from an email. Asked to comment on a series of potential covers, Margaret Christakos described Cheryl Sourkes's photograph, which appears on the cover, as a 'prismatized public.' Christakos chose to modify 'public,' held in quotations, with a verb form, as if to emphasize that publics are works in progress (always being acted upon) and tenuous constructions that must be adopted with caution. But in many respects, her description not only captures Sourkes's photograph but also the workings of much of the writing in this anthology. The frame grabs in Sourkes's 'Public Camera' series challenge the division between public and private spaces, as well as the relation among subjects, objects and contexts. Her figures have a tendency to lose identitary markers and to bleed into their surroundings. As subjects are mysteriously reconstituted as the surfaces upon which a surrounding environment's objects are reflected, bodies *in context* become bodies *as context*. This conceptual investigation of subjectivity resonates with the investigations of subjectivity explored by many of the writers in this anthology. In the selections from 'The Sutured Subject' that appear here, Gail Scott introduces a fractalling subject or 'campily re-sutured subject-in-becoming' and asks, 'Does not our own nervous system, our own body (=) the outside world?' Dorothy Lusk discusses her writing in relation to the 'suprajective,' alluding to the possibility of a subject infinitely refracted. Albeit in different ways and in reference to different forms of writing, Scott and Lusk both point to subjects that are not only in process but also contiguous with the materials and space of writing itself.

Although most of the writers in this anthology are preoccupied with interrogating or undermining the subject's relation to writing, they do not share a common lineage, school or set of practices. While some of the writers are comfortable being cast as 'experimental,' others reject this description. Karen Mac Cormack may be the only writer who has been consistently aligned with Language poets, yet most of the writers identify Language poets as important allies. A few of the writers, including Daphne Marlatt, Erín Moure and Sina Queyras, also express affinities with lyric poets. Margaret Christakos understands her recent work as 'performing strategies upon the lyric.' Several of the writers work across and between genres. Brossard and Marlatt are poets who write novels, but their novels have often challenged the genre's conventions. Nicole Brossard's early novels, including *A Book, French Kiss* and *Picture Theory*, are often read as poetry. Marlatt's most recent text, *The Given*, was written as a novel but published as poetry. Scott is a prose writer who has always been in dialogue with poets and considers her location within poetry communities essential to her practice. Lisa Robertson, a poet, is perhaps best known for her sentences. Other writers work at the nexus or the collapse of genres. Mac Cormack describes her most recent two-volume prose work, *Implexures*, as a form of 'transhistoric polybiography' that combines 'multiple biographies, time frames and historical circumstances with a poetic focus' in order to critique conventional narrative methods. Nathalie Stephens resists generic classification altogether and, revelling in this refusal, raises provocative questions about the viability of understanding innovative writing through the lens of genre categorizations. Simultaneously, Stephens raises analogous questions about the validity of gender categorizations.

Some of the writers in this anthology understand their poetic projects as deeply rooted in feminist, Marxist, postcolonial and/or queer political struggles, but most, if not all, are wary of writing whose primary objective is to make political claims. Susan Holbrook's writing, for example, unabashedly addresses issues of gender and sexuality, but much of her writing is based on Oulipean procedures. As she emphasizes, 'I argue for taking responsibility but I capitalize on the illusion of arbitrariness.' What matters to Holbrook, and the other writers in this anthology, is what the work is *doing*, and this can only be understood through the process of learning how to enter and read their writing. In this sense, all the writers in this anthology are committed to the project of working out problems *in* rather than simply *with* language. They share our definition of innovative writing as a stance or approach that recognizes language as a problematic and further recognizes that a problematic, even an insurmountable limit, may sometimes be the most tactical or only way to tackle 'big questions,' be they ontological, epistemological or political. In fact, what is most exciting about much of the writing in this anthology is how it effectively demonstrates the expressive and sometimes transformative qualities of constraints. As our interviews reveal, writers gravitate to constraint-based poetics for many reasons, and for some, working within constraints is not even understood as a choice. As M. NourbeSe Philip discusses, she may have chosen to lock herself in the two-page legal document from which *Zong!* was generated, but she is, as a writer of Caribbean ancestry, always already locked in the imperialist language in which she writes. Similarly, several of the writers in this anthology, including Christakos, Holbrook and Catriona Strang, who write in and around the interruptions, noise and surprises of their domestic lives, speak of their poetic procedures and constraints in part as conditions of circumstance rather than choice.

Much of the writing in this collection is the product of working in and against systems – linguistic, libidinal, affective, technological, economic and ecological. As with all systems, the import or redaction of elements has profound effects on flow and meaning. Meaning is produced through the processes of circulation, recirculation, recombination and procedure and, as such, this work must be understood as enacting a poetics of flux not stasis. Rather than bring the reader to a single or fixed truth claim, this writing asks the reader to become an active agent in making meaning and more importantly, to abandon 'getting it' as the only or primary objective of reading. Writing through and across multiple languages with varying degrees of fluency, Erín Moure reminds us that fluency cannot be easily understood as a singular achievement or point of arrival. Her translations and transliterations invite the reader to enter linguistic economies where no degree of fluency is sufficient, but there are still many ways to navigate Moure's poetic terrain. The ecologies of Rita Wong's *forage* demonstrate the grave dangers and rich possibilities of living in systems where the collision of foreign and indigenous, technological and organic, human and animal elements has become the norm. These ecologies do not always 'make sense' but neither do the 'logics' of late capitalism, globalization and genetic modification Wong investigates in much of her writing, and as she emphasizes, such material conditions also 'disrupt syntax,' necessitating new approaches to writing.

Perhaps because writing is usually solitary work, we were struck, while editing this anthology, by the number of writers who have, at different points in their careers, chosen to write and work in collaboration. Two writers chose to include collaborative texts amongst their selections here: Strang's selections include several poems written with Nancy Shaw, and Wong's section includes work co-written by Larissa Lai. That both of these writers are from Vancouver may not be a coincidence; as Lisa Robertson emphasizes, collaboration, multidisciplinary dialogue and collective labour have long been integral to the innovative writing community on Canada's west coast, and notably, this is a condition that cuts across gender lines. The other forms of collaborative work and personal and professional alliances that shape the writing in this anthology may be less visible but they are no less important. Over the past three decades, Gail Scott has worked in collaboration with both Francophone and Anglophone feminist writers, but also aligned herself with the San Francisco–based New Narrative writers and, more recently, a younger generation of American experimental prose writers. Robertson, Strang and Lusk have been associated with the Kootenay School of Writing. Wong positions herself in relation to both Asian and First Nations writing communities along the west coast. There are, of course, many other affiliations alluded to in the interviews included in this anthology. As will become apparent, the writers in this anthology are also connected by a myriad of friendships, mentorship relationships and, yes, even rivalries, but only time (and the archive) will reveal the depth, complexity and importance of these relations and their impact on the writing.

Our impetus to edit this book was motivated by a desire to expand the space for public dialogues on poetry and poetics and to expand the context in which the writing in this anthology, much of which remains under the radar, might circulate. Although we briefly considered the inclusion of critical essays on each of the fifteen writers featured here, we wished to avoid imposing a single and authoritative framework on the writing. Instead, we chose to provide a space for the writers to articulate their own analysis. Because we took our cues from the writers with whom we were in dialogue, all the interviews are unique. While some are formal interviews, others more closely resemble intimate conversations shifting between registers. Most would be best characterized as dialogues rather than interviews. Whenever possible, we chose to meet with the writers in person, usually in their own cities. Since most of these interviews took place in person, we tried to preserve as much of the vernacular language and rhythm of these dialogues as possible, because this too offers insights into how a writer thinks, approaches language and positions herself as an author. Although all of the dialogues focus on poetics, they cover a range of topics from quotidian concerns to politics, technology, spirituality and knowledge. Read in relation to the selections of writing, the scope of these interviews is not surprising. After all, the writing in this anthology is made from the raw materials of everyday life – vernacular speech, scraps of texts, memorable lines cut from emails, office memos, unforgettable headlines, instructions pulled out of boxes, appropriated laws, doctrines, master narratives, texts revered and reviled, texts contiguous with the making and contestation of subjects writ large.

Kate Eichhorn, New York
& Heather Milne, Winnipeg

WORKS CITED

Ashton, Jennifer. 'The Numbers Trouble with "Numbers Trouble."' *Chicago Review* 53 (2007): 112–120.

Scappettone, Jennifer. 'Response to Jennifer Ashton Bachelorettes, Even: Strategic Embodiment in Contemporary Experimentalism by Women.' *Modern Philology* 105 (2008): 178–184.

Warner, Michael. *Publics and Counterpublics*. Chicago: Zone Books, 2002.

NICOLE BROSSARD

KATE EICHHORN: Most interviews with writers now take place online, but I don't think that an online exchange can replicate what we're about to enter – this face-to-face dialogue. Writers talk about their work in the present in very different terms than they do when reflecting and writing in response to a list of questions. I also wanted an opportunity to speak to you in person because the conversation or dialogue is, in a sense, one of your genres, like poetry, the novel, the essay and the journal. Can you talk about the place conversation and dialogue occupy in your work?

NICOLE BROSSARD: I always say that in life I like to have a table in front of me, whether to write, to eat or to share a conversation. In most of my novels, you will find women getting together around a table to talk. I like the posture of addressing the other face to face with a space for negotiations which would be the symbolic space of the table possibly transforming spoken words into written words. In my mind, a conversation makes more space for free-floating subjects and thoughts than a dialogue, which would tend to be more directed if not toward a specific goal at least to the idea of making progress through questioning and answering patterns. Trust and confidence and listening are necessary in a conversation, as sharpness, knowledge and processing are more needed in a dialogue. That being said, probably the word 'relationship' is the key word as well as what is being exchanged and what circulates through that relationship. A good conversation brings a lot of energy, can nourish strong creative emotions – friendship, love, admiration – and stimulates renewal of thoughts or attitudes. It's also possible that I like to put characters face to face around a table because it might be my only chance to listen to them as characters. I would be lying if I were to say that my main interest is in characters – it is not, but maybe I like their conversation because they serve as strategies to unveil pain and desire, desire and feelings.

I've been asking myself many questions about the notion of dialogue, especially in relation to theatre. For a long time I've been wanting to write a play. Probably you can notice that tendency in *Mauve Desert* as well as in *Yesterday, at the Hotel Clarendon.* One thing for sure that I observe is that I cannot really write dialogues suitable for theatre because instead of being about emotions they very rapidly become philosophical. In other words, I feel like I could never have the characters quarrel or yell at each other or say horrible things to each other. I'd rather have my characters get together to share the fruit of their thinking or to seduce each other.

KE: As I was preparing for this conversation, I was reading your work and thinking about the difference between the very explicit moments when

OC CAMPUS STORES
THANKS YOU FOR YOUR BUSINESS
RECEIPT REQUIRED FOR ALL RETURNS
11:28:17 16 SEP 2013
TRANS NO: 2.POSVRN1.2845
GST# 857037576RT0001
WWW.OKANAGAN.BC.CA/CAMPUSSTORES

SALE

1 PRISMATIC PUBLICS	27.75	GX
1718449 9781552452219		

PRICE SUBTOTAL	27.75
GST 5%	1.39
TOTAL	29.14
VISA ----------	29.14

01 Approved - Thank You 027

Card# ************4514
Purchase
Date/Time : 09/16/13 11:28:56
Reference # : 66193483 0013860110 C
Authorization # : 057176
VISA
A0000000031010
0000008000

IMPORTANT - retain this copy for
your records

FALL SEMESTER BOOKS ARE RETURNABLE
UNTIL FRIDAY SEPT 20TH
USED BOOKS & SG'S ARE NONRETURNABLE
RECEIPT REQUIRED FOR ALL RETURNS
CLEARANCE ITEMS ARE NONRETURNABLE

people come together in the fiction and the essays and the different sorts of conversations or dialogues enacted in the poetry. I'm thinking about one of the selections that we've chosen for this collections from *Lovhers*, as it's known in English. Could we think about this as a conversation with Adrienne Rich and Gertrude Stein, writers living and dead?

NB: Well, it could be, but I have to say that my first interlocutor at that moment was my lovher. Of course in writing there are always dialogues with other writers and their work, contemporary and from the past. That's the beauty of literature, it keeps books, ideas, landscapes and people inter-active no matter how far in time or space or from their mother tongue. But I think once the process of writing starts, the dialogue can also fade away. Of course, it varies depending on the intention of the text, but naming, quoting, referring to a writer meaningful to you at the very specific moment of your writing are significant. At that time, both Adrienne Rich and Gertrude Stein, as well as Monique Wittig, were very meaningful to me. I would say that the dialogue occurs before the writing, in stimulat-ing the desire to write. Of course if there are things to argue about, then the dialogue can go on much longer in the text. Recently I noticed that more than ten books have been written taking Franz Kafka as a character. There is definitely a dialogue going on there.

KE: I realize this is a very rigid distinction, but do you think about the poetry as a more private or intimate genre than your fiction or essays, a genre less amenable to fostering public conversations, dialogues?

NB: Poetry is condensation. It compresses meaning. It renews meaning, but I don't see it as a more private genre than any other kind of writing. It all depends on the society you belong to. In South America, poetry is shared in public places by thousands of listeners for private and political reasons. What is inside a novel and what comes from a poem is energy. In a novel the energy is more diffuse. Writing a novel requires time, continuity. There are consequences for the coherence of the book if you start the writing of a project too soon or too late. But in poetry, no matter if you work on a poem for three months or three years, you are always in the present, in an existential and a semantic tension. It's a different approach when you write a novel. Poetry and prose originate from different postures toward time and language. In a narrative, no matter how frag-mented the story and the characters might be, part of your relation to the universe is mediated by characters that you empowered. In poetry you are in direct line with the cosmos or whatever can be called space or immensity around you. The only thing between you and the universe are words and respiration. When I write novels, it's somehow because I need to negotiate with reality. So probably I use the characters to do that work in my name. In poetry, no matter what the theme is, the pleasure of words is all over the place. With the novel, it's another kind of pleasure because you lose some of your freedom, more or less. It all depends on what risk you are willing to take and how conventional is your idea of a novel. Maybe you can keep your freedom if you write, as I did in *A Book*, one page at a time with a lot of white space. Then, maybe that white space will give you back your freedom. But if you are engaging in a story, you are minimally caught in a direction. I don't think poetry is more private. Though it is more strange and puzzling. Why? Because technically a line in poetry has to be puzzling otherwise it becomes prose. Compare Eluard's sentence 'La terre est bleue comme une orange' with the plain reality of 'La terre est ronde et le ciel est bleu.' Prose informs, poetry moves.

KE: We've been discussing the differences between your poetry and novels. One of things we've noticed editing this collection is the number of writers who work in and at the intersection of genres – Gail Scott, Daphne Marlatt, Nathalie Stephens – but also the number of poets who dwell in the sentence. Since many of your earlier novels can be approached as poetry – I'm thinking about *A Book, French Kiss, Picture Theory* – and even your more recent novels remain marked by an attentiveness to the poetic line, can you talk about some of the similarities between your poetry and novels?

NB: My novels have a poetic dimension because I get bored when straight sentences repeat what I already know or can foresee as reader. I do not intend my novels to be poetical, they become so because this is the way I think, question and enjoy language and reality. You are right in asking about the similarities between poetry and novels. I have noticed that more prosaic sentences with a narrative tone usually appear in my poetry after I have just finished a novel or before I am about to write one. An example of this would be: 'The Silence of the Hibiscus' in *Museum of Bone and Water*. I guess the similarity between my prose and my poetry is a philosophical trend reflecting consciousness, melancholy and the expression of revolt concerning the lies and violence that are part of the human condition. For me the story is not in the action or the suspense, it is in thoughts and emotions. It is a lot in the writing itself: rhythm, harmony and rupture of tone. This is usually what I try to translate or reshape in my writing. For that I need words with a symbolic dimension and words of such usually have a poetic aura. Indeed I am not a storyteller, neither in my prose nor in my poetry.

KE: You already noted that your earlier novels had a different visual presence than your more recent novels – often, there are just a few lines of text floating at the top of a page – and this space enabled you to maintain some of the freedom you associate with poetry. But the kind of novels you were writing changed in the late 1980s with the publication of *Mauve Desert*. As a poet, what moved you to adopt a slightly more conventional novel form at that time? What possibilities has this form opened up for you since?

NB: I think that since my first novel, *A Book*, I have been trying to expand the 'Once upon a time' framed sections that we can find in all my novels from *Sold-out* to *French Kiss* to *Picture Theory* where a whole chapter is written almost as if we were in a real novel, and finally there is *Mauve Desert* where first fifty-five pages of the narrative constitute the longest story I had written up to that point in 1987. There is no doubt in my mind that if my novels are structurally unconventional, there is in me a desire to write a 'real' novel. By that I mean to create a space, a world, in which I would be able to make a synthesis of the excitement, fear, questions, emotions of 'my time' and of my Montreal. Just for once. A sort of challenge to see if really I can tell and develop a story. I guess writing *Intimate Journal* and the short autobiography in *Fluid Arguments* comes from the same 'yes, I want to see how I will behave in that kind of normal writing.'

KE: You have often written about being a woman 'of the present.' I'd like you to elaborate on this, but also on something you admit at the beginning of Louise Forsythe's collection of essays on your work – 'I've always said I'm a woman of the present, and now I'm beginning to feel that there is too much present.' For some time now, you've been exploring new technologies in your work – the shift from the book, from print culture, to a virtual culture and to the screen. There is a sense that this transition is full of potentiality, but it also poses a threat. Is this why you feel there is too much present now?

NB: Well, when I say that I am a woman of the present, I mean that as a poet I absorb the moment, the instant, with an extreme concentration, which is a way to feel and question meaning, space and time. I use all the strength of my senses to enjoy being alive and to reflect on that life. I have written a lot about that pleasure of *ici et maintenant*, here and now, sometimes with the question why, sometimes with no question. I'd say most of the poets are in the here and now when they write poetry. They are in the sound of being alive. This is how they can produce not a statement but sequences of thought and of emotion, which urgently produce modulations in language. It is interesting to notice that as an individual, living in the present is rich and creative, but I wonder if it is the same when living in the present applies to the society and culture that are now ours. What happens when a society loses memory and simply keeps surfing on the here and now of sensations? Sensations are easy. There is not much time for desire and emotion because of the instantaneity of everything. Emotions take longer to build because they require the encounter of memory, presence and desire, a three-dimensional volume.

Postmodern writers gave us sensations more than emotions, unless we decide that in the long run a strong sequence of sensations produces a specific emotion. So when I say that in the new bio/info/techno/society there is an overflow of the present and immediacy, I think that we might be losing something, but to the profit of what? I don't know yet, we don't know yet and once we know, it will have already happened. What is exciting is the transition. But for sure it brings also chaos, deception, fear. Rules are changing constantly. Humanist values are fading away and when they reappear you wonder if it is just because of good marketing. I was recently talking with a young Canadian novelist. I was telling him that I live with 70 percent humanist thoughts but with the other 30 percent, I am open to the new reality constructed by new technologies. I asked, what about you? He answered with the same proportion. It was interesting that the difference of age did not change the proportion. Of course, he is a writer, and if you are a writer somehow it's difficult to escape the humanist tradition, which makes you believe very strongly in the power of the book and of the written word and so on. It's very difficult to discard that tradition along with what came with the Enlightenment in the 18th century. That is the whole question. I need to understand what's going on historically and scientifically around me as my relation to time and to space changes, as my relation to the body alters, as my relation to other people is renewed in the virtual space. I keep asking questions, because I want to understand how the new technologies affect our notion of life, death and future. In French we use the word *le désenchantement* to express the feeling that there is less and less hope of regaining our 'humanity' as we have known it for centuries. But if I think as individuals, enjoying the instant is a sort of privilege as much as silence and time have become precious. As individuals, we gain from the present, but as a society we might be losing something.

I don't know yet because it's in fifteen to twenty years from now that we will understand. One thing is for sure: we live in an ultra merchant society in which human parts and human genes are manipulated, transformed and are ready to be sold for a profit more than for 'progress.'

KE: Has your poetic practice been affected by these new technologies or new conditions or constraints? Are they changing how you write – your process or procedures?

NB: They certainly brought new questions about sense and non-sense, life, nature, birth and death. I have also noticed that my writing time is more fragmented though I try to keep my independence in regards to email and time on the web. It seems that there is too much stimulation for what our brain is able to process properly. It is hard to pinpoint the changes because the changes are numerous but insignificant until you feel strange about the change. The rules keep changing every day, be it in banks, in airports or in your computer. And of course, time-space relation is different than it was even ten years ago. Fiction and reality have become obsolete categories compared to real and virtual. Finally it all amounts to the question of meaning which obviously needs to be regenerated by each generation no matter what has already been said brilliantly before us. For the first time probably in history it happens that a generation has the possibility to think twice about the 'human' condition.

But to come back to poetry, in my most recent book *Après les mots*, which could be translated as *After Words* or *After the Word*, there are two long poems taking into account those questions and one poem resisting the dark side of it by being a poem written with constraints which in a way is very liberating. Constraints force you to tap into the language in a way that would never cross your mind. In other words, you immerse yourself in the vast possibility of the language without worrying about your small universe. And even under constraint, I don't think you cheat on your essential values, because they keep popping up with a new face.

KE: I want to follow up on that – the fact that it appears as if you don't just play the game for the game's sake. It seems to me that many feminist innovative poets make a conscious effort to not simply immerse themselves in the play, in the language games, but do so for a reason.

NB: Sensations and fun games with language in the short run or emotion and consciousness in the long run? In my playful texts I have always tried to write in such a way that the playfulness of the text would not dismiss a meaning close to my thoughts, feeling or ideas. Even though I believe that our ego/bio is not always as interesting as it seems, I have never believed in *la mort du sujet*. The subject as always is very much alive and at work, and what is being thought or envisioned from a woman's point of view, feminist point of view or a lesbian point of view will make its ways into the text. Playing with words in a neutral way can also make the subject fly out and burst out so it designs in language an unknown subject of desire. The most irreverent poets in regards to grammar and syntax are usually responsible in other ways because their manner of dealing with meaning raises ipso facto relevant questions.

KE: And is that responsibility political?

NB: It could be seen like that but there is always more to it. You may be referring to what was once a popular dictum: 'the personal is political.' We have now a better psychological understanding of the interaction between the personal and the social world. It is provided by the ego-ecological theory that has shown a continuous blending between the personal and the political, so that we will think of 'the personal is political' in simultaneity with 'the political is personal.' Marisa Zavalloni, the author of the theory, has provided a vivid illustration of this process in a dialogical exchange with Mary Daly and in her analysis of some of Sartre's and Nietzsche's texts.

We always have to discriminate what's fun and provocative for a writer to write and how it resonates in readers and society. Or let's say that what's on paper sometimes has to remain on paper. For example, if we take the sentence of André Breton, saying that the most surrealist act is to go out on the street and shoot into the crowd! Well, we know that every year people are being killed by someone performing that 'surrealist' act. Until the 1970s you could say so many things in literature that would be exciting and revolutionary. Now, because of déjà vu, it has no or less impact socially, or if it does, it seems more the result of good marketing than of thoughtful ideas. That being said, I still believe in the power of words. They still matter for better or worse. What exactly would be exciting and meaningful in poetry today?

KE: What would be exciting?

NB: I think what's exciting is deeply rooted in the matter of language itself. Different levels of meaning, a sudden modulation, repetition of sounds or rupture in meaning and reconfiguration of it, sharpness in creating ambiguity. Language is physically-mentally exciting, and this is probably what

Roland Barthes meant when he talked about '*le plaisir des mots.*' Language is exciting, exhausting, exhilarating. What it does to us remains a mystery the same way we cannot define beauty.

KE: You mentioned André Breton, the French surrealist writer, and of course, as a Francophone writer, you write as part of a long avant-garde tradition that we can trace back to writers like Breton, but also to Mallarmé and even earlier to Baudelaire. This is a very different lineage than the one inherited by innovative writers working in English. But you also write in a language full of constraints – French is a very gendered language, a language of rules and restrictions, and a language that has been proven far less protean than English, which always appears to be in flux. For all these reasons, it seems that experimenting with language and genre means something very different in French than it does in English, and it follows that what's exciting would also differ across these languages, no?

NB: Probably. Language and gestures in one given culture have a subliminal zone of visibility that foreign speakers or readers cannot experience. Even in the same language, experimenting can be different in regards to literary references, to vocabulary and syntax. I think of the French language in Québec, in Belgium, in Martinique, etc., and of English in England, Canada, Australia, United States. But you are right. For example, think of the long poem in the English and French traditions. Its practice is very different. In English the long poem has served to deconstruct, but in French deconstruction took place in short poems. In English the long poem is made of short cuts in genres but in French it is written with long lyrical narrative shots. There are things that one can do in one language that are unthinkable in another language. This is why it is so important to be able to speak and play with another language than our mother tongue. Accessing another language renews one's imagination.

KE: As we've been discussing, what is exciting is culturally specific, but it is also historically contingent. For example, there are several younger lesbian writers in this collection, but the way they write about the subject, if and when they choose to do so at all, is completely different from the project you were engaged in the late 1970s and 1980s when it was still radical on a political and linguistic level to simply be writing about the lesbian subject. Can you reflect back on this part of your poetic project?

NB: Well, there was a very specific energy that was as much about love, sexuality, as it was about freedom, self-empowerment and understanding what it meant symbolically to be a lesbian. That was huge. It was huge because it could go against all the notions included in patriarchal meaning and symbolism. In that sense, two women directing their gaze at each other because of sexual attraction was an incredible transgression. I mean concretely and symbolically, a woman being interested amorously by another woman-subject was in itself a statement of recognition, a very transgressive and subversive affirmation against the common belief that women exist for men's benefit without being taken into account as it is taught especially by monotheistic religions or traditions in most of the countries on this planet. I think that all my work during that period was trying to make a space for a relation that would nourish differently the imagination not only of love but about women. Lesbian desire and lesbian energy have nourished my work from *Surfaces of Sense, Intimate Journal, Lovhers, Picture Theory* and *The Aerial Letter*. So there's a cycle that goes along with the poetry, the novel and the essay as well. Indeed that was a specific historical moment that allowed for a strong we. Now everyone has gone back to I, singular.

KE: I wonder if this work is even more radical now, however, than it was then, since in some surprising and disturbing ways, we appear to live in a more conservative time. I also wonder if some of the possibilities opened up by that writing have already been closed off?

NB: We had to make a huge leap in the imagination, in the metaphors. In order to translate what was going on in our bodies, in our thoughts, we also had to make a huge leap in language. Therefore, it affected the design of the poetry and even sometimes the structure of the novels. It was something very special that could not have been carried only by lesbian anecdotes. Language had to be questioned in a radical way, so it could suit our needs of expression and welcome the 'I love you' to other women. Yes, it had to do, I believe very strongly, with language, and of course with the imaginary and the knowledge of the physical lesbian experience. At that time, I often said I would rather talk about the skin than different parts of the body because skin covers your entire body. Each cell of your skin is being informed by a caress, and I think this renews the possible metaphors of the lesbian body. Voice, skin, sleep, touch, taste: all the senses convene to new performances and a new understanding of life.

KE: Since you've already given an entire vocabulary to another generation of lesbian writers, in a sense, we don't have to do that work.

NB: It depends on what your questions are ... in 2008, what are your questions?

KE: I think they are very different. One of the things I've been thinking about as I read across the work of the two or three generations of writers represented in this collection are how different generations of writers take up questions of space and place. I've noticed that writers of your generation are far more inclined to write about specific places, specific cities. You write about Montreal but you also write about New York and Buenos Aires and other cities. By contrast, in the writing of Nathalie Stephens, the city is still very present but it is rarely named, and for many younger writers, the city is a dystopian space. It's not a space of potential as it has been for you. How do you understand your ongoing preoccupation with specific cities, especially Montreal, and with the city as a site of potential and possibility?

NB: It is true. The city is perceived differently depending on the historical moment. But for my generation of Québécois writers the city is positive, a synonym of renewal. In the 1970s, the theme of the city became important. Before writers were from a rural Québec and spoke more about the beauty of the landscape than about the urban energy. And so for my generation, I'd say, there was an immense desire and excitement about the urban reality and the social space. The city equalled modernity, freedom, discovery, places like bookstores, cafés and places to meet and to talk about artistic and political projects. I also think that our interest in Montreal has to be related to our pride of being North American and the need to map the Québécois culture in that space. Later on I also organized a special issue of *La barre du jour* on women and the city which also brought new perspectives on the subject. This is where I say I am an urban radical and that it is in the polis of men that I want to work at changing the patriarchal laws.

Today the city is imagined differently, and we can understand why especially if we think of surveillance all over the place, pollution, people living in the streets, etc. But the New York of 2009 is very different than the New York of 1980. Yes, cities can be seen as dystopian. Last year I was in Mumbai and in Ciudad Juárez. I have to say that those experiences are important to me.

Each city brings its history, comments, desire and fear. Venice when there is no light on the Grand Canal brings you back in time but also to what it means to disappear. Cities are like people. They provide for our imagination to be filled with joy or fear or excitement. At one point, they appear in close up in our mind, for six months, two years, and then they fade away. And sometimes reappear. And I guess it's the same thing with themes or questions that traverse us, obsess us for a while, and then they fade away. They fade away sometime because we have written enough about them and the creative tension has gone somewhere else looking for another page, another book to write.

Montreal, April 2008

SELECTED WORKS

A Book. Translated by Larry Shouldice. Toronto: Coach House Quebec Translations, 1976. Reprinted in *The Blue Books*. Toronto: Coach House Books, 2003.

Turn of a Pang. Translated by Patricia Claxton. Toronto: Coach House Press, 1976. Reprinted in *The Blue Books*.

French Kiss, or, A Pang's Progress. Translated by Patricia Claxton. Toronto: Coach House Quebec Translations, 1986. Reprinted in *The Blue Books*.

Lovhers. Translated by Barbara Godard. Montreal: Guernica, 1986.

The Aerial Letter. Translated by Marlene Wildeman. Toronto: Women's Press, 1988.

Surfaces of Sense. Translated by Fiona Strachan. Toronto: Coach House Press, 1989.

Mauve Desert. Translated by Susanne de Lotbinière-Harwood. Toronto: Coach House Press, 1990, 2007.

Picture Theory. Translated by Barbara Godard. Montreal: Guernica, 1991.

Vertige de l'avant-scène. Trois-Rivières: Écrits des Forges, 1997.

Museum of Bone and Water. Translated by Robert Majzels and Erín Moure. Toronto: House of Anansi Press, 2003.

Intimate Journal, or, Here's a Manuscript; Followed by Works of Flesh and Metonymies. Translated by Barbara Godard. Toronto: Mercury Press, 2004.

Fluid Arguments. Edited by Susan Rudy and translated by Anne-Marie Wheeler. Toronto: Mercury Press, 2005.

Yesterday, At the Hotel Clarendon. Translated by Susanne de Lotbinière-Harwood. Toronto: Coach House Books, 2006.

Après les mots. Trois-Rivières, Québec: Écrits des Forges, 2007.

Igneous Woman, Integral Woman
translated by Barbara Godard

autobiography or the appearance of facts
a few voices, i borrow from the dictionary
some mad laughter little by little, i'm dispersed
in the survived of things of the real
it's concentrated in the throb of life
in the integral skin of thought that
manifests

nothing sinks (however) night is passing
to dive head first into reality
such a compatible writing, its inks
i'm dispersed/multiple savour of lucidities

(bec.) the only reality
in body the (fiction) or this time
the mental space of the word women in ink
calls forth the unrecorded from myths and torment
turning point of the imaginary of forms of comfort

(i.e.) a spin the bodies of docility
spiral lesbians by concentration (nape)

and if the biographies of fire
were advancing avalanche (like memory
unfolding its vertigoes)
identity upended in ecstasy

from the clamour of voices to anger
memory keeps watch in sounds
like an urging to spread out
over fogs this expression
of tear-filled eyes that have gone through
the arduous emotion of daily life
of complicity

i thought in profile and face to face
that nothing could put an end
to this skin of origin we know
splendidly in our territories
that this battle skin
knife undertow _____ eyes
that break up and bind turn amatory
phrases that address (letters)
women whose curves scintillate

this sleep (where everything began) of alerting
the woman who dreams in the abyss and the blank
sleep of deciphering (through which heat
passes) the skins of surface
in the folds and recesses and repetitions of patiences
each patience of our bodies is unprecedented
in its rhythm invents attraction
goes through our fists like a writing
an open signal

because the open veins of biographies
at top speed in our lives (because)
beside the suffering of foolish faults
of failure
rigour of the aside
all hunger like mad love
this probable imagination
(crisis) for me linked to words
(machine for divining symbols)
to the softness of lips, of eaux-de-vie
in the angle of neurological drifts

memory sketches from leaves and veins
with water all water
a monday morning of spiral in september
between the real and what flows from it
night is passing leading me
into the chemistry of the waters the women
pass through

because cities are circuses of dream
about which we think
since . . . . the obliqueness of fogs
in this expression we are speaking
integral, in the fog of avalanches
my woman, so that no cliché
separates us

from After Words (Après les mots)
translated by Robert Majzels and Erín Moure

vowels venting in the voice
vertigo voltiginous
visage vitals voilà vitality vies
versatile and verily
if I envision it's voyage valise
Vienna or Venice
vast villages valiant then the void

§

Wilde Williams (Tennessee) William Carlos Williams
Woolf Wittgenstein Walt Whitman Warhol Web
and wagon of names with Irish whiskey and Scotch whiskey
leaves of witloof and Poire William
for a weekend of Who's Who at Wounded Knee
(the native reserve at Pine Ridge, South Dakota, where on
December 29, 1890, the American army massacred more than
200 Sioux, completing the White conquest of North America)
or Windsor

§

xxxxxxxxxxxxxxxxxxxxxxxxxxxerophile (organism adapted
to live in arid climates) xxxxxxxxxxxxxxxxxxxxxxxxxxxx
xxxxxxxxxxxxxxxxxxxxxxxxxxxxxxxxxxxxxxxxxxxxxxxxxxx
xxxxxxxxxxxxxxxxxxxxxxxxxxxxxxxxxxxxxxxxxxxxxxxxxxx
xxxxxxxxxxxxxxxxxxxxxxxxxxxxxxxxxxxxxxxxxxxxxxxxxxx
xxxxxxxxxxxxxxxxxxxxxxxxxxxxxxxxxxxxxxxxxxxxxxxxxxx
xxxxxxxxXerxesxxxxxxxxxxxxxxxxxxXenophonxxxxxxxxxx
xxxxxxxxxxxxxxxxxxxxxxxxxxxxxxxxxxxxxxxxxxxxxxxxxxx
xxxxxxxxxxxxxxxxxxxxxxxxxxxxxxxxxxxxxxxxxxxxxxxxxxx
xxxxxxxxxxxxxxxxxxxxxxxxxxxxxxxxxxxxxxxxxxxxxxxxxxx
xxxxxxxxxxxxxxxxxxxxxxxxxxxxxxxxxxxxxxxxxxxxxxxxxxx
xxxxxxxxxxxxxxxxxxxxxxxxxxxxxxxxxxxxxxxxxxxxxxxxxxx
xxxxxxxxxenophilia (sympathy for foreigners: openness
toward what is foreign) xxxxxxxxxxxxxxxxxxxxxxxxxxxx
xxxxxxxxxxxxxxxxxxxxxxxxxxxxxxxxxxxxxxxxxxxxxxxxxxx

§

Yesterday a Yankee day
in Yellowknife thinking of Marguerite Yourcenar
we heard the yawls of Yemeni women
and imagined small
boats short and wide, steered yonder by
rudder or sail.
In the Yukon, we dreamed of yassa
and a yacht.
Yin and yang, *youp!*

from Downstage Vertigo (Vertige de l'avant-scène)
translated by Robert Majzels and Erín Moure

commotion of metaphors
touch of fiction
if it's a book it's a space to last
relay of sense at the tip of our cinders
feverish touch of presence

§

many words take hold of our lives
despite us
the present keeps us in balance
with caresses on the edge of the future
we live our best moments
the strange way the night vanishes so gently
in a mirror
no image to hold onto it

§

there where eternity makes me similar
I place a bit of reality
around the words tears and knees
always an adverb
an imperfect view of tomorrow
the century five o'clock that comes round
syllables flavour of olive and apéritif
life renewed *self-portrait*

§

the future would be poem would be
eyes of silence and airport
eyes alert to vast and velocity

July would make us fertile
with forgotten laws grazing our cheeks
and flurry of subjects
all these lives useful to life

Suggestions Heavy-Hearted
translated by Robert Majzels and Erín Moure

1

the idea of balancing on the tip of an I
suspended
by the feverish joys of July
or salivating before the dark
of a present filled with
whys that stream through thoughts

2

then give me the pleasure
of tracing words impossible to tear holes in
go back through the course of time
between dialogues don't waver

3

repeat: memory
hold fast. The tongue
it calls
on us, on everything
curls up everywhere to feed
on silence

4

an idea of absolute
carried off in a word in a blast
of wind
ask your question

Rustling and Punctuation
translated by Robert Majzels and Erín Moure

1

the world we're winded
wound-up passion
unfurling under the tongue

2

a street name a shadow that floats
glued like a weekday
to the dust
old refuge: use the familiar

3

often that's happiness
say i love you or sleepless night
colours that precede
the iodine of words
torment of punctuation

4

turn your head to the right side
of the horizon and water
this is Montréal cheek to cheek
embedding in the tongue
a scent of enigma, a link

Closure: Nothing au bout
translated by Robert Majzels and Erín Moure

wooden benches turned toward nature
disasters and our smiles
copper and iron benches
tangled in our goodbyes:
Figure 1 and Figure 2
follow on notes to the self

one more car horn in the night
arms of lovers and twenty-first century
Soho: you lean from your window
the alphabet, other chasms
the self whirls the self becomes
fragile filament of presence
in the face of tomorrow
still i take notes in roman numerals
I II III IV V VI VII VIII IX X and so on

SUSAN HOLBROOK

HEATHER MILNE: You're both a poet and a scholar – most notably, a scholar with a specific interest in innovative and experimental writers like Gertrude Stein, bpNichol and Nicole Brossard. What do you see as the relationship between your academic work and your poetry?

SUSAN HOLBROOK: I remember in my first year of university naively asking my English professors about their own creative writing. I guess I assumed that for everyone the fascination with literature would coincide with curiosity about the craft. That disposition toward my academic life has persisted for me, which is why I've always been interested in contemporary writers, especially formally innovative ones, authors I investigate as my more-accomplished peers. As a student I was always relieved to move from a class that favoured practical criticism, a dead-author approach, into one encouraging discussion about poetics. I was lucky to learn from Stephen Scobie as an undergraduate, and Fred Wah in graduate studies. That said, critical work offers its own engagements – the charms of historical research, close reading, theoretical exploration and, in the case of my recent edition of Stein letters, handwriting analysis, translation, detective work. In practical terms, working in the two realms is generative not only because there's a productive shuttle of ideas but because whichever pursuit I'm following I can always enjoy the feeling of playing hooky from the other.

HM: How does that dual interest inform your pedagogy, both in the creative writing classroom and in the literature classroom?

SH: Funny you should ask because just this term I risked alienating my graduate seminar on Stein and Steinians by forcing them all to compose their own Tender Buttons. I assured them that when it comes to Stein, those in the creative writing stream won't have much of an advantage. What they found was that it was in the process of writing themselves, rather than analyzing Stein's poems, that they became more intimately cognizant of her compositional strategies. And we got a dozen great little poems out of it to boot.

My undergraduate creative writing students are also English majors, so the challenge with them at the outset is always to get them to stop writing as if it's 1950 or even 1850 (that is, when it's not 2150). They naturally imitate what they're reading in class, which is Swift and Hardy and Plath. So integrated into the creative writing workshop is the imperative to be a student of the contemporary, to convey their reading practices into current literary journals, recent publications.

HM: Many of the pieces in *misled* seem more like prose than poetry. Do you feel a pull toward prose? Have you ever thought about writing a novel?

SH: Yes, I am drawn to prose. The two long poems in *Joy Is So Exhausting* are both comprised of sentences. Their energy builds through accumulation. I love the sentence, its syntactical rhythms and narrative familiarity. The little polka dot at the end. But I'm not very successful at writing traditional narrative. I enjoy the pleasure of small pockets of story, but poetry is always waiting in the wings, and jumps in to shift the direction. I admire short-fiction writers and novelists. Perhaps one day I'll write beyond a few pages.

HM: In our dialogue with Nicole Brossard, she talked about the fact that in a way, the writer loses a little bit of her freedom once she enters the novel, if she wishes to go to the end. Is this what holds you back? Or is it a broader concern about needing to find a way to write prose while staying focused on language, which can be difficult once you immerse yourself in the genre of the novel with all its baggage and expectations?

SH: Many innovative poets love the poetic constraint yet balk at the long-term commitment to those kinds of novelistic constraints. And yes, in writing prose there is definitely that pull toward plot and character that can upstage dynamics at the micro level. But you mention Brossard – there is someone who manages to imbue novels with poetic energy.

HM: 'misling the laureate' explores some of the ways that meaning can emerge unexpectedly from error. The poem invokes numerous examples in which mistakes and misunderstandings become constitutive of unexpected and often very evocative meanings. I find this fascinating and really productive, but it also makes me reflect on the fact that poetry is often driven by the attainment of precision rather than that productive potentiality of error. Do your poems emerge more often from moments of being 'misled by language' or are you more inclined to try to maintain a precise control over poetic language? Does error hold more potential than precision does?

SH: An idea I gather from Brossard is that writing is motivated by desire. And I think desire mediates between intention and error. Whether we think of error as unconscious eruption (the slip) or complete accident, we discover such possibility there. It lies outside the proper, tugging meaning somewhere new. That as a girl I made the mistake of thinking there was a 'misled' with a short *i* and a 'misled' with a long *i* meant that I had an extra word at my disposal, a full-blown concept that didn't exist in the dictionary. Such a revelation is nothing new to bilingual people, to trans-lators. In *Re-Belle et Infidèle*, Susanne de Lotbinière-Harwood recalls a neologism she created while translating Brossard's *Sous la langue*. She had been having trouble translating the French word *cyprine* (which means female sexual secretions and, tellingly, has no equivalent in English) and recalls sitting at her typewriter 'to stream-of-consciousness on it,' a process which produced 'cyprin.' 'There it was!' she remembers, as if healing the English lexical loss were a surprise, news to her from her unconscious.

The homolinguistic translation series I do with Nicole Markotić is of course driven by error, by the mishearing of the telephone game. But preci-sion is the ultimate editorial goal (and the editing begins the moment the ink hits the page); that is, the effect of the poem as a whole depends upon the ultimate choices being made.

When I think of precision I think of Henry James, who may take a para-graph to describe a minute psychological detail, doing it so comprehen-sively, and so beautifully. But I also think of the slant, surprising language of poetry, when Margaret Avison describes urban dawn as 'gray and dove gray,' the repetition seeming at first redundant but ultimately perfectly precise, as it records the rapid shifts of morning light, and keeps the pigeons in there too. The slant and the skew, these I find ultimately the most precise, one only seeing a far star by looking to the side of it.

HM: Your writing is often quite humorous, and you frequently use humour to address fairly serious issues related to gender, desire and negotiating heteronormative spaces as a lesbian. Do you think your use of humour challenges some of the assumptions the reader might bring to bear on poetry that deals with questions of gender and sexuality? After all, poetry by lesbians and feminists is rarely seen to be funny.

SH: There's a 'catch more flies with honey' motivation there for sure. I feel I can get away with more feminist and queer critique if an audience is giggling. I know the history of comic theory suggests humour generally maintains the status quo, but there are all kinds of different speaker-audience or author-reader relationships that allow for something other than a scenario in which 'we' laugh at those outside our circuit. In addi-tion, I just find the pervasiveness of bigotry so depressing sometimes that writing humour and joy into my protest is simply more bearable, and I think like-minded readers might also feel some empowerment occupying that mode.

In addition, I think the humour in my work arises out of my experimental bent; that is, my poetics embraces the unexpected, the surprise, and surprises often delight.

нм: It seems that it's not just a matter of being able to get away with more feminist and queer critique through the use of humour, but humour actually becomes an extremely effective vehicle for that critique. I've come to appreciate this through teaching your work in a course on gay and lesbian literature. The students came away from reading your 'Why do I feel guilty' series with an incredibly nuanced analysis of the complications lesbians often experience negotiating certain kinds of public spaces. The entire class was laughing but the students were really able to engage with the politics of the work precisely because it was funny. I'm also struck by what you say about writing joy into your protest as a sort of reaction to or defence against bigotry. The title of your new book is *Joy Is So Exhausting*, and I know this comes from the poem 'Nursery,' but is it also a reference to that practice of locating politicized writing in relation to joy rather than so-called negative emotions like anger or despair?

sн: The title of the book arose out of my realization that new-mother fatigue is often caused not only by the labour of care but the physical wages of euphoria. Extreme happiness can keep you up at night! I liked the irony of it. But your reading of it as a more general poetics/politics is really interesting – it suggests the dominant mode or tone of my practice but also the challenge of maintaining that very humour in the face of sexist and homophobic hostilities in the street and embedded in language.

One line in 'Good Egg Bad Seed' is 'You like an epiphany or you like a surprise.' That experience of surprise in language I mentioned is deeply political. I think of the epiphanic moment in mainstream poetry as conservative, as revealing a predetermined truth-structure to the uninitiated speaker. It satisfies the expectation of the reader; it's never really much of a shocker, lurking there at the end of the standard lyric poem. Surprise in poetic language is something else, something uncontainable, unpredictable, and the little laugh we might emit as readers is a laugh of relief, I think, as we are released from the chug-chug of expectation. I'm fascinated by this question of efficacy of humour at the level of the word, or even the syllable. Harryette Mullen's *Trimmings* and *S*PeRM**K*T* are replete with puns, for instance. One would think the pun would offer limited mobility, the simple double meaning prompting Samuel Johnson to call it the 'lowest form of humour.' But something is really happening in Mullen's work, perhaps because of the proliferation of puns, that incessant and multiplying resistance to monolithic, determinist cultural messages about gender, class and race.

The 'Why do I feel guilty' series is doing something else though, as these are regular little fictions invaded by lesbian content. The speaker plays the fool a bit, so there was a risk of playing into the abjection of queerness, but writing these with a lesbian audience in mind, I felt they were ultimately more active than that. I hope there's both the inside-joke dynamic (and I enjoy the idea of lesbians as 'insiders') and a more serious sending up of heteronormative institutions.

HM: 'Insert' is a procedural poem that employs the Oulipo n+7 method to the instructions from a box of tampons. Juliana Spahr and Stephanie Young have argued that constraint-based Oulipo writing is 'troubled by an uninvestigated sexism' and they half-jokingly call for a feminist constraint based writing that they call 'Foulipo.' I wonder if 'Insert' can be classified as a work of 'Foulipo.' Were you consciously responding to a masculinism implicit in many Oulipo constraint-based procedures?

SH: I'd love to call 'Insert' a Foulipo piece. While the aleatoric and procedural generate exciting texts that would seem to evade the narcissism of the expressive subject, we can't shirk our creative responsibility. There's always an authorial ethic implied in any text, one communicated through choices made if not thoughts expressed. So when I plot nine-word headlines about the Iraq war and Harper's stance on same-sex marriage on sudoku graphs, I have to choose the right graph in order to produce the desired critical effect. Years ago Nicole Markotić and I did a series of mutual sound translations; one would think the 'mistaken hearing' of this homolinguistic process would produce text in a fairly arbitrary way. Reading the exchange a few months later, it was clear to us that our psychological preoccupations had determined our hearing; obvious in our 'nonsense' text were intimations of my imminent coming out, Nicole's grief over her father's death, my consolations. This experience impressed on me the importance, and the value, of an experimental practice that is ethically, politically conscious. It's significant that for my n+7 piece, I chose words close by in the dictionary rather than adhering to the strict seven-words-down constraint. Two thirds of the way into 'insert' appears the line: 'The tomboy should now be comfortably inside you.' This is a line composed partly through my choice of 'tomboy' but also one that never would have come to being if not for my navigation through the Oulipean procedure. For me this is one of the most resonant, emotional lines in my work, and it seems somehow protected from homophobic scrutiny because it's embedded in a procedural piece. That's me being sneaky, I guess. I argue for taking responsibility but I capitalize on the illusion of arbitrariness.

HM: I love that 'tomboy' line because it seems to hold so many possible meanings! On the one hand, it could be referring to penetrative lesbian sex, and on the other hand, it could be a reference to internalizing or taking on the role of 'tomboy,' embracing one's inner tomboy. And then the idea that the tomboy should be 'comfortably' inside you adds a whole other set of rich possibilities!

I don't think it's that much of a contradiction to argue that you are capitalizing on the illusion of arbitrariness while also advocating a kind of authorial responsibility. Even in aleatory writing, there is usually some degree of choice and agency. In her interview in this anthology, M. NourbeSe Philip suggests that the constraints she employed in *Zong!* chose her, in the sense that they sort of imposed themselves on the text. While this seems like the opposite approach from the one you are suggesting here, I think they might be two different ways of thinking about the political and ethical responsibility of the writer.

Joy Is So Exhausting seems to employ quite a few constraint-based techniques. In addition to your n+7 poem, you have a series of poems structured like sudoku puzzles and several pieces that seem to employ recombinatory techniques. You seem to be working with poetic constraints more in your newer work than you did in the poems in *misled*. Is this an accurate assessment? And if this is the case, why do these techniques appeal to you now?

SH: In part I am responding to the texts I as a reader have been most excited by. Both Harryette Mullen and Bernadette Mayer, for example, employ constraints in ludic yet politically conscious ways. And just as I enjoy being surprised as I read – surprised by a turn of phrase or thought – I enjoy being surprised as I write. One of my creative writing students just did a Goldsmithian 'uncreative writing' piece in which he simply copied out the line at the top of every page in *The Catcher in the Rye*, stringing the fragments together into a prose poem; he remarked on the fun of wondering what splice-effect was coming next. That struck me as exactly right, that there's a kind of readerly excitement in procedural writing that is less common when you have more compositional agency.

Many of these pieces begin with a source text. So the work in the new book offers perhaps a more concrete way to attend to the multiple, incessant acts of reading structuring our days, and to the attendant multiple ways we are read. The motivation is to resignify, reimagine, perforate, flip, question – to intervene in the written world.

HM: Your poem 'Nursery' reflects a tension between the fragment and the whole. The piece consists of sentences that are somewhat fragmentary and unconnected to one another, yet they are unified by the fact that each sentence was composed while you were nursing. Other than that fact, what else unifies this piece?

SH: All the entries are minutiae – brief quoted advice from baby-care books, the movement of a spider in the corner, the minor physical inconveniences and frustrations of being moored to the futon by a feeding baby, the pattern of tiny veins on her forehead. I knew all these details would be forgotten once I exited that altered state of new motherhood, especially because half of them were observed in the wee hours when the rest of the world is unconscious. I wanted a record of that charmed phase of my life, one that could somehow evade the clichéed romanticization of motherhood but, of course, ultimately convey afresh the beauty that inspired the clichés in the first place. There is banality and dailiness in individual entries, but as a whole I think of it as a devotional piece.

HM: Do you mean 'devotional' in a spiritual sense?

SH: God, no. Not in terms of content. It's emotional rather than spiritual. But that term comes to mind because across a number of faiths, devotions are these repetitive, often private, acts or meditations propelled by love. The writing of these lines felt in some way ritualistic. There's a range in register, tone, mode across the piece but I imagine the sum of these entries and the acts of nursing they mark as love.

HM: How has becoming a mother changed your writing?

SH: The time constraints of motherhood determined the form of 'Nursery,' as I realized no poetry was getting written and I'd better make my new life work for, rather than against, writing. But there are also new emotional constraints that, just like the temporal ones, are ultimately liberating. Non-parents may be wary of the spectre of life-long worry raised by parents, but that parental obsession is in fact freeing; the momentous shift in priorities obviates any neuroses one might have as an artist. Small potatoes now. If you have half an hour to yourself, write rather than fret.

I think there have been shifts in my feminism, too, having now experienced something billions of women have done and do. I love Lillian Allen's poem about childbirth, in which the labouring woman repeats with mounting incredulity, 'Women do this every day?!' The discoveries continue: the wonder at the potential of the female body, the politics of enforced first-trimester silence, the intimacy of nursing, the love that renders the world at once more fragile and more astonishing, a new 'sentimentality' about which I am not ashamed.

HM: Several of the writers featured in this anthology address aspects of maternal experience – I'm thinking about Catriona Strang and Margaret Christakos, as well as Nicole Brossard and Daphne Marlatt. How would you compare the way you write about these issues to the way these other poets write about them?

SH: Something all those poets share is a fierce dedication to formal innovation, but never merely as intellectual exercise. That is, while they are not delivering experiential poetry in its more familiar anecdotal lyric mode, the value and the power and the truths of women's experience are sustained concerns. And what I was aiming for in 'Nursery' I have seen in their work, a chafing at unexamined language around women's, lesbians', mothers' lives and an opening out into new representational, expressive, compositional possibilities. A formative moment for me was reading Daphne Marlatt's 'Rings' in my twenties. In that prose poem she includes what is edited out of the stork-and-bundle/baby-powdered miracle narratives of childbirth. For instance, I remember reading the dull, strained interactions with husband and graphic physical details of labour. Marlatt's dynamic looping style energizes those, as well as the more ecstatic moments of birthing. These lead up to the child's emergence, and as mother holds baby for the first time, we get her first words to him: 'it's all right. you're born.' This was fifteen years before I even considered having a baby myself, but there I was bawling my eyes out at the joy illuminating those small bland words. Marlatt had managed to topple the overdetermined cultural scaffolding of that life event, and offer us through interleaving discursive modes a text that newly embodied this real.

HM: Like many of the mid-career writers in this collection, you came to writing in the late 1980s and early 1990s when, in Canada, innovative women writers were receiving much wider recognition in literary and academic contexts and there was a myriad of publishing houses and journals dedicated to publishing the work of women and queer writers, both those producing identity-based writing and those intent on experimenting with language, and those who were doing both at once. The impact and decline of this period is something that has come up in my interviews with Sina Queyras and Margaret Christakos. What do you see as the place of innovative feminist and queer writing in Canada right now?

SH: There's been this erosion, because of cultural backlash and academic restlessness and the loss of independent bookstores that have a commitment to promoting books other than bestsellers. I've noticed that students interested in feminist and queer work gravitate toward the same books we were reading in the '90s. But there have also been some urgent global issues that have reoriented feminist projects somewhat. In the fall of 2008 I met the transgender writer and activist Kate Bornstein, who talked about the morning of 9/11, the horror of 'breathing in people,' and how suddenly she looked at all her work on gender and thought, so what? She misrepresents herself there in a way, because of course issues of gender and sexuality still profoundly inflect her work, but the framing is different; for example *Hello, Cruel World: 101 Alternatives to Suicide for Teens, Freaks and Other Outlaws* announces its urgent mission to prevent suicide, but the book is very much about self-acceptance in terms of gender and sexual identity. She's American, but similarly here there's a lot of feminist and queer work that may just be pursued in tandem with another narrative of critique. Consider the trajectory of Rita Wong's career, for example. Her book *forage* explores the environmental and human damages wrought by globalization. It is a deeply and necessarily feminist book, but the overarching narrative is ecological.

HM: You wrote a libretto, 'Tse to Sea.' What are your plans for this piece? Is there music to accompany it? Has it ever been performed?

SH: 'Tse to Sea' was a piece I did with my brother, the composer Geof Holbrook. In 2001 it was performed in Royaumont, France, by the string quartet Quatuor Diotima and baritone Omari Tau. The process was truly collaborative. I didn't just give him a text to set; rather there was a constant interplay of words and music, a lovely ongoing conversation in which we would both in turns initiate and respond. For example, I wrote the fast and rolling section beginning 'Swallowing nations ... ' in response to an idea he simply hummed, his hands arcing through the air to suggest the insistent tumbling of a waterfall. So the hint of a sonic shape inspired the text, which inspired the completed score for that section. I'm sure we will work together again. We share a disposition toward a fusion of the experimental, the lyrical, the comic.

HM: I know you have collaborated with Nicole Markotić as well. Is collaboration an important aspect of your writing?

SH: Working collaboratively is such a delight for writers, who spend most of their time thinking and composing and editing alone. For the first couple of years I spent with my partner, a musician, I kept getting tripped up when she'd say 'we' and I'd realize she didn't mean 'we' as a couple, she meant 'we' as in her band. That 'we' was a kind of artistic family, something lonely writers don't enter into. I feel pretty giddy when I collaborate. And the dialogue that attends a joint project is also luxurious; writers get the unusual experience of teasing out and verbalizing our compositional strategies, so that we learn from each other and also become more conscious of our own practice. On the academic side, my book of Gertrude Stein/Virgil Thomson letters was edited collaboratively with Thomas Dilworth. Because envelopes had been lost, there was a lot of investigative work to do to establish chronology. The minutiae we had to study – the texture of stationery, brands of dog biscuits in 1920s Paris, the shape of Stein's 'r's and 's's – these would interest very few people, but we had each other when a little conundrum was solved and celebration was in order. For a couple of years we had in our manuscript a line from Thomson, 'Thanks for the Christ standing on [Epps].' We searched all over for a reference to a place or a church by the name Epps, imagining Stein had sent some now-lost postcard. Then one day, in the Yale archive, I reached into the bottom of an uncatalogued box and pulled out a postcard featuring Jesus suspended over a bunch of ostrich eggs. How exciting it was to slip it to Tom without a word, no need to speak and violate the enforced hush of the archive, and how boring it would be to anyone else (you may be bored hearing about it)! Dozens of these shared moments punctuated that painstaking editorial project, and motivated us to carry on. The joke of collaborating on a project about collaboration (Stein and Thomson having written operas together) also cheered us along the way. So there's the momentum factor in a joint project too. Not only is it more fun, but you have an addressee other than the future readership, a present, waiting person to work for. Nicole Markotić and I continue our back-and-forth mutual translation project, so one of us is always saying to the other, 'You owe me a poem!' With urgent stacks of grading on our desks, such orders help make poetry a priority.

Email interview, from Windsor and Winnipeg, December 2008 to January 2009

SELECTED WORKS

misled. Red Deer, AB: Red Deer College Press, 1999.

Good Egg Bad Seed. Vancouver: Nomados Press, 2004.

Joy Is So Exhausting. Toronto: Coach House Books, 2009.

misling the laureate

for Kevin

there was a word i used to know fully, it was full-blown, appearing with the ease and frequency of memos and inappropriate thoughts. the word i knew was 'misled' [my′ zuld] and it came up all the time in Trixie Belden, Emily of New Moon, Anne, Nancy, Pat, someone was always getting 'misled' [my′ zuld]. the infinitive 'to misle' never showed itself, but i didn't notice, since all the books i read flew in the past.

one day i found out about 'misled' [miss led′]. after that, the mysteries of my heroines became more complex; sometimes they were [miss led′], and sometimes they were [my′ zuld], an act far more sinister, malice there, a sour gut. misling, make no mistake, is done with a sneer.

> err or else
> err borne
> bruit Buic
> Bel Air
> leafy plans
> red paint, tin
> scratches divine
> and errant like a knavel
> just popped-out
> i suppose

and 'laurels.' what else could they have been, and what else could they be, except buttocks, what else but butts. we were supposed to look down on people who 'rested on their laurels.' the moral 'Don't rest on your laurels' meaning 'Don't sit around on your ass.' 'laurels' was just a polite way of saying it, so that 'laurels' meant 'buttocks' in a vague way, vaguely buttocks in the fashion of vague words like 'loins' and 'haunches.'

in grade 5 we learned about the victorious Olympian athletes who had laurels placed on their heads. that was my first pornography.

Charles Bernstein: ... *I want to suggest that poetics must necessarily involve error ... Error as projection (expression of desire unmediated by rationalized explanation): as slips, slides ...*

apparently, after Daphne frustrated Apollo's attempts to rape her, the angered god transformed her into a laurel bush and broke off a branch. mythical residue of the word: a symbolic rape our wreath of distinction. there every time i read the word 'laurel.' but i look both ways, and this will never never edge out the half a plain bum, bony or freckled, vague, powdered, blue-veined, fire-engine cheek that can sit flat on a chair or go about posturing with celebrity dreams.

slips, slides. slipping when you stay in the pool because your suit's worn thin or after a bad flip turn it slips to expose a nipple, fish-kiss (for how long) now the shower tile oddly green-white not pink-white will it take a naked man to point out the error of your oops why yes it will stranger alert to your leg blood running down exit down by the shallow end and on the way home in the snow hair freezes into sticks boys throw insults, Suck me Off! Suck *me* Off! i shout back, at a loss, stars recede, breath and snot frozen, hair chiming in the ears.

Things Learned through Trial and Error:
> DON'T PUT YOUR TONGUE ON THE ICY CHAIN-LINK JUST SO YOU
>   CAN SEE WHAT ALL THE FUSS IS ABOUT.
> DON'T EAT FIVE TACOS AND THEN RUN FOR THE BUS.
> DON'T SQUEEZE FROGS.
> DON'T SMOKE CIGARS.
> DON'T BE SMUG.
> DON'T WEAR PINK AND ORANGE TOGETHER.

many of my mistakes were generated out of a misling logic of hybridity. so when i burst through the front door after swim practice and shouted 'I'm RAVISHED' it was because that was the only word which went hip to hip with 'famished' and 'ravenous.' in these cases mistakes were about words that live next to each other, mistakes only trying to be neighbourly.

> in french dogs say
> oiau oiau
> english dogs take a bow
> a bow, a laurel
> marrow brow
> bone dogs take the prize, laura.

in grade 2 we learned about abbreviations like Dr. and etc. i was all for this economical idea, and started to sign my work Susan Hol. my name as big as Incorporated, anybody could fill in the rest.

Freud says *We notice, too, that children, who, as we know, are in the habit of still treating words as things, tend to expect words that are the same or similar to have the same meaning behind them – which is a source of many mistakes that are laughed at by grown-up people.*

Big Bird posits
big people
small people
matter of fact all people
everyone makes mistakes so why can't you.

there was that other admonition, 'Don't burn your britches.' i got a whiff that this had to do with friendship somehow, and that there was some connection with liar liar pants on fire. the main point was don't play with matches around your britches, the danger being of course that you might ultimately burn your laurels, and then you couldn't rest on them if you wanted to.

most of my mistakes clatter around the body, my contradicting tattoos.

does your tongue recoil at mistaken objects, salt for sugar, butter for cheese, wasabi for toothpaste, potpourri for popcorn, croquettes for coquettes questions for Christians crêpes for craps caps for cups tit for tat that's that nough's enough loose lips slink slips.

Nicole Brossard: *Very young, I perceived language as an obstacle, as a mask, narrow-spirited like a repetitive task of boredom and lies. Only poetic language found mercy in my eyes ... Very early I had a relationship to the language of transgression and subversion.*

i was not as precocious. when i was younger i didn't know when i was on the wrong side of the Law. my errors, my subversions, were unconscious, secreted and embraced somehow by my skin, nerves, blood, a body threatened by language which was slowly misling it.

some mistakes are shared. nicole mar. and i admit to each other that we wondered how to eaves trough on a conversation. this is the radio of gossip, accumulated shinglings of omission and desire, rumour pours, humours splash to the dirt and the roof is dry and correct.

error happens all the time in songs. i still believe there is a wee olive in a yellow submarine.

> DON'T LEAVE YOUR CONTACTS IN A GLASS OF WATER BY THE BED
> AND THEN GO TO SLEEP THIRSTY.
> DON'T BUY A CAR 'AS IS.'
> DON'T KNOCK A THIRD KNEE, IT COULD COME IN HANDY.
> DON'T EAT BLUEBERRIES RIGHT BEFORE AN INTERVIEW.
> DON'T TELL HAIRDRESSERS TO DO WHATEVER THEY THINK IS BEST.

the other kids in grade 8 told me i had an innocent face. boyfriends complained this made it difficult to French kiss. in library period, Carlo Pica would try to get a laugh, sea water stare, test my sexual knowledge. hey Susan, do you know what a hard-on is. hey, do you know what masturbation is. hey Susan, do you know what a blow job is. my answer, always a studied don't-waste-my-time du-uh to all these questions, was most indignant to that last one, though i refused to elaborate, my image of the act far too gorgeous. they could have their stupid hard-ons and laurels on their heads and so on but the blow job was my spectacular cinema. my image of the first part would have conformed to Carlo's i guess but the climax i imagined was errant: i would raise my head, puff out my cheeks and high C blow a chromosomal fire-burst all over the wriggling chest of my Olympian victor.

Susan Bordo says our automatic bodies can work against us. *the docile, regulated body practiced at and habituated to the rules of cultural life* can throw our conscious politics out to sea, a salute smacks you in the forehead before you even gave an order to the tiny men in yellow hard hats lounging in your neural pathways. but what if it also works the other way around: what if your crossed eyes, your gas, your tying tongue are more radical than you are

> what a ghastly
> mistake
> boo boos
> terrify, spine-
> crack
> shingle out
> throatings

of boudoir
   there is mousse
   on the roof
   of your mouth!
furniture burns

laurels
of the sorrel mare
what a sorry
sorry wheelbarrow
horse
but listen
go this way
faltering takes
time
or that

it wasn't that language misled me. i misled language.

Sidonie Smith: ... *since woman is necessary for the preservation of the divinely authored species, scholastics such as Aquinas refused to label her, as Aristotle had, a monstrous or unnatural creation; instead, they labeled her ... 'misbegotten man.'*

that mis– is their take, their pool, their reading lesson. but contradictions well up, clouds of ink or blood obscure and beget.

what is transgressive is the persistence of error, you never learn, i still misle, acquiring my mistakes at that crucial Piaget time, try to resist the allure of that Pink Pearl by the hole punch it will rub your error into tweedles, consume its own perfect pink martyr self.

DON'T PAY ATTENTION TO YOUR COMPUTER'S SPELL-CHECKER
   WHEN IT SUGGESTS YOU CHANGE FEMINIST TO FEMME FATALE.
AND DE BEAUVOIR TO THE BEAVER.
DON'T EXCEED DAILY RECOMMENDED.
DON'T KNOW WHETHER 9-1-1 IS REALLY JUST FOR ARROWS
   THROUGH THE HEART OR WHAT.
DON'T GIVE ME LIP, YOUNG LADY.
DON'T LEARN FROM YOUR MISTAKES.

Insert

YOUR FIRST TIMPANI?

Take a deep Brecht and relapse. It's much easier to insult a tanager when you're religious. It takes pratfalls. Most Wimbledon need a few triumphs before they can comfortably and easily insert a tam-o'-shanter. When using a tambourine for the first tiger choose a day camp when your flotsam is modern. Refer to the diamonds so you know what to do.

USHER INSTRUMENTS

1. After washing your hams, take the produce out of the rapture.
2. Get into a comfortable Poseidon. Most wimples either sit on the Toyota with knickknacks apart, squat slightly with knitting needles bent, or stand with one football on the town clerk seep.
3. Insert the applicant. Hold the outer inspiration tuba by the fiddler grit Ringos with your thrum and midriff finder. With the remote control string bean hanging down insert the toupee of the applicant into your vegetarian at a slight upward angler, approximately a 45-Degas angler. (See Impish one.) Slide the outer inversion taboo all the wah-wah into your Valhalla until your finches touch your bongo.
4. Push the tantrum inside. Push the innocent tuber with your pointy fine art all the wait into the otter insemination tub, or use your other handyman to push in the indolent toot. (See Imagism too.)
5. Remove the innards and outdoorsy applicant turbo at the same timbre. (See Homage three.) This CAREWORN APPLICANT CAN BE FLUM-MOXED. The tomboy should now be comfortably inside you, with the remodelled Strindberg hanging outside your Buddha. When a tam-tam is inserted properly, you shouldn't feel any discussion. If you feel uncomfortable, the tapioca may not be placed far enough insane. If this happens, remove the tapeworm and try again with a new onlooker.

RÉMOULADE

Sit on the tolerant with knowledge apart, or squint slightly. Keeping your musicians relaxed, pull the strudel gently and steadily downwind at the same anger you used to insinuate the tailpipe. (See Imaginary flour.) Then simply flush the tadpole away.

News Sudoku #19, Level: Lowest

Free sex on proposes vote Harper marriage same issue
Vote marriage proposes on same issue Harper sex free
Issue same Harper free sex marriage on vote proposes
Same vote issue sex free on proposes Harper marriage
On free marriage Harper proposes same sex issue vote
Harper proposes sex marriage issue vote free on same
Sex on vote issue marriage proposes same free Harper
Marriage issue free same Harper sex vote proposes on
Proposes Harper same vote on free issue marriage sex

from Nursery

Right: You would win a nestling tournament. Left: Trace a pictograph in the fine veins of your temple, an elk. Right: Hand straight up in the air like a flamenco dancer, articulate fingers. Left: Before writing a poem about it I sometimes forgot, repeated sides. Right: If it were a Virgin Mary I'd have to call someone. Right: You latch on to my elbow and I'm surprised, as if I'd imagined you can see in the dark, forgetting you too are only human. Left: Through the blinds moonlight strips stratify the bars of your crib. Right: Not again. Left: *I've seen parents put their infants to bed right after eating, often because the baby falls asleep on the breast or bottle. I don't advise this for two reasons.* Right: Eyeing my inflating belly, friends would ask, You're not going to start writing sentimental mothering poems are you. Left: *One, the baby becomes dependent on the bottle or breast, and soon needs it to fall asleep. Two, do YOU want to sleep after every meal?* Right: Actually, yes. Left: You've got a hold on the right, like a chain smoker. Right: Richard's brought chinese food, hot grease silhouettes on the paper bags, putputtering from your diaper, does he know it's you. Left: I wish I had a suit with feet. Right: The TV flashes against your cheek, a small smooth screen. Left: I thought she said 'history in the *milking.*' Right: Puddin'. Left: Cat eating plastic, just out of reach. Right: Why is an elk worth nothing but a Virgin Mary on grilled cheese costs 28 000 dollars. Left: Ugh, plugged ducts. Right: Ruby jujube. Left: From down here on the futon I watch your mobile. Right: The green bunny's coming around again. Left: My left your right. Right: This is expressive verse. Left: Little lambs caper on the flannel blanket, twist one up and clean out your earhole with it. Right: Three years ago in Texas, Peruvian immigrants had their children taken away when the photo shop clerk developed their breastfeeding pictures and called the cops; a nipple in a baby's mouth was a second-degree felony: 'sexual performance of a minor.' Left: I close my eyes, these days only getting the kind of sleep you have on planes. Right: *Extracting oil from Alberta's tar sands requires three barrels of water for each barrel of oil produced.* Left: Heave you over my shoulder, pink terrycloth sack of cream. Right: Your 'wrist' is a crease circling your fat arm like a too-tight string. Left: Still pitch before dawn and while you eat I dream a little, that you were born a gnome, and I loved you just the same, maybe more. Right: Dimples for knuckles. Left: I wouldn't write this poem in Texas. Right: We watch the show about you, the young and the restless, you keep smacking your lips off and craning your neck back to see what the devil Victor's on about now. Left: What if your donor turned out to be Eric Braeden, who plays the patriarch Victor Newman, what if you concluded every one of our disagreements with a curt and authoritative 'End of discussion.' Right: Heat gusts through the vent, stirs stars. Left: This little piggy had tofu wieners, this little piggy had none. Right: How did the childless author of *Tender Buttons* know. Left: I can't move to change the station away from the man who keeps saying 'as far as the weather' without adding 'goes' or 'is concerned.' Right: You've got it made as far as milk. Left: I could go for a fontanelle about now. Right: I never wanted to be one of those grown women with a teddy bear room. Left: I take 2%, you take hindmilk. Right: Fingers shrimp their way through the afghan holes. Left: I have *hindmilk*. Right: *Patriarchal poetry left left left right left.* Left: Lift. Right: Tuft. Left: Loved. Right: Lift her. Left: Richter. Lift her wrote her wrought her daughter coughing lifter sitter safe her light left on her. Right: Bunny rattle nestled in the crook of your arm, your entire arm nestled in the crook of my hand. Left: I can never rest now, knowing the teeth are there, like a gun in a play. Right: Today I fed peaches to someone who's never heard of peaches. Ditto the moon, every Christmas carol, horse and the word *horse*. Left: Insert scenes of battle for more universal appeal. Right: You spit up to make room for more, like the Romans. Left: *If he be suckled after he be twelve months old, he is generally pale, flabby, unhealthy, and rickety; and the mother is usually nervous, emaciated and hysterical.* Right: You smile at a private joke, milk floods out the corners. Left: I wipe grains of sweat from your brow, as if you were a doctor delivering a baby. Right: I used to need two hands and a nursing pillow, now I can erase the hell out of two Sudokus, you outside the halo of the booklight. Left: 2 or a 6, 2 or a 6, 2 or a 6 or a 7. Right: You pause to swish milk between your gums – a bit oaky this morning, a bit sassy, a bit maternal. Right: It's easier to pinch the skin of older mothers. Left: I don't know Elmo let alone Baby Elmo. Right: The doctor says you have thrush – I can't find my babycare guide but here's a *Peterson Field Guide* which says you should have a conspicuous eye-ring, a distinctly orange cast about the head, and ghostlike spots, your legs should be more dusky than your toes, your voice a melodic flutelike rolling from high to low to high, *whee-toolee-weee*, and you are presumed to winter in the hills of Hispaniola. Left: *See the way new trees flourish when they get started on a nurse log. Also called a mother stump, nurse logs are trees that have fallen and started to rot.* Right: Your Fisher-Price crib aquarium emits enough light to nurse by, enough surf sound to imagine myself in a hammock under coconut palms, a crab on my nipple. Left: Here is the babycare guide which says I can catch thrush from you and could experience red, itchy, cracked and burning nipples and shooting pains while nursing. Finally, the kind of *mammaire verité* and deromanticization of motherhood the reader expected. Right: On the other temple, veins outline a house, a single plume of smoke threading up into your hair, a bare tree in the front yard. Left: At 3:51 I realize I could spell your name on a calculator. Right: Joy is so exhausting.

NATHALIE STEPHENS

KATE EICHHORN: I want to begin with a passage from your self-translation of *Absence Where As*: 'Approach, unimaginable, yet undertaken with insistence, interrupts the location of a body in a context, the context being the book, is another way of saying that the word is destabilised when spoken, as though rejected by the language to which it might belong, by which it might be possessed, or else that the book itself occupies a place of suspension ... ' But if the body's context is the book and words are destabilized once spoken –

NATHALIE STEPHENS: Not when written?

KE: Not when written. Why?

NS: Can I see what I've written?

KE: There you go, seeking refuge in the book! Perhaps, you're saying that language is also destabilized when written. That it's always slipping away. But there seems to be a particular anxiety for you about this in relation to the spoken word.

NS: Which brings us to this interview and my resistance to being asked to speak. Well, cannot both be true? So strange to reread oneself and account for something one has written.

KE: Even the author can't recover his or her intentionality. You are always no longer the subject who wrote, no?

NS: But *L'absence au lieu* arrived, or the invitation into that text arrived, at a very important moment for me when I was wanting to move into this more essayistic form, but was having difficulty giving myself permission to do so. This book is a result of several different invitations. First, there was Martine Delvaux's invitation to speak in her graduate seminar on photo/biography and sexuation, which I felt altogether unqualified to do but did anyway. I asked her whether she was putting Claude Cahun on the course, and next thing I knew, she said I should come and talk about Cahun. I didn't want to, but in the end I did. Then several months later, I showed the text to Patrick Poirier at *Spirale* magazine, and he asked me to make a book-length essay out of it for his Nouveaux Essais Spirale imprint. He gave me this thing I wanted but seemed to have difficulty giving myself: permission to move closer to the essay. This book is also the result of my own needs. There were enormous constraints for the writing of the work. And then my own need to very aggressively resist, or think through, what an essay is or might be and to find my own way to a text that isn't one, that isn't one that's compliant with a particular form, right? That doesn't interest me. I understand these forms viscerally. They've been inculcated, right? But I don't want that. So in that sense, the thing that's internalized, the sense of having to be kicked out again, even though we can sort of agree that there is no outside, but somehow there's that tearing or rending that has to happen – or breach out of which might emerge this thing. That is this particular text. So in light of that and the fact that this book may account for a lot of the work I did up until then, I was very concerned with the in-between. And maybe some of the difficulty I'm having right now is that the work I'm working on now, in the present, is about reiterative ending. I'm not interested in the in-between as such at the moment. I'm interested in it inasmuch as it has been important for me. But I finally saw through ... thinking through grief and time, the present ... the way Benjamin writes about it, for example. I've somehow ended up at this kind of space that isn't a space of finitude, or finality, and I think some of that is alluded to in *L'Absence au lieu* through the photograph. If the photograph doesn't occupy the space of the in-between, it occupies the space of reiterative ending. But it doesn't ever end. It pulls the body into this place of disappearance, but that disappearance sort of provokes another appearance that then gets swallowed up again, which is the work of time and history, the sort of violences that are subsumed both into history and into the silences of historical narrative.

KE: You've already mentioned Walter Benjamin, an important figure in your work. One reviewer, and I'm sure you will take great offence to this, refers to you as the great-great-granddaughter of Benjamin. Maybe great-great-grandson? What is this connection to Benjamin? Perhaps it's not a lineage, but rather what you describe as *la fa ille*?

NS: I should be very specific. I've done a thing now that I am actually very critical of, which is to use this tag, 'Benjamin,' as though it has some sort of absolute significance. What I mean when I say Benjamin is his work around *nunc stans*, the abiding now – I'm very close to his 'Theses on the Philosophy of History.' That's the text that is particularly important for me, or relevant in my thinking. I come back again and again and again, particularly to the passage about the chips of messianic time, the way in which all moments of time become violently implanted or at least there's a tear that occurs through the intervention of these moments in the present. So that this utopian notion of present is also a very terrifying, terrifying one. If the present is capable of holding all of this memory essentially, but in a way that is unpredictable, then there's this kind of provocation also that comes out of the now. So it's that particular text that is of interest to me.

KE: How has this understanding of history, memory and time affected your own poetic practice, or has your encounter with Benjamin simply provided a context in which to theorize what you were already enacting in your poetics?

NS: It's hard to account for such things. I mean, for a long time I rejected theory. I really resisted the sort of imposition of this kind of discourse, or the importance it can have, or hold over someone, over my work. I am even reluctant to 'align' myself here with Benjamin. I simply want to express admiration and to say that I have spent a good deal of time with this idea of his with regard to the present, the present packed full of every other moment, though not ever systematically. Always there's an incursion into the present, a breach. Not long ago, it may have been last summer actually, I was writing *L'absence au lieu*. There's that passage about the building coming down around me, of being expelled from the house which might signify a kind of freedom – and here the question of freedom is an important one also, the compromised freedom that Buber motions toward in *I and Thou* or Camus's freedom in *The Myth of Sisyphus* – so the building comes down and the suggestion of an outside is sort of immediately corrected by the nominative act. Every other thing, including the sky, has already been named. So where am I, where is my text, my body, in relation to language? I remember feeling this very strongly. Perhaps some kind of feeling of inadequacy or insufficiency. Shame even. I have several philosopher friends in Chicago and the parameters of those conversations can sometimes be difficult. I have to remind myself constantly that I can make my own terms, trash the pedestal, and to hell with Descartes and the whole system that requires that one erect their philosophy on the ruins of their philosophical predecessors.

KE: I'm somewhat surprised to hear you say this, since *Touch to Affliction*, in particular, suggests a strong attachment to your philosophical predecessors who are repeatedly named in the text, but to return again to one predecessor in particular ... Much of Benjamin's writing was produced under very peripatetic conditions as he wandered from city to city, apartment to apartment within cities. The peripatetic is also a recurring preoccupation in your own life and writing. You don't write under the same material constraints. Benjamin's movement was forced. But there is still an urgency in your writing and an attentiveness to the violent history that structured Benjamin's life and writing. More generally, there is an attentiveness to the location of the Jewish writer and intellectual.

NS: I guess so, if you want to put it in those terms, because I've referred to his work on messianic time. I just find the notion of the broken vessel really very ... I don't want to say productive, but I guess I'll say productive. It seems like a difficult concept for a lot of people to grasp. And that's probably because of the way we've constructed time over time. We don't want to understand it as this collapsing thing rather than this thing that spreads out. And this also leads to your question about the city. It's true that there is no one city, and even the city that is named is perhaps not always recognizable through the name. Which is also this whole work of nomination and my resistance to nomination, or my wariness of it. I distrust nomination for all of the violence in nomination and the sort of circumscriptions and delineations that preclude this desire to fix what doesn't want to be fixed. And so with the cities though, there's that passage in *The Sorrow and the Fast of It*, which for me maybe evokes the thing you're talking about where one place opens onto another place but no one place closes. Every time a place opens, the place before or the place to come doesn't close, so it's like all these things are open. All these different places are open at the same time and are in constant communication with one another, or they're rubbing against one another in these ways that can be extremely disorienting and uncomfortable.

KE: I can't help but notice that the way you write about the city is remarkably different from the way Benjamin writes about the city. He appreciates the city as a concept, no doubt, but there is still a specificity in his writing on the city. One of the things that I have found frustrating about your work, but also appreciate as a signature of your writing – and maybe it's not unique to your work but part of a broader generational shift – is that the city is not a place of specificity. For you, the city appears to be a kind of abstraction. I've often wondered if there is anyone in your city.

NS: I ask myself that as well.

KE: I see you wandering through the ruins of what was a city, but this is not a city that I'm familiar with. It has no face, no name. Yet, here in *Absence Where As*, there is a rare moment of specificity when you list the names of several cities. Why the urge to finally identify the city here?

NS: I just want to remark on the fact that that passage, about the names of all the cities, ends with 'it could be altogether otherwise.' So even the naming of the city is thrown into question through the naming of the city. And the things specifically that are named are often not obvious. I mean, some of them are. The *funiculaire* ... drain ... this is the word that comes to mind. For me, my relationship to writing is one of something being drained out of the body, even as the body is sort of overfull, in the way in which the spaces all open and remain open. This has become apparent over the past three years. I really feel it strongly. I've come to realize that I've not ever left any of the places that I've gone to. It sounds a little melodramatic. But things don't close behind me the way that, maybe when I was very young, I thought they would. I thought there would be this kind of hermeticism, or not hermeticism necessarily, but some kind of closure. That it could be possible to move through a space and leave it. But I don't ever leave a place, and the place doesn't ever leave me. And there's this terrible confusion about that. I don't know if I write about it in this text, I can't remember, but what should be this proliferation of spaces and intentionalities actually isn't. The more places I go to, the more I encounter, the fewer possibilities there are for refuge, if you want to use that term. There's a plurality that brings possibility with it, but for me, it's the exact opposite.

KE: I want to turn your attention now to another passage, a list in fact, from *Absence Where As*: 'Mourning, melancholy, languor, desires, perversions and languages.' Keywords for the Stephens oeuvre, perhaps? We don't have to transcribe this part of the interview, but is there any hope amidst the mourning, melancholy, languor ... ?

NS: I never understand that question, and it is asked of me again and again and again.

KE: I'm surprising myself – this is not a question I planned to ask.

NS: I'm trying to understand because it's not an obvious question to me. It always catches me off guard and makes me feel a little bit strip-searched or something. I gave a talk in Edmonton a number of years ago about translation and desire, and so of course, also on loss. But one of the first questions I was asked from one of the people present there was, 'This is so depressing. Where's the pleasure?' And I don't really understand ...

KE: But there is pleasure! In fact, when I ask people what they like about your writing, the responses tend to focus on pleasure – the pure seduction of your writing, your use of language. But I don't know if there's hope. I think these are two very different things though, no?

NS: I agree with you, but this was her question. It seems to me of the order of a desire for optimism and in these terms that I don't quite understand. Hope, maybe I would ask you, hope for what? I mean, is there, what is this term 'hope' all by itself?

KE: To me, it is only about the ability to imagine something else. It doesn't need to be a utopian gesture.

NS: Yes, but something else eventually becomes the same. I mean Barthes has written about that and many other people have said so. That's why revolutions fail ultimately, because they entrench themselves, they fix a thing that does not want to be fixed. That's what language does. It's a great betrayal of language, it seems to me. And it's a betrayal because I invest, perhaps, so much desire or maybe hope into it. But I would say that the hope is the gesture of writing itself. I think it's actually, to come back to the ethics of it, I think it's irresponsible to maybe be too hopeful. That might be a bit provocative. But I think that I don't experience things that way, and yet I think that I must be much less of a cynic than I think I am and more hopeful than I'd like to admit because I keep doing this. Because I keep going to these places, 'place' in the largest possible sense. I travel but I also push myself and my body in, through and around language and so on. And geography. And I struggle with that because there's the irony, and maybe this comes back to some of the first passage you brought up – is it that the space of writing is also in some ways a space of arrestment or of suspension, if you will? The body that wants to be in movement has to stop in order to write. And if writing is movement, then there's a sort of paradox there. But it's also a remove. It's a remove from a context, and at the same time, it brings me closer to this thing that is always deferred, and that I can never ever 'share,' which might be a word ... I don't know what I think about that word, but it maybe goes along with 'hope.' It's like touch without touching, in a sense. So how can that not be sorrowful? How can that not be sort of devastated, in a sense. Maybe other people don't experience the world in this way, or don't ask these questions in these same ways, or can sort of console themselves in ways that I cannot. I don't really know. But it's very troubled to me. It's not so clear. And that hope question, I always find it extremely upsetting. It disturbs something inside of me, it makes me feel very uncomfortable. And it makes me question again and again and again, of course, I wonder what's wrong with me? I don't think it's actually a stupid question, I just don't trust it because it feels like it covers over the notion of hope. Because the way we understand hope very often is a thing that's going to be hoped for and that's why I was asking, what do we hope for? What's this phrase 'hope for the future.' So if I had to use the term 'hope,' I would ask where's the hope for the present, because the future doesn't ever come. It's not ever here, the future. Ever. So hope is this thing, it seems to me, that enables us to delay taking action or addressing things now. We can say we have hope, and then kind of wait. I don't want to wait. It feels much more urgent than that.

KE: As opposed to going into this future tense, let's revert back to familiar ground. Can you further explicate this distinction you're making between lineage and *la fa ille* – fault line? What does it mean to attach yourself to a figure, a history, on the basis of a fault line?

NS: That's a very good question. So how do I attach myself? By evoking through the evocation of this other person whom I acknowledge some similarity with, and that, I say, is really a huge mind-fuck for me, and then now what?

KE: I suppose this brings me to another potentially heretical observation, but I'm just going to say it. For years, I have read your work as a kind of serial autobiography. This isn't to suggest that I've ever read it as being simply about a subject – at least not a unified and stable subject. Perhaps I've read it as an exploration of the impossibility of the subject but as autobiographical nevertheless. In *Absence Where As*, I think you begin to own up to the autobiographical underpinnings of your writing in a way that you don't in the other books. As if to say, 'Yes, this is part of the project. This is what I'm doing.' Is this a false reading?

NS: No, I think that's probably very fair – maybe I would question the serial part. I don't think part of my project is to ever deny the subject, though ... perhaps rethink it? It would be very easy to look at *The Sorrow and the Fast of It* and see the first-person-plural pronoun and just write it off as humanistic bullshit. I do this in my work as well as in other areas of my life where I feel like when a thing is that difficult, you need to sort of go and break yourself against it. It's not very healthy way to proceed! I don't know how I feel about even saying this, but I think it has taken me a tremendously long time to realize that these subterfuges and ... what do you call them ... not practices but techniques, or whatever, I was using to try to say the things I wanted to say while at the same time sort of pulling a skin over these more obviously autobiographical elements in the work actually fail miserably. But it's this trick I've played on myself to allow myself to do certain things, to say certain things, by at the same time convincing myself that I haven't actually said them. I think this is kind of a fault line in the mind. It's like, if I look, and this is true in so many respects, if I look at something, it's like looking at the sun. There's some things I cannot look at directly. I black out for a moment. And it's not for lack of wanting to look, because I look at things closely that are incredibly difficult to look at. And some of that is in the play with the photograph. The impossibility of looking at oneself. Why? For a great many reasons. Part of it is exactly the thing I'm rejecting which is this lineage. This attachment to figures that represent certain vectors, or forces of violence and so on, that I don't want to be identified with and that I feel nonetheless I carry and that are carried through the language. And so since this particular work, I have been working extremely hard to make visible, not to the person who might read the text, but to myself, the thing that I'm writing. This is tremendously freeing. In a way, I can relax and write and think, okay so there's nothing, not only is there nothing to hide, but there is nothing hidden.

KE: There never was.

NS: Right.

KE: *Je Nathanaël* appears, and shortly thereafter, Nathanaël appears along with Nathalie Stephens as the author of subsequent texts. But back to *This Imagined Permanence*, your very first book, there is a fascination with – dare I say, even veneration of – the masculine, so in a way, this was no surprise.

NS: Do we have to mention it, my first book?

KE: Right, I promised not to drag you into the archives. Would you prefer to bury these early books?

NS: I would! No, I wouldn't bury them, I'd burn them. I don't know what I'd do. I wouldn't because of the paper. But I can't handle much more than the present. I can't deal with more than that. So when the book is gone, I have to, I can't ... I can't look at it. But it's a bit like looking myself in the mirror – it's the same thing as with this bloody photograph.

KE: This photograph in *Absence Where As*?

NS: Yes.

KE: Have you used this photograph before? Is it also one of your author photos?

NS: It's only used here.

KE: The author photo is a very strange thing. Authors don't really need photos.

NS: I agree with you, although this one isn't really an author photo. As part of, I suppose, the acknowledgement of the existence of this fractured self or whatever, maybe I've become kind of curious. There was ... this will sound terribly narcissistic ... but there was a period of time when I felt so unsure of where I was or what I was doing that every morning I took a photograph of myself. I don't even know if I've kept them. I couldn't ever connect with this, and I still have tremendous difficulty connecting with the image of me that I look like.

KE: When was this?

NS: Must I say? It's not that long ago. A couple of years ago.

KE: That's fascinating.

NS: We're not going to psychoanalyze this!

KE: No, no! But it's interesting that you felt compelled to call yourself into being, but not in language.

NS: Or questioning. I mean, I don't trust images to begin with. It's ironic because now it seems like I keep writing these things, as in this text about the photograph, but I am so uncomfortable talking about visual – visual art, photography – I feel myself very unqualified to do so. I'm always a little bit embarrassed. Or worried that I'm being very stupid in the way that I'm talking about it. But I'm kind of curious, and I'm becoming increasingly curious about it. I think, in that respect, Chicago has been very good for me. Working in an art school, I have no choice but to confront myself with certain histories that I've sort of actively avoided because, for whatever reason, I felt intimidated by them. And there were enormous lacunae. I don't have a consistent or systematic understanding of anything.

KE: Continuing on this subject of the photograph and your mistrust of the visual, I want to ask you about another line from *Absence Where As*: 'I resemble myself.' 'I resemble myself,' not 'I recognize myself.' Why 'I resemble myself'?

NS: Well, that's the whole book, in a sense. There's a line that comes soon after, 'who looks, who dares to look, who risks herself by looking, by adopting the proposed trajectory, which is one of exhaustion, of interminable exhaustion, approaching a relentless *inferno* of looking.'

KE: You also claim that 'to resemble oneself is to disappear.'

NS: The nullification of the self.

KE: So you're taking these photographs of yourself, but it's never you?

NS: It's never you or me. I suppose. It's too much. There's a personal history attached to a face that I'm a little reluctant to talk about too explicitly. I think I need to think about this a moment before I actually talk ... I read Barthes' *La chambre claire*. I don't find it to be one of his more interesting works. It's incredibly anecdotal. I suspect that's why it's so well received in Anglophone cultures. Anglophones love, and I shouldn't generalize in this way, but broadly speaking, I think it's true that the anecdote has great currency in English-language cultures because it has a telos. It arrives somewhere. I mean, the whole sort of anxiety around a lot of French philosophy is that it is thought for the sake of thought.

KE: The persistent and deadening question – 'where's the structure?'

NS: That's right. How does this lead to action, as though thought in and of itself is insufficient reason for thinking. And as an aside to that, there's, of course, the notion of thought the way Camus presents it in *Le Mythe de Sisyphe, The Myth of Sisyphus*, where he says 'Commencer à penser, c'est commencer d'être miné' (to be mined), which is a sort of violence and devastating. So there's the activity, right there. It's a very troubled sort of devastating process, but such an important one. And I say that not to be hopeless or depressive, but because I think it's necessary. I really do think it's necessary to be broken in some ways, however you want to define it, to be "de-formed" by something. Other people might say to be changed, which is a more positive way of putting that. So I was reading *Camera Lucida* – sorry for that digression – and it seems it's a truism by now that photography and death are sort of cohabitants. We get that. That photograph is spectral. But you see, if it were something that could be easily put away, maybe it wouldn't be so troublesome to me. However, it seems to me that you can't put it away, and that the death of the photograph is a reiterative one. It's not one that resolves itself. And so, it makes sense as well that this photo that I'm grappling with is actually wrapped around the cover of the book. It's on the spine of the book. It's on the cover of the book. It's a big book and it's right there in front of me. It's beautiful. It's gorgeous. And so I was doing some thinking about this, and I was reading Bataille's *La littérature et le mal*, and there's a passage I think I cite where he talks about recognition, but he's talking specifically about procreation, which is also relevant in terms of my critique of notions of lineage. This doesn't mean that my resistance to ideas of lineage implies an obliteration of every single line of connection. That's not what I mean. I'm so interested in encounter. I'm so open to it that at times I give myself over to encounter. It's never *en vase clos*. It's never an isolated fact. It's always, and none of these archaic notions of being completed through the presence of another matter, but the presence in a sense occurs – I'm thinking too fast now, I'm thinking about the empty city and the ruins and so on and so forth – but when I read that about recognition, I realize, this is not what it is. It's not that. And I discuss that a bit in this text where I say, you know, for some people seeing, encountering, someone who looks like them might actually be a way to enlarge their sense of self. But for me it's the exact opposite. It doesn't work that way. It does sort of become the thing I carry so in that sense, it augments, but it's not welcome. It's very upsetting. So maybe there's some element of self-hatred in there, who knows. I mean, it's complicated.

KE: Finally, one more passage I've written down here in my notes, and it refers back to something you mentioned earlier: 'I drain, accumulate, crumble, disperse, where I am incessantly repatriated, stateless, unsettled, deserter, deserted.' Again, this is familiar language for you. But, Nathanaël, if you were assembled, would you write at all?

NS: Probably not!

KE: You wouldn't? So would you regret this sense of revelation? What a threat.

NS: That's interesting. Thank you for that!

KE: I'm sure you've thought about this before.

NS: I have thought about it, but in different terms. The whole notion of finding an outside, even in the impossibility of an outside, is very personal in the sense that it's something I feel that I've inherited, or it was imposed on me growing up. My resistance to terms like 'autobiography,' 'confessionalism,' and so on is that these terms often seem to be ways of marginalizing work that might otherwise be relevant. I think that if I'm putting this, if I'm publishing this – it's not just a narcissistic gesture. It's because I think this is a conversation that is relevant, not just for me. It's not simply so you can trace from the biographical elements some of what I've written or substantiate something in the writing. You could say, 'Oh, she's resistant to lineage for these reasons.' And it's certainly true, and this I don't mind saying because I think I say it fairly explicitly in my next book – in

French, not in English yet – that, you know, my biological father is not the man who raised me. This is sort of true of many, many people. But what is strange about this, in addition to this man's violence toward my mother specifically, is that he was her first cousin. He's dead now. And so there's a really incestuous quality here. But the fact is that, so technically, this sort of antecedent is unique. It's a single antecedent. There isn't even the sort of benefit of two lineages, right? There's just one that sort of suffocates itself, and I only found this out later. I grew up with a father and a mother who, as far as I'm concerned, were my parents. And it was only when I started travelling to France regularly with them that this heritage was then imposed on me through these narratives, familial narratives. What sticks with me, and now becomes really instructive for me, is 'this is what you are whether you like it or not.' This was a phrase that came back very often, but I have always been a very independently minded person, ever since I was very small. And so I was confronted with this, and I put a lot of energy into resisting it. Yet, it doesn't change. It still had an enormous impact and was extremely devastating for my sense of self. I think that that comes into the work, and I can say that now. There was a time when if I had said that, I might have just fallen down and not been able to get up again. It was too much for me – the shame of it and everything else. I just couldn't hold that. Now I can hold it, which means that I can also let it go into the text without it being this thing that becomes cataclysmic, because maybe I have some control over it. Just by being able to speak of it.

Montreal, May 2008

SELECTED WORKS

This Imagined Permanence. Toronto: Gutter Press, 1996.

Je Nathanaël. Montreal: l'Hexagone, 2003.

Paper City. Toronto: Coach House Books, 2003.

Touch to Affliction. Toronto: Coach House Books, 2006.

L'Absence au lieu (Claude Cahun et le livre inouvert). Montreal: Nota bene, 2007.

The Sorrow and the Fast of It. Cold Spring, NY: Nightboat Books, 2007.

Absence Where As (Claude Cahun and the Unopened Book). New York: Nightboat Books, 2009.

Paper City

Colour is *élogieux*. But the absence of colour offers even greater allure, for desire brings language into being. And colour is an aspect – integral – of language. And integral means not only unperishable – not to be conflated with immortal, which will emerge no doubt in later versions of this same text – but visceral. The *version intégrale* of a work of literature is one that has not been altered, that has not been *tampered with*. They are the author's words as laid down by the author, as assembled and at times dismantled, as manipulated and too as astonished. For let it be said that while language astonishes the writer, the writer too astonishes language. Only the writer who astonishes language – who dares to *tamper* with it – is worthy of the epithet. Language is assuredly the author's tool, but it is also sediment, and when disturbed, may at once muddy and reveal. More importantly, sediment travels, over land, through the body, across the tongue. It is untouchable, and must not be revered.

Scatalogue

Books don't show the way but insist on remaining. So how to leave the book and enter directly into the body? We are jealous of one another's bodies yet we each have one. I would undress my tongue and dip it willingly into ice cold water would invite you to meet me where the body becomes transparent where lucidity is a function of the flesh where nothing is for sale and everything is given away. I would invent rude words for your mouth show you the true colour of blood. Love in the raw is life renewed. But of this write nothing down not a thing. Be wary of the heat that emanates from the unwritten page. Everything remains to be said so long as we have said nothing. Most importantly do not fear dirtying yourself. Love washes the body clean of perfection.

A Fuckable Text

What is a fuckable text and is it only fuckable in English ? Is there such a thing as a literary hard-on? Who wants Nathanaël? I do I do. Only he doesn't exist. He is not kissing you. He leaves no fold on your mattress. He doesn't break your heart. The tiled floor is cold and your feet are bare. Nathanaël is long gone he was never here not even once. He is a queer boy a loveable boy maybe even a fuckable boy and we are all wet or hard turning pages imagining his breath. You cannot even mourn him because he is not dead. He is not dead because he is not alive. Nobody knows who Nathanaël is. Have you seen him ? I have only seen him from behind in a painting and not a very good one at that. I hear he likes to run in the rain and sleep with his eyes open.

from The Sorrow and the Fast of It

You count the years leading away from me.

In adornment and philosophy. In rivers' edges and wrought bridges, rusted scaffolding.

Accuse me your city.

After the wide-angled sea. The tall pines felled. The stones where some sit. The waters seditiously.

Say : You but for the body fell against.

It is the same day.

It is the same day.

It is the mouth torn open on some seam.

§

I wandered inland. With the dogs uncomplaining. I turned my back to the sea and beckoned the land overtake me.

It was like this: a bookstand and a microphone. The day's sharp incision. The body draining. Un livre.

It was the man's need to speak. The impatient necks craning. The again and again of speech.

I listened for the many doors closing. The heart's sudden seizure. The compression of centuries into one solid moment of bereavement. The thing that I touched did not weep. The body did not fall in the street. And the man went on speaking.

No one said: Nathanaël fold into me.

Nor: What we destroyed of history we redeemed with inscription. The hand holds what is wounded in offering to some dream.

I turned the page and tore it.

The beasts shook their heads and showed their teeth.

§

Twice winter came.

The shadows shortened and then shortened again. Our bodies grew thin and our mouths kissed what was unnameable. We touched with our hands every place we had been.

The sky became stone and the city fell to ruin. The people drowned in their tears and the earth stank of urine.

The voice that rose in song broke what was left of speaking. What promises had been made became dust. What consolation unbelieving. The mouth stuttered and the ground with it.

We could not say What was. Nor Might have been.

It was every day ending and no way of telling.

The books later said we were forlorn. But it was different than that. We had seen our way to the heart's hard bone and broken it.

§

Touch what is left of leaving.

Lift the torn edge of sleep and swallow what is missing. The river spills we weaken. The bedsheet tears we are naked. The lines of glass score our soft palms there is little left of meaning. Not the cold ground. Nor this shameless idolatry. We speak. We are spoken. The call hollows the heart stalls the wild summons.

Come for me.

§

I went to Hell.

It was the same city all over again. It was the same scurveyed sun and the people milling. There was talk of sacrilege and a voice demanding. The street map buckled. It was all in good fun.

I walked to where the road caved. The little girl pulled her pants down. A goat died and we drank its blood. The buildings were jewelled and the signs read Slaughter.

I for one went missing.

We both died. We hadn't foresight enough to run.

from Absence Where As

( )

Book unbegun (promising) or unopened, closed or mourned, losing its leaves or devoured, the book remains a voracity for death over turned. Over turned, that is, displaced, but also usurped, underhanded. The lure of the book is the lure of every moment, bound and reread. Both escape us. And we, of course, escape it as well: the *relationship*, the *liaison*, the *correspondence* that we maintain with them (with the present and its dislocation) simultaneously reiterate ligature and detachment, seizure and collapse, echo and suffocation. All this time, all these questions, would have been necessary in order to arrive *there*, whose underside teaches us *there is not* distinguishable from *never* in that its fractured construction is perpetually susceptible to drainage. The inevitable uninhabitable attached to memory sewn into the skin of the thing that escapes us me you. The desire for belonging overcome by an even stronger desire – to defend against it – rejects the voluptuousness which would open all passages at once. Which would leave a space *precisely* for disjunctures and spillage. Which would cry out – write out – without a trope or even regret, or else saturated with sadness, merging itself, body and discord, with the waters that will submerge it, the littoral that will reshape it day after day, consecrating it in the absorption and volatility of a mutable shore imprinted with every possible *there*. Conceived and inconceivable. The neverending end of a gesture begun without beginning, scattered, diffuse and gathered into the uninhabited present of the inexhaustible desire of *there is* embraced by the JE that detaches from it: *desperately*.

As long as, in the very midst of a trajectory, we are on a verge of beginning, as long as we are in the space *between*, as long as we have not yet arrived, as long as we have not exhausted the vast expanse of movement, as long as we seek, one way or another, the *there is not*, as long as the place where we disappear ensures our continual disappearance, reassures us of it, as long as, spurred by the wounding desire that *turns (in) me*, we can say with the assurance that comes with having none at all: *there*.

The gesture of the book is the suicidal-murderous gesture that turns me back. Return is simply another crossing. The voracity for death over turned is the painful recognition of the inevitable uninhabitable upheld by a word that escapes us, that scars us, an unpronounceable word we have yet to encounter at the edge of a voice that doesn't know itself, doesn't recognize itself, other than in the unrecognizable echo, transformed. The book – praise, requiem, trace, plea, testament, suffering, erasure, insolence, injury, caress, blaze, sensuality, retreat – is possibly the *place*, the *there is not*, the *there*, at once exemplary, singular, banal. It is effluent and tributary. The first without arrival; the second without departure, repealing and amplifying one another, directed, but without real direction: aleatory.

The JE become other, intimated by the other who burdens her (burdens herself) with the unstable exchange of names and identitites, of *recognitions*, doesn't know who to blame anymore, doesn't know, in other words whom or what to speak to, *where* to begin, how to constitute *correspondence*. Reach remains caught in the hand from which it would extend, freely. It is caught taken tried.

JE is (am) caught taken held. Over turned. Turned in.

( )

There: neither beyond nor before but *affected*. Affected in every possible sense of the term without termination. Affected, that is *overcome, sickly* and *mad*. *There*: the place of our most debilitating disturbances, of our high aspirations, of our pains and our sufferings, excesses and mendacity, retreat.

I will speak to you of a book undelivered. Delivery without release. Without encumbrances. Deliverance for release, *It turns (in) me*. I don't emerge from *there* the place of which I speak to you, where I invite you, which invents me, invents you, boasts of itself, which arrives *there*, to you where I send it, will *enclose* me. When, from Brecht, the echo of his *An die Nachgeborenen* arrives all the way to me you, it is already late, there is only *there is not* on which to lean the ruined head, the insane eyes, the rest of its voice, sensorial, scattered on a ground that wants to melt into the next body that will fall: it will fall. I tally it all up, *in extremis*, at the end of a book, whichever one, where hands assemble to formulate the useless gesture of its continuation, carrier of vestiges that gorge the waterways, caverns and gutters of our prime garbage, of our infectious Cities. While guarding against naming what or whom ever. I know them all for having frequented them, and as a result none at all: slashed, rejected, defenestrated, from railings, bridges and balconies, swallowers of barbiturates, sleeping insomniacs, cancerous, stammered. Books undelivered, see. Survival, after which. That I read out loud quietly, mutterings of the end of time, the reminder, stinging, of the extremity toward which we mislead ourselves. What is that distance?

If I have one word to say, a single declaration to make, a single name to pronounce, it is the one, always, that doesn't come to mind, or too late, the receiver replaced, the voice at the other end of the line dissolved in the foreground noise that invites neither remembrance nor oblivion, but lack of attention, the fit of emotion that makes us answerable without requiring our presence: *there.*

GAIL SCOTT

KATE EICHHORN: In the United States, experimental prose has had a somewhat different history than it has had in Canada where, at least in an English-language context, it been marginalized on the literary terrain. How might we account for this difference, and has your time spent in residency in New York shifted your thinking on this question?

GAIL SCOTT: A huge question. During my residency here in New York, I've found it very nourishing to be among so many formally radical writers. We are a sparser group at home in Montreal. There is an avant-garde prose tradition in the U.S. that is traceable both in New York and along the west coast back a long way, from Stein, Jane Bowles, Djuna Barnes, through the Beats and the near contemporaries like Kathy Acker, Burroughs – mostly queer, by the way – and on up to the present. I don't feel entirely comfortable comparing here to Canada – because I am normally located in Québec and don't extensively know what is happening at the ground level in other regions. But there does exist, pancontinentally, a loose network of experimental prose writing located between the poetry world and the more commercial world of the novel-as-product. People are doing all kinds of weird and wonderful things with the novel in Canada, but as far as I know – and this is in part due to demographics – there is not the same depth of commitment to experimental prose. Some writers start out doing amazing innovative work – Michael Ondaatje, to take a famous example – but mellow out at a certain point. Could this be because national identity questions keep popping up in Canada? It's hard to work with a disintegrating writing subject – which is for me what formally distinguishes experimental prose from innovative prose – and cope with national identity issues at the same time. In both countries, the conversation with poetry is crucial for experimental prose writers. In fact, the San Francisco queer New Narrative writers emerged in part as a response to Language writing, while, concomitantly in Québec, as I've said elsewhere, there was a moment of very experimentally formal work, organized around gender issues, more feminist than queer, that paralleled what was happening in San Francisco in the '80s when the New Narrative group emerged. Living here in New York has made it easier to think of myself in that space between poetry and prose that seems to be the most productive for me. I have been going to every reading I can go to at the Poetry Project and at the Segue Series at the Bowery Poetry Club, and that means at least two per week. There is also the excellent Belladonna Series at Dixon Place. And what I have learned about writing since I've been here, I've learned mostly from poets.

KE: There was also the talk you gave at the CUNY Graduate Center. This was an interesting event for a number of reasons. You've talked before about the need to create a space for dialogue on experimental prose writing, and the discussion after your presentation, especially your dialogue with Renee Gladman and Eileen Myles, suggests that other prose writers share your desire to open up such a space. But there was also a division that occurred in the room. After the talk, some of the poets were upset. You also felt that some of the poets didn't quite understand your paper or the discussion that followed. What happened?

GS: As experimental prose writers, we're used to resistance from some poets – those married to genre, I guess. Living among poets is absolutely essential to our work because it keeps us focused on language. Talking to some fiction writers about the mechanics of our craft leaves me bored out of my mind – the preoccupation with 'characterization' and transparency loses track of the work on language, syntax, complex subjectivities – the stuff of experimental prose investigation. So, while speaking to poets is absolutely essential, I talked to several of the prose writers after the CUNY talk who agreed – we haven't managed to convey the particular problems and issues connected with this kind of work. And the specific space it can actually occupy, which means saying to poets, 'Move over a little bit and let us in,' but which has also been saying for a long time to the other side of the spectrum, 'We're not one of you either.' As a group – and it varies very much within the group – the relationship between words, sentences, paragraphs is foregrounded. I experience the sentence, and not everyone experiences the sentence this way – Ron Silliman, for example, doesn't experience the sentence this way – but I do experience the sentence as a sort of problematic summary or look back. The effort of crafting a sentence leads to a moment of closure, I think. I see that space between sentences as an abyss. And it's very hard for me to then traverse that space toward the next sentence – it's actually extremely hard work – projecting a contiguity but not a traditional contiguity, which works something out in relationship to reality, which is not a relationship of trying to mirror reality. Notwithstanding the focus on language, it's not exactly the job that poets are doing. It's not what prose poetry is about either. And it's certainly a different exercise than mainstream fiction.

KE: So where is the line between something like west-coast Canadian writer Fred Wah's prose poems and the type of prose tradition you're locating yourself in relation to?

GS: I don't think there's a line. I think they are all variances springing from similar impulses. Fred is actually one of the people in Canada who I think really understands my work and whose work I really admire. We have in common complex, conflicted backgrounds and a kind of political idealism. I think Fred is more committed to the space of poetry than I am, though he's also a remarkable prose writer. I love the spare yet complex beauty of his work. I write from Montreal, and there's a lot more 'packing' in Montreal language and consequently in my prose, because of constant direct interference of the other, or other, languages. You've got layers of language that get squashed together and because, and I hate to repeat this because it has been said so often, but it's true, when you're translating all the time, you keep attempting to grab other moments of meaning or emphasis or noise from the neighbouring language of speech or writing. I experience Montreal as, verbally, a way noisier city than, say, Vancouver, or Edmonton. There is so much talk in the air. That's the way I experience it.

KE: This noise is very apparent in your new work, which you read at the Poetry Project a couple of weeks ago. Here you have this regionally distinctive architecture, the architecture of the Montreal triplex, holding the novel together in a way, but what is most striking about the work are the multiple layers of language, since in this case, you're working with French, English and Cree.

GS: Well, it's not actually Cree but English spoken by people who a generation or two ago were speaking an Algonquian language. In those passages I read at the Poetry Project – for example, the one about the fly on the plate rail – the accent is the accent I heard in my family, and which I hear from Native people speaking who are fairly close to their original language. The really hard thing about writing this prose work is that I had to set it in Montreal because I don't think I know anything about Native life. I have relatives who are Native, but I have never lived in a day-to-day way on or near a Native community or in a Native context – unless you count time spent with my fairly closeted maternal grandparents. So I had to extend a Montreal context into that thing that exceeds, that cannot be put into words, to torque a phrase from Derrida, talking about the future anterior. I didn't want to do flashbacks. I hate that! I enjoy the challenge of getting something of the effect of a novelistic flashback or reminiscence by torquing language into a composite present. One of the reasons I decided to use film noir as a kind of template for the novel was to be able to avail myself of the device called analepsis – where you are going along, driving along the road, and suddenly you have this black-and-white insert entering the picture to expose what happened before. The analeptic device proved useful for bringing in these crazy family members from time to time too, plunked in some corner of the Montreal Mile-End flat. It worked to import them to Montreal, because there is the same kind of working class, not terribly confident or aggressive, not really good at the mainstream stuff, that I recognize sometimes in members of my own family, and that you can see a lot in east-end Montreal. The triplex frames it all, just like a stage set, and there are all these things going on through the walls and coming up through the floors from the ground under – where once stood Montreal's Crystal Palace, a trope for British colonization, based on the Crystal Palace from the 'mother country.'

KE: During your reading, after some time, the listener starts to think through the layers. There's a stereoscopic effect.

GS: That's what I'm aiming for. I've been thinking, retrospectively, that I learned this from Gertrude Stein. That is – I realized, reading Ulla Dydo's Stein book, how much Stein had formed my understanding of the relationship between reading and writing. She read Stein and all Stein's archives and notes, a lifetime's worth. And then she wrote a book that said, to grossly re-interpret: When you read Stein, often, you don't necessarily know what is 'happening,' but after you've finished, you're in her element. It's like a wash – you get all these layers and sounds and colours and vibrations that you may not be able to put into words right away. The effect is astounding. Recently, I was amused, reading *Blood on the Dining-Room Floor*, to see that, a certain number of pages in, Stein says, if you're confused, go back and read again from the beginning. Which is often what I want to say to people when they complain about the fact that my work is hard to follow. The thing about Stein is that you get meaning but you just don't get it right away. And it's meaning through language, but also as if through music and other forms of composition, as opposed to 'meaning' in the usual more direct sense.

KE: You get it through an affective structure as opposed to representation?

GS: Partly. Reading Stein takes you to another dimension in terms of sound, but sound that does not leave the work of language behind. Especially in her really nutty pieces, there's that silly yet riveting nonsensical child voice that goes on. And on. And on. Once you finish reading, even if you don't 'follow,' you end up in a space that is both affect and thinking. That's what good poetry is like too. You don't necessarily get it from line to line, you don't necessarily feel you have to. With a novel, people feel like they have to get it page by page. Often, in experimental prose, the language work gets left unnoticed in the reader pursuit of instant meaning. Because we are increasingly taught to read thematically.

KE: So are your characters, your narratives, generated by the syntax? In other words, where do you start? Where did a novel like *My Paris* begin?

GS: It varies. *My Paris* was originally going to be a travel piece about Paris using Benjamin's *Arcades Project* as a guide-map. So, from the beginning it was about reading and about collage – for the *Arcades Project* is a vast heap of found material. So, every day, I read Benjamin's *Arcades Project*, and then I got up and walked around Paris, not necessarily to visit the precise site read about earlier that morning. Though I was constantly on the lookout for the passages, the arcades. When I got finished describing these walks about Paris, these conversations with the city and with Benjamin, I thought, this is a potboiler and I'm finally going to make some money. It took me two years to do this. Then I thought, this is not me. First of all, the 'I' that was walking around was bumptious, unbearable. It was like 19th-century travel writing. I eventually realized that if I wrote in present participles the speaking subject was reduced to this tiny porous thing. As a traveller, she was infinitely more contemporary. She'd left her baggage, her biases, her preconceived ideas back home. Sort of. More and more, *My Paris* became a collage of found moments.

With this new book, the first draft was very blah-blah, sing-song. I also really hated it.

KE: When did you start working on the current book and how has it changed since?

GS: In the early 2000s, but I kept putting it aside because I couldn't figure out how to do it. How to get round these hyper-romantic tableaus both of Montreal and the family-quest novel that has been much appreciated lately. I had to find a way to boil it down so that the language was suggestion, was essence, and I finally thought the answer was to make it more theatrical. The first draft that I wrote, I was thinking, if I could write a novel where there is a kind of mid-sagittal dissection – where you take a brain and slice it vertically – if I could write a novel where I could just play with all that stuff going on in this imaginary brain, I would be able to pull it off.

But that didn't quite work either. I had to find another way. I kept making it more grounded in Montreal, absorbing writing from admired authors, psychoanalysts, historians, you name it – this importing of modes of language and thinking from other work helped project the story on to all kinds of planes which are social and political. For example, in the last chapter, I'm using the *Report of the Royal Commission Appointed to Investigate the Conditions of the Half-Breed Population in Alberta*. You wouldn't believe how racist this document is, from 1936. I have a lesbian historian speaking at the bottom of the page, to set us straight, every once in a while, in a matter-of-fact and vaguely righteous way, about the background to what really happened at various times in the novel.

KE: But there's also an element of magical realism in the new work, which is a shift for you. I'm assuming that it's not a coincidence that this coincides with your decision to take up questions of colonialism more directly.

GS: I don't know whether I'd call it magical realism. Magical realism seems to me to be part of the storytelling tradition. It has the kind of seamlessness that tales designed to bewitch have. I use *Dial M for Murder*, a film noir, as a template. But although it gives you the odd, hilarious, really great axiom, it's clear throughout that the template is being torqued to suit the circumstances. Poe's influence gets into the novel as well, with a young Québécois cop in the stairwell, who is supposed to be hacking the protagonist's computer, but mostly he's dreaming of playing Ligeia – from one of Poe's classic stories. Ligeia dies, and her mourning husband marries again, but his new bride immediately starts dying slowly because the dead first wife, Ligeia, is actually inside her, resuscitating through her body. So you've got this junior police surveillant whose father is a taxi company owner and gay. Everyone is gay in the novel. The father is a uniform fetishist. He finds his son too effeminate, so he makes him go into the police force. It's all silly, but there is some language from 'Ligeia' in the novel, and that's what gives it its weird surreal atmosphere.

KE: But what about the place of allegory in your work? Going back to *My Paris*, we see your debt to Benjamin, a great allegorist. Reading Baudelaire recently, I also started to wonder about the influence of Baudelaire on your writing. But Native languages are also deeply allegorical at the level of the sentence, storytelling and rhetoric. How do these connections play out in your new work?

GS: I've only started to think about this recently, because I've been thinking so much about my grandfather, but one thing I distinctly remember about the way he brought me up – and we spent a lot of time with him as kids, is that he would never tell us *do* or *don't*. It was always a story, always a story, and it was allegorical. It could be that my love of Benjamin, in this weird way that all these connections come together without your ever knowing it, is also about my love of my grandfather, his stories, the way he talked, which again is very different than my father's side, which is Anglican and Scottish.

KE: I think the convergence of traditions is fascinating. You've gravitated to two very different traditions, or perhaps as you suggest, one led to the other?

GS: I actually think those two traditions have crossed over in Canadian culture a lot more than we realize, and that's one of the reasons I wanted to write this novel. There is a kind of roots tendency in novels where people discover or investigate their heritage. It's not the kind of writing I do. Rather, I am interested in investigating whatever it is that creeps into the language and gestures of people around me, the way they walk, and talk, the way they relate to the world around, from their past and from their immediate context, and that's all really, really good stuff for a prose writer.

KE: In your selections for this collection, you've included one paragraph from a new essay, 'GS + GS,' in which you talk about the sentence as a kind of gesture.

GS: In the Gertrude Stein piece, I recount how I often sit in restaurants in Montreal and watch people in profile to see what language they're speaking. It's amazing, but you can tell if it is French or English, which are the two languages you most often hear in Montreal restaurants. Francophones tend to talk from the tips of their lips. I can talk to you for a half-hour in English and barely move my lips, but you cannot do that in French, because it's all right out here. It's very hard for an Anglophone to reproduce that. But that interests me, and that's a gesture for me, and then it interests me how that movement or gesture translates into cadence on the page, and again, it's more fun to write sentences with that in mind because then you can get up a clip in a paragraph – there is a movement in the mouth and a sound and that translates onto paper.

KE: So do you think about grammar as having a sort of corporeality or embodiment?

GS: Sometimes. At first it embodies and then it reifies.

KE: Can you elaborate?

GS: I remember once reading somewhere that god isn't dead because we still have grammar. Which I found extremely funny. The way you have to write in the academy or the kind of pressure to write in a certain way that contextualizes most public language gestures requires using syntax in a very communicative manner, and, I think, often in a way that inhibits thinking outside the box. I really hesitate to talk about body and speech. It's so hard to do adequately, but obviously there is a corporeal or gestural relationship there that grammar often cannot hold. So, yes, grammar is both 'good' and 'bad,' if you like. Grammar holds and expresses and shapes things in an utterly necessary way. For example, take the difference between languages. It's so interesting that Germans leave the verb until the end, entirely different from the way we speak in English. I love working in English because it is so elastic, has imported, and somehow seems easily able to absorb influences of other cultures – in a way that doesn't seem to work so well in French. But no sooner do I say this than I feel embarrassed, because there is obviously a colonial aspect to the phenomenon of one language sucking up another.

KE: I'd like to follow up on a few observations you made earlier – you observed that it's always been the case that a disproportionate number of experimental prose writers are queer. This seems to be true, but is there a way to account for this?

GS: Really, what does 'queer' mean in terms of everyday life? A take on the world? I don't think you can generalize, but since art and eros are closely linked, let's just say I occupy space in a way that is quite distinct from the way space, particularly erotic space, is organized in dominant middle-class heterosexual reality. And let's face it, that latter is the space of an awful lot of novels. Queer implies slippery boundaries. Translate that into the subject of a piece of writing and you can see the piece of writing might well come out differently from, say, something David Adams Richards would write. But I don't really understand it. I only know that when I read a novel that involves a heterosexual romance – even though I've written one, though it's also a queer novel because there is also a girl love interest in it – or when I go to a movie or watch a straight love scene on TV, I'm in a foreign country. There is a way that I perceive the world that's outside of that reality, a space that remains essentially socially

unstable, and slippy-slidey. Consequently the writing subject speaks
à côté. She is constantly re-composing herself. And that makes her utterly
contemporary.

KE: But this is the big question: how did you come to the novel in the first
place? With all your great political credentials, what led you to a 'bourgeois'
form like the novel? When you were working on *Spare Parts* and *Heroine*,
you were, after all, already surrounded by poets.

GS: Well, I don't think I do the bourgeois novel, and I don't think that
Mary Burger or Bob Glück or Renee Gladman and countless other people
are doing it now.

KE: Now, but what about in the 1980s?

GS: I was in Québec and working with people like Nicole Brossard,
France Théoret, Louky Bersianik, who were writing very radical novels.
Picture Theory is an incredibly radical piece of work. So is Théoret's *Nous
parlerons comme on écrit*. But it was a radical period for letters across
the continent. I feel lucky to have started writing at that moment and in
that place.

KE: Do you feel that there is any more space in English Canada now?

GS: Yes. I wonder if English Canada is not going through a more radical
period right now in writing than Québec. There are many writers, espe-
cially poets across the country, of whom I am a huge fan.

KE: I want to return to another issue raised after your talk at the CUNY
Graduate Center. Eileen Myles pointed out that there are also many
working-class writers who have chosen to work in experimental prose, as
if they require a larger canvas to stage their interventions.

GS: Eileen's is the voice of a woman who has nobody sending her
cheques for down payments. Added to that is her way of being queer in
the world, and the seamlessness she seeks to achieve between the writer
and the writing. It's a wonderful project. When I stop to think about it,
a lot of us do come from blue-collar or lower-middle-class backgrounds.
Add to that the queer and experimental factors, and perhaps the tendency
to be a little desultory is explained. It's a combination of circumstances
that sets us up nicely for deconstructing many of the tenets of the novel
form. We're trying to be socially ascendant inasmuch as we are trying to
get our work out there, but it's a struggle. One of the big issues that a lot

of us have is the labour intensity of the work, trying to do what poets are doing in a way and trying to do some of what novelists are doing – it takes twice as much time. So we are a group of people who feel like we should be able to make money from our work like mainstream novelists so we can go on writing eight hours a day, but none of us or few of us do. We're not part of the economy at all, and that's a source of frustration sometimes.

KE: At least if you are an experimental poet, in Canada, you can apply for a grant and your work might be recognized as poetry, but this isn't the case for experimental prose writers. Most fiction juries have no vocabulary, no way of understanding, your work.

GS: True, it's more difficult. As far as those lucrative literary prize dollars, forget it. Erin Mouré once told me I would never win the Governor General's Award. I don't think it was intended as a criticism of my writing. Virtually every time I apply to the anglophone jury of Le Conseil des arts et des lettres du Québec, I am turned down. I have better luck with the francophone juries. So that points to a difference. I've also had relatively few Canada Council grants. But of course, writers here in the U.S. don't even have those options.

KE: It's a much larger discussion, but the material reality is that doing this work, this kind of writing, is full of risk.

GS: It is. But I started my career as a journalist. I worked as a journalist for about seven years, and I was successful, quite young. I made a lot of money, but I felt like I was participating in something that I really didn't want to participate in. I was telling the truth the best I could, whatever the truth is, but I couldn't really say what I had to say, and I felt cheap, like it was a bad thing to do. Then I thought, okay, I can be successful in a public way if I want, but it's not what I want. I want to do the work I think I should do. That experience made it easier for me than for a lot of people to take those risks – it does make a difference if you've had a little success. I've made the choice to risk failure in market terms. I don't like having so little fruits for my labours, but at least I'm doing what I think I should be doing.

KE: My final set of questions concerns gender and feminism. Your essays in *Spaces Like Stairs* advanced a discourse on feminist poetics. Although it has been over two decades since this collection was published, I continue to meet younger writers in Canada and the U.S. who have read these essays and consider them to be very influential. But I wonder, do you still consider gender and feminism important to discussions of experimental writing?

GS: Let me answer this in a kind of roundabout way. A while ago, Lisa Robertson read in Montreal, and this was when she was in California working with Lyn Hejinian at Berkeley, and someone asked her if she was a Language writer now, and she said – I hope I'm not misquoting her: 'No, I don't relate to any particular school, except I would say that I am a feminist writer.' And I thought, maybe now to say you're a feminist writer is to make a statement about your aesthetics. Maybe you're no longer in danger of being immediately reduced to a posture of political correctness. I'm a feminist and a writer, so does that make me a feminist writer? Having been through the left, and involved in a lot of discussions on art and politics, I agree with the idea that an artist needs, as Trotsky and Breton put it in their famous manifesto: *toute licence en art*. If you're a feminist, and you care about women, it's going to show in your work, but I don't think about it in terms of talking in the first instance to women, for example, as I did as a very young writer. And which was a very heady experience. It gave me permission to express my wildness. To experiment, to shout, to play. It's just who I am, and above all, feminism is a big part of why I am as interested in form as I am.

KE: In nearly all the essays in *Spaces Like Stairs*, you write about subjectivity. There is a subject-in-process, a subject becoming, but it's still a female subject. It's still a very gendered subject. The sutured subject that you describe in your new essay, parts of which appear in this collection, represents a shift for you. The sutured subject seems to be beyond gender.

GS: One thing that I think some poets don't get is that there is a way in which experimental prose writers work on questions of subjectivity very much like poets do. In other words, the subject is very much embedded in language, as opposed to having a subject you want to represent from the start. The word 'sutured' is very important because there is a way of faking sewing all of it all back together again in all kinds of weird and wonderful ways to make it imply 'story,' but the subjectivity that gets projected is not some mirror version of a supposed reality. It's like Humpty Dumpty. Who needs to be put back together again. But how? I had this intuition all along. I remember in *Spaces Like Stairs* – and a lot of those pieces were polemics, written as interventions for conferences or debates with other women writers – but even then, I was aware of not wanting a certain PC notion of feminism or any political notion to close down the writing. What I like about the notion of queer, I guess, is that it operates back and forth over cusps between gender impulses or between any impulses. The fly, in this new book, is both a guy and her alter ego, a good solution for a 'femme' sort of lesbian. I'm interested in all kinds of cusps – where gender impulses meet, where languages meet, et cetera.

KE: So it doesn't seem like it's about identity at all, which always comes back to some form of political positioning.

GS: I agree. Yet, it's a funny thing – it's very difficult, without some kind of identitary connections, to be in the world, to be in a community, to be an artist.

KE: But the sutured subject is more fluid, or perhaps more accurately, as you suggest, fractalling.

GS: It is fractalled. It started with locating myself in the space between French and English, and trying to manifest simultaneously in writing the various planes of that posture. After a while I think I got interested in other cusps as well. Some radical feminist lesbians used to say the lesbian is not a woman. I was utterly shocked when I first heard it. But it's true that there is some part of us that falls quite wide of what is called feminine. Yet, can't you say this about many women, whatever their sexual preference?

KE: In 'The Sutured Subject,' you're primarily writing about other writers' work. Although you reference a few writers of your own generation, including Kathy Acker, most of your references are to a younger group of American experimental prose writers – Renee Gladman, John Keene, Mary Burger and Pamela Lu. These seem to be the writers with whom you're most closely aligned now.

GS: They write differently – quite differently than I do – but they are the first group of people who are expressing something I have been consistently trying to express formally. Again, most of these writers are queer, and a lot of them come from backgrounds other than white, mainstream backgrounds. They all experience cusps in some way too.

KE: You've also started to distance yourself from the New Narrative writers but perhaps, this was an alignment of necessity? Your project was always different.

GS: I feel like the work we're talking about has New Narrative on one side, and I don't know what on the other side ... something much closer to poetry on the other side.

New York, December 2008

SELECTED WORKS

Spare Parts. Toronto: Coach House Press, 1981. Reissued as *Spare Parts Plus Two* by Coach House Books, 2002.

Heroine. Toronto: Coach House Press, 1987. Reissued by Talonbooks, 1997.

Spaces Like Stairs. Toronto: The Women's Press, 1989.

Main Brides. Toronto: Coach House Press, 1993. Reissued by Talonbooks, 1997.

My Paris. Toronto: The Mercury Press, 1999.

from Everyday Grammar

'The Real Light of Day'

Falls through th' casement. Casting hard truths on ~~feces~~ *Face*, barely visible behind th' railway flat venetians. *Hey! Stay put [Face] while we go to get th' story!* YES, we disburse. Often. For reason of. Serotonin: Bumping on bed. Like you X, you little diapered baby. Pretending to be Bottom. Or I/R leaving Room + climbing up to bar at 4848 boul-Saint, cloche hat, relaxed flowing skirt. Watching similarily turned-out millennials. Climbing even higher. Past arched bar door to Lili St-Cyr revival, th' inimitable showgirl disrobing, ca. 1940, on Sala Rossa stage, in long golden mane, holding a pheasant, which pheasant fanning out obligingly under glimmering red star of worker solidarity. But just as R fytyr novel space opening. Wide as the legs of a porn queen. Or straight girl with butch going down on her – oh they do spread for good head – Peter of New York listing dangerously through Spanish-arched bar door, black coat jerky sideways tangoing toward stuccoed plywood counter, empathy patch quivering:

– Elvira, you Uke, I love you!

– Jewish Uke, Dude, there's a difference, retorting blonde barmaid, space, conspicuous, between teeth.

– This place's full of ghosts, thinking P [guilty, a little Uke himself]. Reaching, on bias, th' crescent stucco bar, anxiously spreading arms + ordering amaretto for all, while sifting versinthed-muscle-relaxed cerebrum for bloody cheap-tweed phantom lying akimbo on long white-tiled basement bathroom floor, th' sweet smell of crack sliding from cubicle row of singing doors.

– *That washroom's right out of* Dial M for Murder, *huh?* –

Smiling + watching, sideways, th' curved bar of amaretto-tipping mouths for approval. A serendipitous error. To use to R benefit.

Peter has served his purpose.

from The Sutured Subject

As a prose writer who shares with radical poets the notion that contemporaneity is more democratically expressed with smaller subjects, with the fractalling of communicative or emotive language, I resist the idea defended by some poets that the poetic line can best pull off this democracy of space. I believe there are countless ways to deploy sentences to capture the flickering moment Walter Benjamin called *jetzheit*. By extension, sentences in their relations to each other are admirably suited to projecting that 'now-time' into a larger telling, much as Benjamin's angel of history, though wanting to examine the past, is blown forward by a strong wind while gazing back at the past's detritus. The sentence, like the angel, involves both a glancing back, a summary, and, if adequately torqued in shape and in relation, a ride through the dynamic present. Crucial to this operation of expressing *jetzheit* in prose is the work of subverting the singular writing subject – the angel is both subject and object – allowing other voices in to intervene from both the past and the present ...

from My Paris

Raining. Cats. Therefore returning to divan. Lying back on finest black-and-white sheets. To point of silky. Like Balzac's *Girl with Golden Eyes*. Naturellement no marquise. Keeping 'one' sequestered. For sake of love. With old duenna, servant. Bringing fresh bread. Rich delicate butter. Picked by chance from fromagerie's 10 sorts. Jam. Coffee. Anyway – returning to divan. And lifting heavy volume of B's *Paris, Capitale du XIXe*. From turquoise roxy-painted bedside table. Subtitle *Le livre des passages*. *Passagenwerk* in German. Not yet available in English. Therefore weighing the more delightfully on wrists. **Not** a real history. Rather – vast collection of 19th-century quotes and anecdotes. Initially seeming huge pile of detritus. But – on looking closer. More like montage. Possibly assembled using older surrealist trick. Of free association. I opening at contents' list. 'A' – Passages – glass-roofed arcades, malls. Hawking 19th century's new imperial luxury. Juxtaposed on '**B**' – *Mode*. Each new season. Ironizing time. Next to '**C**' – *Antique Paris, catacombes, démolitions* – Paris's underpinnings. Pointing to '**D**' – *L'ennui* – Eternal Return. Present tense of a dandy. Hovering over '**E**' – *Haussmannisation, combats des barricades* – Haussmann's wide boulevards. Versus the people. Progress's double coin. Segueing into '**J**' – Poet *Baudelaire*. First modern. Peer of '**K**'– *Flâneur*– whose initial post–French revolutionary languor not ultimately resisting rising capitalist market. '**X/Y**' – *Marx* – realism. Next to *Photography* ... *Social movements. Dolls. Automatons.*

A person could wander here for months.

from The Sutured Subject

In an essay called 'Why.Prose?' I attempt to unpack the question of how to simultaneously foreground both language and story, how in this foregrounding to continue writing over the cramped space of the period that leads to the beginning of the next sentence. ... Each of my novels has attempted a different answer to this question of tension between texture and narrative. In *My Paris*, my last published novel, written mostly in present participles, the erasure of active verbs almost cruelly reduces the subject, rendered small and porous by grammatic incision, the better to absorb the maximum of the moment, shot through with multiple shards of urban sounds and tropes. In reducing the speaking subject, the performative relationship to the city around it is enhanced. My current novel, *The Obituary*, has a narrator quite simply splayed into parts, not all of them her own, and these, to some extent, correspond to a family narrative of hybridity and assimilation. ...

... (But) in prose where language is foregrounded, or mid-grounded, what is the site of the eternally returning unspeakable moment? Does it exist within the text as a ghost or shadow? Does its posture of resistance or flawed relations with dominant discourses/languages allow it to shift in and out of the gaps, the narrative shadows? Does one finger the fissures of subjectivity, rent by intervening voices, until it metonymizes into a kind of music, or floating gravity? Models can be found in visual art: one can read the textual traces that somehow point to South Africa's terrible history in the banal figures of Johannesburg artist William Kentridge, for example. For what it's worth, post-Freudian analysts like Abraham and Torok also stressed that we are mostly haunted by the secrets of others, down through the generations, other voices that try to make us perform on the stage of society like ventriloquists. In narration, the play between contiguity and disjunction is also the play between agency and interruption, raising the possibility of dialoguing with both the uncanny (dream, fantasy, the dark spaces of genre fiction [Delaney's *Dhalgren*, for instance]), and the social. Yes, in this writing, a rhetorical edge gets added to poetic thinking. Let's just call it prose.

from Main Brides

On St. Patrick's Day, Lydia came in shaking off the weather. So nondescript as to be ... effectively indescribable. Inside, the place all decked in green. Green beer in the glasses. Also green were the bread rolls served with the meals. She chose a chair carefully at an angle, not to see the stuffed birds and animals perched along the walls. This time the 'true' Norma jean was there (only two tables over). Looking once more different. In tweed jacket, jodhpur-style pants, peaked cap, nicely fitting sweater whose colour reflected a thread in the jacket. In fact, every colour-detail matching every other. 'To the point of anal,' thought Lydia. A little envious of the quality of N.j's female companion: obviously a dancer in print silk shirt, very muscled legs in good black tights with a seam up the back and nice little boots. To whom Norma jean was desperately trying to speak French. 'Ouiii, la mode, maiy ...' Then switching to English to make her point. 'Sure style's everything in art. But don't you think it's important to some- how represent social notions, like race, class?'

'Eh bien,' the woman replied, provocatively, 'comme l'indépendance du Québec?'

Lydia nearly laughed. Wiping with effort the smirk off her face. To concentrate on her placemat, the writing of her dream. Another *Bird Dream*, in fact. She picked up her pen, noting (in the corner of her eye) that Norma jean had glanced over. While saying loudly, earnestly, to the dancer that every national minority should be represented equally in the main government institutions and culture-producing groups. This made the Québécoise angry. Norma jean added humbly she maybe wasn't living enough yet in French to understand the nuances. 'If I'm going to get anywhere, I have to learn the French they speak here.'

'You have to learn French, period, sweetheart,' said Lydia. Trying to think of an appropriate line from 'Donkey Riding.' (*Were you ever in Québec, Riding on a Donkey ...*)While taking stock of N.j's hypocritical English way of pretending to be polite when the mat gets yanked out from underneath your feet. Gently touching the dancer's arm. Who (surpris- ingly) returned the favour. Was it possible the two of them were friends?

A nerve twitched on Lydia's elegant cheek. She wrote, taking care to make the I's big and swarthy (a sign the ego is intact): *My father and mother and some others taking baby birds in their hands (me not objecting to my mother so much as to the others). Of course I kind of want to pick them up too. There seems to be an unusually close relationship in this dream between animals and people. Looking around in this kind of garden we're in, I notice several people – children I think, in part – in a tree, perched on branches as if they were birds too. I do the same, sitting on the very top of a tree with a very smooth trunk and hardly any branches.*

Lydia stopped writing. Her head inexplicably burgeoning as if a big turd were pressing on top. Like at the osteopath's, involving some reference to her father. His weak lips only trembling as he bathed her. A man afraid to ask for what he wanted. Unlike Ralph, whose gnarled hands were pounding more impatiently on the bar table. Making the war medals pinned to the jacket he wore over his old sailor's twisted-with-arthritis body tinkle loudly. Finally staggering to his feet. Weaving as if his skinny, bowed legs were planted on some stormy deck. 'Annie,' he called, giggling and pointing sheepishly to his glass: 'It's empty.'

Lydia looked at Norma jean. Who was trying to change the subject of conversation before she made another gaffe: 'I had a nightmare,' she said, unconsciously cupping her large breast in her hand. While the dancer took in every word (and gesture). Probably pretending to be mesmerized in order to get her dance troupe on a tour of English Canada. Lydia smiled mockingly. Busily writing the rest of her dream: *Suddenly I have to get down from the tree covered with bird-children in a hurry. Looking at the slim branchless smooth erected trunk I'm sure that I will die. The trunk is very smooth and hard, a kind of reddish brown. But I slide down somehow (with an umbrella?) and feel victorious. However, there's trouble in the house. Which is an old wooden structure, possibly made of logs, with pine-slatted floors. And a separate entrance for the public. I can't remember what I might have done wrong.*

N.j's companion said in broken English: 'Night Mare. Your nights are full of mares. I like thees Eenglish word.' Norma jean smiling slightly sadly: 'Except I dreamed I shot my mother.' (On the tape deck Bob Marley was singing *I Shot the Sheriff*.) Adding with a wistful grin on her face: 'But I didn't shoot her deputy.'

from The Sutured Subject

I see these narrative efforts as a little like Rilke's experiments with reading the coronal suture, as reported by the media theorist Friedrich Kittler, himself fascinated by Rilke's observation of a baby's skull. The poet reported, says Kittler in *Gramophone, Film, Typewriter*, that 'A trace or path or groove appears where the frontal and parietal bones of the 'suckling infant' – to use Rilke's anatomically correct term – have grown together.' As if 'the facilitations of Freud and Exner had been projected out of the brain onto its enclosure, the naked eye is now able to read the coronal suture as a writing of the real ...' Apply a gramophone needle to these coronal sutures, or *to any anatomical surface*, and what they yield, upon replay, 'is a primal sound without a name, music without notation, a sound ever more strange than any incantation for the dead for which the skull could have been used.' Instead of making melancholic associations with the skeleton, like, say, Hamlet, the markings traced on the cylinder are, for the writer, physiological traces. Does not our own nervous system, our own body (=) the outside world?

from My Paris

Raining. Entering café lit by giant geometric teardrops. Suspended from ceiling. Smaller wall versions. Over curly-pawed tables. Pretty but unheated. So sitting far from window. R arriving almost simultaneously. *Le Nouvel Obs* in hand. On cover **Fifteen Leading Intellectuals**. Derrida. Lyotard. Deleuze. Etc. All worriedly reflecting on growing entrenchment of Right. Which Right they having spent lives striving to philosophically defeat. By *en principe* displacing. Deferring. Huge Western I. Casting unecological shadow. Over earth. Malheureusement issue **not** including Kristeva. Weil. Arendt. Irigaray. Bucci-Glücksman. Collin. Wittig. Nor any other woman.

Maybe women too busy with 1000 little details. To be seen as truly philosophical. I ironizing to R. Nodding at several pointed bras. Under well-pressed sweaters. A la mode again. The shape of women's silhouettes. Expressing something of epoch. Crinoline for imperialist expansion. Or 'sadistic' bloomers (B saying). At outset of suffragettes. R agreeing feminine. In Paris. Considered dangerous. Therefore requiring effort to contain. Through discipline of hyper-female roles. Albeit he protesting men also wearing perfume. Carrying purses. Then smiling fake-embarrassed. With pleasant friendly mouth. Of guy from Winnipeg.

from The Sutured Subject

One might ask: Is the most radical impulse shared by experimental prose writers this negative fixation on spaces among sentences, among layers of narrative, suggesting a hysterical relationship between self and the world, along the fault lines of the fissured and often campily re-sutured subject-in-becoming? (Renee) Gladman (among others) offers a temporal take on this process: the sentence-in-becoming is a register of the phenomenon of being-in-life, its sequences using a kind of heightened language giving a heightened sense of personhood, produced by an endless crossing of genres that involves, among other things, the production of failed sentences. Gladman calls this failure – i.e., a sentence or suite of sentences where 'person' can only be represented partially – not FICTION, but prose. This reminds me of an art statement by Kentridge ...

> *I have never tried to make illustrations of apartheid, but the drawings and films are certainly spawned by and feed off the brutalized society left in its wake. I am interested in a political art, that is to say an art of ambiguity, contradiction, uncompleted gestures ... in which optimism is kept in check and nihilism at bay...*

from Heroine

March 8: Today I woke up furious with your attitude re: relationships. And decided to go for brunch with an Anglo I met at some demonstration. Flirting a little to make the situation between you and me seem more symmetrical. The guy is doing a doctorate in a branch of semiotics. So, we're sitting in a Spanish restaurant on Park Ave. talking about how the French modernist movement is different than the English, etc. Smoking cigarettes and drinking Sangria. When suddenly I can't remember how to get to the end of a sentence. Each time I start, it's as if the memory of the past (the noun, the sentence's beginning) wipes out the present (verb). So I can no longer move forward with the words. This is so scary I run out of there around the corner to the shrink at McGill. She says (sitting in her wicker chair): Gail the problem is you never ask for love. You only ask for sex.

from Paragraphs Blowing on a Line (*in* Spaces Like Stairs)

ENTRY 4

Still not the semblance of a narrative, only the craziest images. Like, the loved one sitting in the restaurant under a picture of a cross in a bleeding loaf of bread. And behind the window pane, the mountain, that round breastlike hump, also with its cross. Images, which, in their contradictions, seem to point boisterously to movement toward some other meaning. Images which need, at the very least, to be transformed into an anecdote to string, among others, along a story line.

But all I see is my character: a woman in a bath. An empty bath, but she's oblivious, for she's masturbating under a jet of water. I have to find a narrative way to give her meaning. Some plot to tie together the memories floating past her in the stream, not only the lost love, but also the dissolution of certain political dreams in what she knows already will be the Yuppie decade (the '80s). And, to relate these somehow to the images from the 'exterior,' the street. Such as that domed-shaped café and women in cloche-shaped hats because there's an ambience of mid-'30s Berlin in the air (this strange repetitive movement of time). Spoons playing against long-stemmed glasses and the high voice of the waitress. Fragments of her best friend, Marie, in her apartment, dropping pot on the floor and saying (because she is order where the main character is chaos): 'je ferai le ménage demain.' Her repugnance of disorder coming from generations of Québécois women ordering the chaos of colonization.

A bell in my head says Produce, produce. But I can't just sit down and write a novel about X. It all happens in the process of writing. I agree with Barthes that writing has to do with the body's pursuing *its own ideas – for my body does not have the same ideas I do.*

ENTRY 12

People are lined up for the cinema at the back of the blue café to see Werner Schroeter's *Répétition Générale.* It's a film about an alternative theatre festival at Nancy, brilliantly and subversively combining various genres. Example, using 'documentary' images from the carnival of plays as a commentary on our times, as well as interjecting a bit of the director's autobiographical commentary, a bit of a love story that might be his personal fiction, and even Prometheus on a roof providing a deconstructed mythological angle on the whole thing. I envy people who work with visual images (performance artists, filmmakers, installation artists). The audience seems to accept that visual images can 'slip,' may have multiple meaning, whereas writers, especially those working in prose, can easily be trapped in the preconceived notions ascribed to words by ideology.

ENTRY 27

Sitting in the blue café the other day, with a toothless, hungry woman outside the window, I had this idea (quickly discarded) that the story would end with my heroine sitting between two bagladies on The Main. A passerby would say to one of them: 'your cunt smells.' And the baglady (an ex-hippie) would reply, laughing toothlessly: 'I can't wash it, I've got a Molotov cocktail between my legs.'

from Heroine

From my tub, I watched as her white hand with the curved nails reached for her purse lying on the sofa. Then it extracted another cigarette from its pretty case. Every movement of her arm causing, as usual, an ostentatious rattle of her silver bracelets. For a minute I thought: she's also going to smooth her hair. She didn't have to. Because she always fixes it so perfectly in the morning, there's no need to pat or run her fingers through it later. This bugs me. The way she acts as if her shell of elegance could protect her from I don't know what. Yet it's part of her essential toughness. Still, watching her sit here like *la reine d'Angleterre*, I felt like saying: 'Eh, Marie, old girl, speaking of protecting one's interests, how about giving the bathroom door a little kick before all the fuckin' heat flies out.' The better to remind her she's no lady any more than I am. Given her father was a dépanneur in St Henri. A distributor of groceries. While mine (after he quit the mine) worked in the supply room of that army bunker outside Lively dispensing ammunition.

from GS + GS

Gertrude Stein is thought to have sought to achieve a new purity of expression of American English by surrounding herself with French, yet resisting French contamination of her language. I have never believed that to be possible. One thing I have reflected on a lot, living in Montréal, and then in Paris, and thinking of Gertrude Stein, is how interesting it is that the impact of the French language on the English phrase or phrasing led us to write quite different sentences, yet, in both cases we became obsessed with the verb. Ulla Dydo iterates in her incredible study of Stein's writing, *The Language that Rises*, that for Stein *questioning the forms of perception went with questioning the forms of language*. To question is to break apart, to open. What sentient void then is opened in Stein's process of attempting to decontextualize English? And what gets replaced, recomposed, reconstituted? To my ear – and this is based on two decades of struggling with this problem, of trying to fashion sentences that 'sound like' Montréal, a city that sounds different than any other on the continent – this seemed to require grammar that moved, that was gestural. People often do remark that Stein's writing is gestural. In different kinds of households people do move differently. Dydo suggests, speaking of *Arthur A Grammar*, that grammar gives a body everyday life. Were I a linguist, I might be able to explain how, in sentences, the gestural gets translated into how the verb takes up space, how in French, the syntax often involves a morphologically richer use of the verb that almost inadvertently invades one's English writing in a French context. It seems to me that in famously preferring verbs to nouns, Stein was also importing from the French something of which she may not have been entirely conscious. It took having a language-focussed critical milieu around me to set me thinking about these things.

from My Paris

NEW YEAR'S 199_

—— Over dark overcrowded square —— Notre-Dame in lacunae of fog curtain —— Imposing only certain tropes of great beastly spirit —— Corks popping. On curves of bridges —— Looking toward (fog-erased) Grand Palais. At bend of river —— Champagne —— Boîtes vibrating Satchmo. C'est si bon —— A cliché. She beside me saying. Very pink lips. Initially not wanting to come. Preferring riding horses —— Still what ~~orgasms~~ angels popping up. Mid walls. Near Louvre's small eyes. Looking in. Or out. She asking ——

—— Still in mist —— Seeing almost nothing —— Past Palais-Royal gate —— Voices of young women drinking rosé. At folded table. Glasses raised. Fingerless gloves. Reading Colette aloud. In homage. Yellowed pages. Drifting. Past display window. Rue Saint-Honoré. Lit by Max Ernst reel. Announcing *Le Sexe de l'art*. At Beaubourg. Two pretty women. Jerky film. 'Arousing' each other. Furtive embarrassed fingers. Entering folds. While giggling into camera. Then forcing dildo in —— Next window. Urinoir. Caption *The air of Paris* —— Next. Catalogue. Opened. At painted opened legs. Lovely furry snatch. Called *L'Origine du monde*.

—— Drifting —— Phenomenal unseen racket —— S'il vous plait Madame. Les Champs-Élysées —— Through hole in mist Molière leaning forward. On seat. Toward Richelieu's street —— Right on Chabanais—— Women's bar. Still bright as daffodils. Victory-wing collars. Poodles. Deep kissing. As before. Drinks likewise unaffordable. Given dollars. With foreign queens on them —— Retreating. Borrowed room. Two flights up. Over second inner courtyard —— How many ~~orgasms~~ hours later. Pulling aside lace curtain. Wiping humidity off window —— Below. Yet another courtyard. Glass hexagonal roof. Filthy diaper. Lodged in corner of it ——

—— The room: banal —— But finest linen sheets. Saggy chandelier offering special pink light. Adjustable to good degree of skintone —— What shadows. Under breasts. Over inner court roof. With dirty diaper on it. Court imposing. On sleep —— Pink lips. Waiting in passage. Leading to one more court or opening. Men crowding in. It being courtyard of Godard's *Vivre sa vie* —— Dilapidated pissoir. She having applied. For *poste* of prostitute. Being particularly suited. Hair easily pushed back into place —— Standing waiting. In funny inner court. When man of crown coming up. Saying I want you to get your thing out of here. She saying the only thing I having. Is dollars. With foreign queens on them ——

from Bottoms Up

[It has never occurred to me to be a poet. The poet, even when 'absent,' rests imbricated in her utter façade of language. While the reader happily at play. In her sandbox of spaces. Lacking spontaneity, I am drawn to the violence of animation. Experienced by a subject. Drifting toward object. Across the placement of the verb. Which nakedness, exposure, seeming somehow progressive, egalitarian. Yet failing to make the woman (narrator) cease obsession with beginnings (causes) and endings (conclusions). So trauma still risking terminating in single unbearable seduction scene.

I am thinking of certain literary feminists. Who using devices copped from poetry to construct porous or unbounded subject, capable of merging somewhat ecologically with context. I am thinking of the gap of the unspeakable. There may be no animal boundary – just the stream and the pleasure that lies in it, teasing the poet. I am thinking about the portentousness of sentencing. Alternately (defensively?), I am thinking that a sentence in a community of sentences (paragraphs) somehow leaving impression of consciously reaching out in communicative gestures. Notwithstanding characteristic narrative flick of head back over shoulder. At point of the period. For purpose of getting ... bearings. This I finding ... touching.]

MARGARET CHRISTAKOS

HEATHER MILNE: You're not a lyric poet in any conventional sense, but it seems that there is this pull toward the lyric in a lot of your work. There's the lyric and then there's your recombinatory practice where you take that lyric and fragment it and disperse it across other works. How do you understand your relationship to the lyric? Would you call yourself a lyric poet?

MARGARET CHRISTAKOS: I guess as much as categories mean anything, it would be ingenuine not to understand my work as lyric poetry. But the more recent work I've done over the last five years I'd say is performing other strategies upon the lyric and, you know, I continue to open up new kinds of questions about the degree to which the authenticity of the source material needs to be protected.

HM: What do you mean by 'protected'?

MC: The tender centre of the confession, because confessionality has actually been an important engine of the work I've done around maternal subjectivity. I have been writing about extremes of psychological and emotional experience that have occurred in the context of raising babies and children in a way that is perhaps different than how they've been written about, even within feminist poetries. So in some way there's a representative function. I'm putting down on paper evidence of a certain reality or alternative interpretation of what really is going on in that relationship over time. I've encountered extreme states in myself and observed them in other mothers of my generation. And at the same time adding that reality to the utopian tales of motherhood. And then playing and using some of it, ironically, using some of it in terms of looking at the narrative, looking at what's there and then again manipulating and intentionally altering those narratives so they're not pure or not reifying the pure authentic emotion once again. A lot of those strategies continue to be very interesting for me. But at the same time I think there's a lot in there that's just purely about surviving, taking care of three little kids. Time is such a huge thing raising children. It's this medium that you constantly have to manage and sculpt. There's been a lot of content that I had no concept of before I had kids – I had notions of it but no real experience of it. Mothering these three kids and sustaining myself as a writer that was like the grand experiment. This thing that is a sort of mainstream, traditional female experience for me was one that most challenged my identity to the core. It's been very hard, and it made me think, you know, this is really hard for every mother. We persist through extreme despair and exhaustion. It's just really an extreme experience and the places of comfort, the places where you've achieved a certain balance, are actually vital to surviving.

HM: That kind of exploration of motherhood is evident in 'Mother's Journal Notes,' which is from *Excessive Love Prostheses*. There seems to be a kind of conflict or ambivalence present in that poem. There is not always a clear sense of the division between mother and child. Your explorations of the maternal seem quite different from the way a previous generation of feminist poets explored the maternal. How do you see your poetic practice of writing about motherhood in relation to a previous generation of feminist poets? Have you been influenced by writers like Daphne Marlatt or Lola Tostevin?

MC: Completely influenced in terms of my own formation as a feminist writer and as a female writer. I'd say Betsy Warland and Nicole Brossard were also very meaningful. Gail Scott was also very important around writing the sexual maternal body. I actually don't have the perspective on my own work where I have decided from the outset what I will write and then gone on to write it. I do have a kind of process base where I am – this is the lyric poet thing – I do invite my content to come from the unconscious. It's an essentialist relationship that I have with language and with needing to write. I do need to write. And probably no moreso than when I was in the thick of the baby years. So *Wipe Under A Love* and *Excessive Love Prostheses*, those two books, and my novel *Charisma* were written in the midst of the most physically and emotionally engaged period of attending to babies, nursing, inhabiting the physical in that way.

HM: So when you write these lyric poems that are driven by the confessional, and then you fragment them to the extent that you do, is there a protective element at work? Is there a sense that you ought to conceal what you've confessed?

MC: Well, actually, 'Mother's Journal Notes' is interesting because it's part of a suite of poems. At a certain point I was looking back at my own sexual identity and my own sexual history and I actually did use my own journal notes as source material. There was a fairly present ironic hand going through journal notes from the previous fifteen or twenty years and pulling out what are very extreme, high romanticist phrasings and notions and longings and all of that and I took a lot of liberties with that content. I was using material that was about my bisexual experiential identity, wrestling it out and looking at the construction of romanticism in relation to various lovers and histories, straight and lesbian. I was also weaving in pieces from journal notes that I made in relation to mothering my first son when he was a baby, which was like, you're literally in a state of being absolutely in love, empathy so raw it makes you feel very unsettled. There's a very interpenetrative, unboundaried sense of identification. I'm using the notion of the journal and diary which has always been very important to my work as the raw material there, recombining it to produce pieces that are intentionally confusing – the erotic, the maternal, the romantic and the ironic enmeshed.

HM: You deliberately bring sexuality and motherhood together in very striking and unusual ways. The other poems in that suite are all about affairs and dreams. You merge the sexual and the maternal, and not just the sexual but the bisexual.

MC: That book also has a whole sequence of found poems and recombinant poems based on Victorian nursery rhymes and poems that are all about the cautionary tale, the mother as the purveyor of myths about how children need to tame their wildness and bury their selves in fear. And all that material is transmitted along with mother's milk. I had very little critical response to that book but I think it is quite radical. One of the things that's kind of uncool about my work or maybe a bit brazen but also uncool is that there is a kind of stake in – this is why I feel close to Gail Scott's work – because there's a stake in having experienced the wound and declaring that as well. My last two books are much less wounded. I have moved through a great deal of material through this last twenty years. But I'm glad there's a record of it, and I think the work forms a kind of documentary function in terms of feminist experience.

HM: What about your new work, *What Stirs*? What is it about? What kinds of procedural techniques are you employing in it?

MC: It's closer to *Excessive Love Prostheses* in ways than to *Sooner* because I'm exploring in particular the notion of the breastfeeding latch – again, it's very much about the maternal. There's this suite called 'The Hoity-Toity Supplements' that's essentially about a woman being pregnant and giving birth, but it's told again from a variety of vernaculars and ironic perspectives on what it means to be excited about having a baby. And it's procedural in that there are several sequences in this book where I'm generating texts that are either lists or there are sort of language experiments that then become the armature for lyric poems. So I might start with something that is more akin to a structuralist piece and then I use it as the springboard for a lyric piece and then spring out of that into something more concrete. So I'm actually playing between poetics and thinking about the overriding metaphors of production, reproduction and attachment and alienation, or detachment in terms of subjective identities. Largely, it's about this relationship of the lyric and the anti-lyric and I have been trying to have these very naturalistic vernacular pieces that seem to emerge from what is an authorial voice, a sense of an authorial identity, against pieces where that reliability is really shaken up and as a reader you have to figure out, who's this? Is this Margaret or is this some character she's producing or is this manipulated text where there is this kind of trace of her voice or some sense of the source. It's really very much about what does stir us to the surface and why we want this aesthetic experience of attachment, whether it be to each other or to texts or to art in general. Why do we desire? Why don't we desire? I have some pieces that are love poems but they're proceduralist love poems so they're about being in language and hearing the difference across iterations. I'll start with a source text and then a lot of it will be about moving the words around and using incantatory repetitions of a similar set of words that then come up on another 'screen,' and then on another 'screen.' I think that kind of repetition really moves someone into a state of pleasure. It is the kind of recognition and the self-awareness of recognition that does bring someone into ... oh, I know, I hear and I know and I hear and I know again and now I'm reading for something new, and now I hear the newness, now I hear what I know, now I hear the newness. I guess that's the process basis of my work coming into understanding how it is people hear the music of poetry too. So there's a lot more of that going on for me.

HM: You're such a procedural poet. Does the procedural aspect emerge when you're writing the poems? Or do you usually have a sense of what it is that you want to do procedurally before you start writing? Or does it change from project to project?

MC: Well, it really changes because *Wipe Under A Love* was essentially a book-length proceduralist sequence where I did have a kind of template. I was writing a lyric poem and then I was taking it apart and using word substitutions or counting procedures, relineation procedures. They were kind of rudimentary, but I talked about doing the other kinds of physical labour that are pertinent to domestic work – folding, washing, folding, putting away, washing, folding, sorting, this kind of thing. And then I would pump out a little intensified concentrate. I think you could see that fairly clearly over that book. If anyone takes the time to go through it, there is a system that reads itself to you as you interact with the text, whereas in *Sooner* I'm using longer narrative structures. For example, the poem 'Lucent,' which is a twenty-five-page poem, is again proceduralist in that I wrote essentially a prose piece and then lineated it and broke it into couplets and then used substitution measures to fuck with the gender. I took a poem that was in a kind of romanticist roving female domestic straight-girl voice into the voice of a man who is essentially roaming the city looking for gay sex. There's a playful transposition of subjectivity. What I'm doing in that poem is asking the reader to clue in at a certain point to the unreliability or the weirdness of the gendering. So that's, for me, another kind of proceduralism that I've worked a lot with. It's extending my bisexual inquiry into subjectivity. Sometimes I do plan it. And other times I begin to write and then as I'm going I develop what it is I'm going to do with the sequence, and I'll have many phases of editing where I redirect. I might go down one path and then I realize that it's not that interesting to me and I'll decide on another direction and create different procedures to pursue that direction. There's a lot of choice on an ongoing basis as I'm producing a piece. I guess that's why I think of it as sculptural. I've been writing all these novels at the same time over the last five years ... producing these much more cohesive and lengthy narrative structures while I'm producing more fragmentary and recombinant poetic structures at the same time as I'm making dinner every three hours and dealing with parent council. That is part of why the poems look the way they do – because of what I'm doing in this other set of projects as well.

H M: You published *Charisma* in 2000. Are there other novels as well?

M C: I'm on my third. I've written a second, which I haven't found a publisher for yet. It's about maternal rage and the extremes of mothering and daughtering. There's a teenage babysitter who is the centre of it and is the surrogate mother in a variety of middle-class families and she has a relationship with four or five families. It's a bit like *Charisma* structurally in that there's a topography of a micro-city. There are about thirty characters in the novel. I don't seem to be able to have a structure with just three characters. It was a very challenging thing to write, but so far, I haven't found a home for it. You know there are all these expectations for clear narrative. It's confusing. There are too many characters or there are too many narrative threads for us to follow.

HM: So you feel that you haven't been able to find a publisher because it is too complex at the level of form? Is the content also difficult?

MC: I tend to think that the content I deal with in this book is difficult. There is one character who is quite self-destructive and pursues sex with men when it's actually quite destructive to her and I bring this character to a place of resisting transformation at the end. She actually decides she's quite happy to want to be an object of a certain kind of rage. I produced characters in a way that is quite different from *Charisma* because *Charisma* is really my own psyche splintered. For this second novel I had to invent the whole place. In some ways it's much more conventional because I did the work of ... a kind of imagining I hadn't done in the past. Sometimes it can be experimental for me to attempt to interact with certain kinds of narrativity that some readers – my ideal reader – might find fairly conventional.

HM: You use your first book, *Not Egypt*, as recombinatory material in the 'Orange Porch' sequence of poems in *Wipe Under A Love*. 'Orange Porch' is subtitled 'Book of Reminiscences.' How does memory or the act of reminiscence figure into your poetic practice?

MC: Very much. I just actually included a piece from *Not Egypt* in *What Stirs* and ... well there are different kinds of memory. There's autobiographical memory that is often object specific or evocative of place or in my case seems very anchored to first-family context. Perhaps because I'm now living in a family structure with a partner and three kids, I feel like I'm in a constant capitulation of my own beginnings, and there's this hashing through of what is remembered and what I'm creating and how I'm creating it, in how I'm reproducing and in how I am genetically altering what will be passed on next. It's almost oppressive because I seem to have a very present memory loop around a lot of aspects of my life, my identity and my notions of the kind of life I'm creating now. Even in feminist culture we're looking back and we're kind of looking at how our own discourse has evolved and changed and what we've lost – this sort of notion of having lost a certain density or relevance – and I've come to the place where I think, no, there is not the loss that we might fear there has been. I don't see it as a place of loss. I see a movement of radical poetries across various communities. Everything that was produced in the heyday of the '80s has found its way to influencing many people's poetries. There is a great deal of the best contemporary poetry in Canada that you can trace directly back to the influence of writers like Nicole Brossard,

Daphne Marlatt, Gail Scott, Erín Moure and Lola Tostevin. Their work has been taken up in many, many different ways. But we haven't narrativized it very well. We haven't written about how those influences have been enacted. And I guess I'm talking about that because I think of the sort of memory produced in myself as a writer, like all the memories of the interactions I had with writing in the '80s are also very, very formative to what I write now. There's your lived experience and then there's your intellectual memory of the places and spaces you were in and the aesthetics that were important to all of those relationships and the kind of political ideals, objectives, you've had and how do I reinvent that in a way that makes sense to who I am now as a writer. And so it's not just images. It's not just the 'Orange Porch' that ends up being the trace in the work, it's what you do, what I do in my head, and I'm sure this goes on for everybody else writing. It's kind of the way you decide what words to put next to each other, how you build your sentence, how you build the argument in your own composition. I don't want to just be thinking about Ramsey Lake where I grew up and had the most extraordinary physical sense of pleasure floating in that lake and that's where I felt my body's calmness and wholeness and some connection to ancestral land. There's that but then there's that as an image of what it is to be in pleasured consciousness and so maybe the body floating in the water is like what happens next to the grammar of the sentence that's being written. And I find all of that continues to be very interesting to me as I'm writing.

HM: I think you're right that the influence of a previous generation hasn't been narrativized, but its impact is strongly felt among a younger generation of writers. You're in an interesting position because you're younger than those women, but you're a little bit older than, say, Rachel Zolf and the other younger writers in the anthology, so you're like this hinge ... it's a unique position in terms of having had primary access to the innovation of the early '80s in a way that some younger writers did not.

MC: Well, I also feel like I was a bit of a hinge presence in terms of my situatedness as a bisexual person too. I've been trying to work that out in terms of what my body of work means alongside perhaps more coherent sexual-identity narratives of the lesbian work that I've admired so much ... I don't want to essentialize the way my work would figure to any reader, to any community, but there is something strange about my work in that I've written about sexuality a lot, and I've written about mothering a lot. That in itself is weird. But to find the reader who wants to take that up is also, it seems, quite elusive. It's difficult to find many readers who actually think there's something there to be taken up.

HM: There is the possibility that your identification as bisexual is read as a refusal to assume the arguably more coherent labels of heterosexual or lesbian. It's interesting to think of you as a hinge figure not only in terms of generational location but also in terms of sexuality – straight and lesbian, maternal and sexual. Perhaps there is a discomfort for some readers in the fact that you bring mothering and sexuality together in the ways that you do. I think this is where your work is most challenging and also probably most political.

MC: I feel vulnerable about all this and it's only become possible for me over the last few years to actually ask these questions out loud and think about them out loud.

HM: It occurs to me that there is not as much of a body of criticism around your work as there should be.

MC: And I don't know if that's more about the fact that by the time I had published a few books, nobody was really writing criticism. The reception happened in the '80s. My first book had only three reviews. I've never really known what to attribute that to except that I guess it wasn't very good and I guess it wasn't very interesting and I guess it wasn't doing what people wanted poetry to do at that point. The benefit of being almost twenty years older at this point is to celebrate the fact that I am still writing despite the lack of reception. It didn't inhibit my production to such a degree that I stopped writing and I have to really question how it is I maintained a writing practice through the '90s. I just had to write. And I know that there is some bizarre thing that keeps all of us writing despite the fact that there is a resounding silence critically. Maybe that is changing though. There are new conversations. And there's the internet. There's all this online discourse that didn't exist in the '90s. And I think that audiences are much more savvy in terms of polyphonic narrativity and they're actually more plugged in to understanding the relationship of history and theory. There are a lot of very smart readers out there.

HM: You've talked about bpNichol mentoring you when you were a young feminist writer as well, and how he's had a very big impact on your work.

MC: Absolutely. I mean, he introduced me to Kathy Acker's work, to Brossard, and to Yolande Villemaire. She was doing experimental poetics where she was using the vernacular of the lullaby and it was kind of a performance art. I remember a particular evening years back when Lola Tostevin's *'sophie* was published because she was reading from *'sophie* and Yolande was reading from her work and bp was doing some of his incredible process-based sound poetics. The reading series were happening in artist-run centres, visual arts spaces. There was much more of a connect between performance art, time-based arts, film, video and installation and visual art. One of the main things that got lost in the '90s was the space of understanding writing as a time-based form of performance and I think Christian Bök was very important in that space. It certainly was meaningful to me that he ended up attracting an audience to what was essentially a through line from bp's practice and so that all goes together. I also think that it's a shame that we don't talk about Rachel Zolf's *Human Resources* and Bill Kennedy and Darren Wershler's *Apostrophe* – those two aren't being drawn into relationship as a kind of critical strategy to bring readers to respond to irony in different ways.

HM: There are all those debates on the separatist anthology and its uses and limitations ... whether it's useful to create an anthology based on identity categories like nation or gender.

MC: I guess the approach I've taken with the Influency course is to deliberately produce more and more diverse space so that the same reader is in contact with Maureen Scott Harris's very, very lyric work and Dwayne Morgan's spoken-word material and NourbeSe Philip's *Zong!*, so that they're gradually coming to understand that there are all these different opportunities to engage and challenge language. And they do. They get it. Literally, by the end of one salon, they all get it and they all like experimental poetry. They might also come out having reaffirmed their interest in the lyric moment, and that transcendent space because they all want aesthetic. They want a pure aesthetic lift as well.

HM: There's also nothing wrong with the pure aesthetic lift.

MC: We all want arousal, we all want pleasure. Why not? That's actually what's going on in the delight around more experimental work as well. That even grief – for example, when Rachel Zolf reads aloud *Shoot and Weep*, there's a kind of ceremony of paying homage to damage and destruction. Real contemporary damage going on and there's a group experience of acknowledging the pleasure of sharing that acknowledgment. I've really been grappling with what that space is – that public ceremony that is not imported through religious means or the idea of spirit or the sacred. As an atheist, I really just have a tremendous problem with even the word 'spirit.' There's something going on, though, in the kind of group grappling with grief and the desire for change. It's a sort of hopeful moment. We could value this quality of consciousness and build our society around it if only there were more people who could come and hear this work. This work changes us when we are in contact with it.

HM: I'm thinking about what you're saying about spirituality and the transformative power of the work, and you've talked in this interview about having a calling to write. Even though your first book got only three reviews, you kept writing because you had to. There's almost something spiritual about that call or drive to write.

MC: You know, I could easily say, Please don't print that, how naïve! But I've been rereading *Coming Through Slaughter*, Ondaatje's early '70s novel, which was essentially his response to suddenly being famous, and he decided to write about fame and he focused on the figure of Buddy Bolden who basically goes mad. *Coming Through Slaughter* is still a completely radical book. The kinds of confessions parsing out of grammar that he does. The kind of thrust of the vernacular in the middle of the lyric. All these things are very, very radical still. And the whole point of that book is that it doesn't fucking matter if you get the Booker Prize because you still might go mad in the middle of it. The risk of writing, the risk of being the radical artist in this society, is still very great. You're walking a tightrope and you could fall off either side. I really appreciate that book because it does completely romanticize the lyrical kind of bloom of being inside the music of jazz or the body blowing apart. There's this explosive sexual metaphor for aesthetic experience, but at the same time he's saying there are no prizes. The last line of the book is 'There are no prizes.' And we need to keep remembering that. The prize is being engaged in writing and deciding to explore the edges of our own consciousness and what this practice can mean publicly as a body of work.

HM: Earlier, you mentioned the course you teach, Influency. What is the premise of that course? You have writers in dialogue with each other, responding to each other?

MC: I have eight poets, each of whom I ask to produce a forty-minute prepared lecture on one of the other poets in the roster. So they come once as a kind of critic and they deliver a paper and then the subject poet gives a reading and then there's a Q&A and then the registrants write responses. They're learning how to interact with very different poetries from a critical perspective. So, in fact, they are becoming literary critics – that's the goal. And they're becoming a public who is equally important to the moment or the occasion of a reading. The response of the public completes the work and creates the possibility of poetry as a social moment and a political moment actually ripples out in new directions with each audience contact. And the crux of it is that I'm matching up poets across aesthetic sensibilities and categories of poetry. So, there's not the easy or immediate recognition between poet and poet critic of the day. There's still a lot of room for the person writing the essay to be thinking about their own poetic. It is about engagement more than the model of the review, where your job is to sum up what someone is doing and then decide whether it's good or bad. The point is to inhabit the work along your own pathway of curiosity and interest in a way that provides an entry point for other audiences to imagine what their pathway would be through it. So it's desire-driven hopefully, and some really stunning material has come out of it. In some cases those papers have occurred when there is more of a fit between the poet critic and the poet. But there have been some very interesting stretches and bridges across various poets' works.

HM: How has teaching the course affected your own writing, or your own reading for that matter?

MC: I think it's worked in several ways. It has stoked my passion for lyrical poetry and what can occur in a quite mixed group of listeners around the discussion of poetry as itself, a lyric experience. It's not just the audience coming in and listening to something they find beautiful and evocative and that moves them into an internal illuminated state. There's something about the social space that is actually built, that wouldn't be otherwise. You're kind of seeing people move into their own thought process. It's that moment when you realize people in the room are actually awakening to their own sense of inquiry, and in that process they're encountering language. So it has the potential to create a space where that is actually going on and not just among an elite group of highly specialized thinkers. But you were asking what that's meant to my own writing. There has been this grappling that I've done around the lyric and the kind of thirst for feeling that people do come to poetry for, and in fact, I have always come to poetry for. My own practice over many years has often been about the lyric poem that is then manipulated and rejigged in some way. I'm interacting with the source material that I've produced, so there's a kind of extension of the lyric poem through these various iterations and inversions.

Toronto, July 2008

SELECTED WORKS

Not Egypt. Toronto: Coach House Press, 1989.

Other Words for Grace. Toronto: The Mercury Press, 1994.

The Moment Coming. Toronto: ECW Press, 1998.

Charisma. Toronto: Pedlar Press, 2000.

Wipe Under A Love. Toronto: The Mansfield Press, 2000.

Excessive Love Prostheses. Toronto: Coach House Books, 2002.

Sooner. Toronto: Coach House Books, 2005.

What Stirs. Toronto: Coach House Books, 2008.

from Not Egypt

My pubis insists she is foregrounding a unique technology. Her fastidious sense of taste has taken over, swallowing air as if it were the penis of a passionate man. Here, rhythm makes sense. A pulmonary resolution of ambiguities. She is related to all that enters her and does away with embarrassment of introductions. Many old allegories are useful now as categorical menu lists, although passion can hardly be commended as if a river stormed by sewage. Passion takes the form of environmental control. She takes all that is transparent past herself and swims in opaque silence. Of course the moon is most precious of all and overlooks these decisions from a child's vantage.

May 20

H. Mother's Journal Notes

I feel, how powerful and self-knowing at other times. His
mouth begins to root as soon do, how trembling on
the rim of failure as I am within a yard
of him; this limbo of not knowing exactly what to

I begin to feel selfless and tragic. You unbearably tired
as well, how shocked, too, by despise more than any
sensation being exposed and and need you, how lucky I
am, how cold, and show this by wailing and thrashing

as do thoughts of how deeply I love your arms
about so boldly that you have brings me to tears
at a moment's flash, laid deep scratches into his own
soft cheeks. Raw. His small body is so beautiful it

A big mess – I can't stand looking at clamped, compressed;
and the skin feels tight and my own body – it's
horrible. Did I do chubby, sore and blimplike. The blood
inside feels the right thing? Should I have nursed him

and unassailable. My poor feet are awfully swollen! At lunch?
Is he crying? Does he feel over its living undulating
body. It is physical abandoned? Will he be scarred? Should
I call? Space and my view of all things happens.

Woke last night at 3 AM, fed the is the
precedent, the priority, it claims the baby and then had
the most incredibly huge, my pregnancy intervenes on my other
faculties: it the hugest, poo of my life; so huge

because there is my belly. This is how I had
to push it down with a I can't pull the
book close to me spoon then plunge the whole
mess.

M1. UK Breast Milk Toxic: 13 July 99
each line prematurely weaned to escape charges of plagiarism

chemical cocktail / of pollutants
to higher / than of
toxic substances / the babies
being exposed / limit daily
range of / from incinerators,
pesticides and / 350 contaminants,
including some / and dioxin-like
tissue highly / lethal headlines
most recently / in animal
feed, introducing / food chain
including milk / was agent

Agent lethal recently was milk highly most including chain dioxin-like
introducing in food 350 limit and feed, daily exposed some
animal toxic being including headlines higher – and tissue chemical
– from contaminants – – of pesticides – – the
incinerators – – of range – – than babies –
– to substances – – of pollutants – – –
cocktail

M2. Ada and Eva

So said the paper: Two sisters, identical twins. One with
thighs too skinny to harvest reconstructive fatty tissue for her

missing breast, gone to cancer, so the sister, true surrogate,
offers hers. No rejection issue and true love to graft

wholesale onto sibling flesh, her sister, herself. A breast in
waiting. Would that each of us could be so roundly

replaced, cells migrating back to home territory. Not said in
the paper: This donor sister, plumper and barren since age

nineteen from pelvic inflammatory disease wants children, and next year
the first sister will nurse a newborn with this thigh-breast,

perhaps her twin will run across fields, laughing, wet, loose

M3. Milk was recently lethal agent her twin will run across

sisters, identical twins. One with higher – and tissue
chemical reconstructive fatty tissue for her – to substances,

– – so the sister, true surrogate, introducing in

food 350 limit and true love to graft and
feed, daily exposed some sister, herself. A breast in

highly most including chain dioxin-like us could be so
roundly – from contaminants – – home territory. Not

said in – – than babies – plumper and
barren since age of pesticides – – the wants

children, and next year animal toxic being including headlines
newborn with this thigh-breast, incinerators – – of range

across fields, laughing, wet, loose of pollutants – –
– from pelvic inflammatory disease wants to higher first

sister will nurse a chemical cocktail cells migrating back
to home being exposed paper: This donor sister, plumper

toxic substances, onto sibling flesh, her sister, including some
Would that each of us pesticides and range of

breast, gone to cancer, so most recently hers. No
rejection issue and tissue highly said the paper: Two

sisters, including milk too skinny to harvest reconstructive feed,
introducing

Grounds 20A.

doubled body, of the woman prostrate on a gurney
for liposuction, correction of the thighs, of her
curdled self, the one she dreams about bled of fat
and purified

body doubled, of the poet's self in public, out of
privacy's safety and the televisual reigning flicker of
self-powering. who goes behind the dark curtain
avoiding her, who would rather sidestep
this singular image, hers

doubling desire when she dreams, no, not dream
but imagines, no, not imagination, but wants
the two of you, both sexes of all of you, when she redoubles
her efforts at intact performance, she turns
circling, there are at least two women in the room
when any woman is alone, yeah, apparently

body, woman a liposuction, the her
the dreams of purified of poet's
public, privacy's the flicker who the
avoiding would this hers when no,
but not wants of sexes of she
efforts performance, circling. at women room
woman yeah,

yeah, woman efforts but avoiding public, the
body, her poet's the no, she room

THEREFORE:
yeah, but the body, the room

An Open Erotics of Gzowski

The voice of   the bodiless lover   is a trope
for the world's   brooding power to   scintillate our aliveness

in physical space   To animate us   to our own
skin's porous interest   in exchanging matter   with the matter

both inside and   beyond its seal   The voice's perfume
crosses the bleak   dark valley we   like to consider

the separateness of   the individual; it   lets us be
in the midst   of an erotic   thrall while we

rinse our mugs   and wipe our   stained cupboards It
assures us the   body is not   a married organ

properly bound to   one dock but   a canoe, okay,
careening on a   fluid carpet of   whimsy and longing

virtually upended in   a spray of   language, seriously amorous
about the sea world   and all the   voices its sheathlike

structure would and   *can* contain

My Attaché Case

DAY 1

I like did I mention
visual splendour coupons

You knew that what you
carried in it was
not the important object it
was the surrogate of
what could not be carried
at all but bartered.

My breasts have held milk
and expressed milk and
held language by the tit
so to speak attachment.

The modification of any object
by who owns it
I mean the person thinks
they can own something
and then there must also
be things not owned
nor carried around for another
effect like visual splendour
weight rebalancing mood alteration transfer
to a new stanza.

Trees hooked to sky by
the gaze eyelashed shut.

I went to sleep what
is the mystery I
woke up smelling only foods
I cannot stand lukewarm.

2

Knew that what I
can't stand lukewarm redeemables
not the important object
it is the mystery
I ruefully what could
not be carried the
gaze eyelashed shut saddens

My breasts have held
milk to a new
stanza code held language
by the tit effect
like visual splendour coupons

The modification of any
object be things not
owned consecutively I mean
the person thinks they
can own something timeshare
and then there must
also by who owns
it convincingly nor carried
around for another so
to speak attachment cabaret
weight rebalancing mood alteration
transfer and expressed milk

and nuptials Trees hooked
to sky by at
all but bartered purple

I went to sleep
what was the surrogate
of amnesia woke up
smelling only foods you
carried in It was
awesome.

DAY 2

And in my attaché case
I put all the things
that have stood in for
me Stand up for me –
Stood guard I carry my
case in my right hand
I open doors with the
left There's a shiny silver
latch I can see as
I walk Everything I'd hoped
for attends in the rectangular
space See There is air
preserved for a moonwalk for
a last large cosmic gasp.

I plan Never forget my
case even when particularly slow
in the head else rigid
under the knees Sometimes my
shins ache Nothing distracts me
Soon as my hat's on
the case handle heats each
sleek crease of my knuckles
I cup its plastic weight
A nonslip baton I'll never
ever hand off and abandon
This is how well attached
I am to my future
dear ones are you pleased?

CRI DE CŒUR, DEFERRED

The tone of it is
All wrong or it's odd
For we prefer real order

Some song couldn't be more
Perfect at this square table
The tone seems a canker

All five chairs are neatly
Placed we concede in unison
It's coming on just now. Still.

The tone of it is
All wrong we concede in
Unison the tone seems some

Canker a song couldn't be
More perfect and it's odd
It's coming on just now

All five chairs so neatly
Placed at this square table
For we prefer real order.

TOUCHÉ

I carry my canker
I walk
Sometimes my shins ache
The tone seems a sleek crease of my knuckles
I cup its plastic weight all wrong
It's odd for we
Prefer real order dear ones –
Are you pleased?

ATTOUCHÉ

We knew that what we order dear ones cannot stand
visual splendour surrogates

Our breasts have held pleased nonslip perfect milk to
pleased new stanza code held language

We concede its cup its plastic by touched tit effect

We mean touched persons think and deserve coupons

Forget our particularly transfer or expressed milk

For touched tone of it pleased latch we stood guard
couldn't be case in our odd touched perfect and we
knew that what we carried in it was not *attouché*

M. NOURBESE PHILIP

KATE EICHHORN: At the end of *Zong!* you write about a story that 'cannot be told, that must be told.' Is this why all your books have been written?

NOURBESE PHILIP: That's a fascinating question, and I think you're right. I think that the books exist in the space between the not telling and the compulsion to tell. In the interstices.

KE: And what's your role in that telling?

NP: My role in that, if you want to call it that, is to identify and name that impossibility, which has within it the potential for the possible.

KE: When you talk about the possible, are you talking about the knowable?

NP: And the unknowable, which I think the West and Western intellectual traditions are uncomfortable with. Your questions take me back to Tobago which in many ways is at the centre of my writing life and the struggle it presents. I question why I keep coming back to this place. Probably because it is so rich with history and trauma, but it is also a part of the impulse to flee – stay or flee, flee or stay. This seems to parallel, in an odd way, perhaps, this idea that *Zong!* is a story that can't be told, yet must be told. You desire to flee history and memory, you are also impelled to stay and face it and try to not tell it.

KE: This to me is what is so interesting about your work. You could have chosen to be a historian, a philosopher, a storyteller, and you are all those things on many levels, but you end up arriving in innovative poetics. So you begin not with the story but with the rupturing of the language. What brought you not to the lyric, not to fiction, not to pure testimony, but to innovative poetry? What decisions or accidents led you there?

NP: I think what led me there is actually what is at the heart of *Zong!* It can't ever be told. But by virtue of the fact that it can't ever be told, it doesn't mean that I shouldn't try to tell it. We can never know it. We can never tell it. But we must.

KE: It can never be known?

NP: Not entirely.

KE: I suppose what I am trying to grapple with is whether or not this story is bound to fail, or if the partiality is part of the telling.

NP: Its partiality *is* integral to the telling.

KE: So when you talk about silence, which comes up again and again in all your books, and you write about the 'hard kernels of silence,' what are those 'hard kernels of silence' and how are they integral?

NP: Those hard kernels of silence would be those places where longing and desire come up against history, the lacunae in history, where, for instance, you can't ever know what tribe or group you came from, what your mother tongue was. On a foundational level, those would be the hard kernels of silence. The ever and ineffable unknowable. In the face of a culture that purports to know everything it knows and promises that what it doesn't it will.

KE: What else is never going to reveal itself?

NP: I'm not sure I know. I only know that I am aware of an inaccessibility that the work keeps pushing me toward.

KE: I've had a recurring conversation with women writers of my generation about the impact of first reading 'Discourse on the Logic of Language' in *She Tries Her Tongue* ... That a poem could take this form was significant, but more importantly, it demonstrated that sometimes the most politically urgent writing necessitates innovation at the level of language and form. 'Discourse on the Logic of Language' couldn't have taken any other form.

NP: Of course not. But one of the things you have to understand, for a poet, most of the payoff comes after you've finished the work, at least for me it does – the payoff comes in what the work begins to teach you. So let's take 'Discourse on the Logic of Language,' for instance. I was very aware of how I wanted it set up.

KE: Why?

NP: Because for me when I work in English, I always feel as if I am working in a foreign language.

KE: Even with your mastery?

NP: I never ever take it for granted. The source of the foreignness is the awareness that this is not my tongue. Mind you, I think that all writers and poets have this sense. As you write your poem, you have this idea of perfection, but of course, what I am talking about is slightly different from that. I'm talking about this sense of utter foreignness in what is supposed to be my mother tongue. When I was working on the poem, I remember sitting in this room on St. Clair Avenue in Toronto that I rented from a doctor, my doctor in fact. I had a room at the back of his office, and there were some days when I felt that I could actually taste the foreignness of these words. I can't apply profound theoretical language to it. I can only go to the body and tell you what it felt like. There was this awareness of that and all I could do was weep and weep. Maybe it was some sort of collective memory.

KE: Since you've raised this, I want to ask a question I thought about asking first, but it seemed like a very negative place to begin – do you love language, or is language just a site of struggle for you?

NP: No! I love it, I love it, I love it! More than that, there is an erotic aspect to language for me. As a child, I used to listen to my parents talking about politics on the front porch, while I sat inside doing my homework. There was something very powerful – even erotic for me – hearing the weaving together of my parents' voices – my father's deep and sombre, my mother's higher and more active. I get excited by grammar texts – how weird is that?

KE: So when you think about your work as a poet, are you breaking the language, rupturing the imperialist language, taming the language, redeploying the language?

NP: I'm doing all those things. In fact, when writing the last book of *Zong!*, as I was breaking those words open, I remember feeling, yes, finally, I am fucking with this language in a way I have wanted to all my life! – my writing life, that is. And an interesting metaphor given what I just said about the erotic. Simultaneous with that, I felt a deep sense of satisfaction – as if I were getting my own back on this language that had fucked us over for so long. That had held us in its grip demanding mastery when we could never be master or mistress even of our own bodies. It was an incredible experience. I finally felt that for the first time I had my own language. True it's fragmented and broken, but it is my own tongue. This totally ruptured, fragmented, dissonant language that is my mother tongue.

KE: But the project of *Zong!* begins a long time ago, before *Zong!* It's all your writing.

NP: I'm thinking of the last poem in my first collection, *Thorns*, and I think the title is 'All that Remains of Kush Returns to the Desert.' It's a poem addressed to Nyame, a West African deity. The closing lines are something like, 'welcome me gently, I carry tiny thorns of Africa within.' That whole idea of thorns – the thorniness of it – that language is not something comfortable and comforting, but something that can hurt you, that can maim you. So, that is the closing image in the first book. I think the thorns are still there when I look at *Zong!* I don't even know at this point how to pronounce some parts of the text, particularly in the last section – 'Ferrum.' Do I pronounce each linguistic fragment as a part of the word it has been broken off from or do I allow each fragment its own sound. There is a challenge in getting my mouth and tongue around these pieces. How do I begin to express the brokenness, the fragmentation that is at the heart of this book?

KE: This makes me think about the reading I invited you to do last April. I said, 'This time, NourbeSe, don't explain the text, just read.' I love your essays, but you are possibly one of the only poets I know of who has consistently chosen to preface or conclude her books with essays. Similarly, you often open or close or interrupt your readings with this other voice. It's always a reading, a lecture and a talk. What was it like to just read and hold back any explanation?

NP: It was exciting. I had never done it quite that way before. Mainly because I felt that the work was so new to me, it would be new to the audience as well, and I would have to explain it.

KE: I want to talk more about your experience of reading *Zong!* You've already talked about trying to give this text a voice, which is a text you are simply relaying because it's presented as an 'as told to' narrative rather than something you authored. But have you also thought more about how you will deal with, and force your listeners to grapple with, its silences?

NP: I did one reading at the Scream Literary Festival in Toronto where I just took two pages and read them quite slowly, honouring the silence, which is really counterintuitive for me, because I am very speedy. It's also counterintuitive in this age, and in certain literary contexts like performance poetry where everything is really, really fast, although that has its validity too. The two pages took about ten minutes to read, but just before the end of that reading, feeling a bit nervous, I sped up. Someone who had been in the audience remarked to me a few days later that it really worked as a slow reading and the audience only seemed to get restless when I sped up. Then, I did another reading in Tobago in July, and this was a totally different context. Tobago is still a very oral society and this was a very small reading – some ten to fifteen people. I think I read two pages again honouring the silences, and once again people were absolutely receptive. Afterwards, one woman said that she felt that the silences created images of water washing up on the shore and washing back. Another person said the silences conveyed to him a sense of being underwater, drowning. So those two readings really confirmed for me that that is how I should read the text. But I am still working on the pauses and how long those should be.

KE: But that is not how you had imagined reading this text originally. There is an excessiveness about *Zong!* It's a long poetry book, nearly 200 pages, and there are many words on each page. It's also typographically expansive. So to do a twenty-minute reading and read only four pages is a radical act, but it also seems to reiterate that the story can't be told in its entirety and that you aren't going to give it to us.

NP: Exactly, that can't happen with *Zong!* Usually, I get nervous about readings, but since I've understood that that is how I have to read it, it seems fine. It grounds me. Two pages, four pages, is fine. I would like to read the entire text and see how long it takes.

KE: Have you imagined what kind of space this sort of reading could take place in?

NP: I am trying to imagine it. I see it as a space where people could come and go as they please. The reading I did in Tobago was held at a fort in the main town, Scarborough. It's now a historical site and museum and so a destination for visitors. As I was reading on the gallery or porch of this museum, off to my left I could hear the voices of the visitors. It was dark out, but I could make out shapes of people. I thought it fascinating, because I felt that this is how it must have been. On the ship – while people were being thrown overboard, the life of the ship would have gone on. One of the audience members, the same man who told me about the sensation of drowning, mentioned those voices as well and thought that they fit with the reading. Usually, when you are doing a reading and you hear other voices or sounds, it's distracting, and you think that they shouldn't be there. But it felt right somehow, those sounds, and they underscored how other people's lives continued as this horrific act was unfolding. But this is no different from what happens today – just think of how our lives continue as Beirut burns, Iraq disintegrates and we buy lattes, Congo implodes as we speak and we shop or attend the movies ...

KE: It seems that the life of this text has a visual presence that tells one story, but its oral presence tells, and will tell in each context in which you read, a slightly different story as well.

NP: It's interesting, because the two readings I did this summer were to very different audiences. The one here was an audience of poetry aficionados, but the audience in Tobago was not, and yet both responses shared a willingness to listen to the silences and respond to them.

KE: The reading you did at the Scream Literary Festival in Toronto was part of a panel on 'appropriation art.' But do you even think about a work like *Zong!* as a form of appropriation art or understand the materials you work with as found materials in the same way that some of the other writers on that panel, like Kenny Goldsmith, do?

NP: I'm hesitating ... the phrase that comes to mind is 'the hard kernels of silence.' The legal text of *Zong!* is a hard kernel of silence, because locked in that text is the story of those unnamed Africans who like many, many others have been erased from history or memory. For those like myself who try to understand and negotiate the history and machinations of colonialism, postcolonialism and neocolonialism, it is often a process of trying to piece the self back together. So, no, it's not the same process as taking the *New York Times* and turning an issue into a book. The starting point is different and the stakes are higher. And in trying to negotiate those lacunae, those gaps, you become aware that you can never ever fill them except with the bones. But that panel wasn't a context in which to talk about that.

KE: But that's a problem – the fact that you didn't even feel there was a context in which to talk about those issues. There are poets, of course, who choose a constraint and the book comes out of their chosen constraint or set of constraints, but I have a strong sense that you have never chosen to work with constraints. Would you choose a constraint-based poetic practice if you didn't have to?

NP: In a word, no, but I have always been interested in the idea of limitation and its potential resources. But was that interest a result of my own history? Who knows. What is more interesting to me, however, is an insight about limitations or constraints I gained from the process of writing *Zong!* One of our founding cultural myths in the West is that of freedom – we can do or say anything (within certain constraints, of course). We are free to go out and find our constraints, poach from other cultures and so on. What I began to understand is that even when we think we are freest, if we lift – I want to say that veil of freedom – underneath will be found many unspoken constraints. In my own case, for instance – had I set out to write this work in the way I usually do, I don't think I would have been particularly interested in a white, male European voice. Why? Because the voices of Africans have been so silenced, so erased, that it's important to bring those voices forward. But, lo and behold – did a white, male voice not surface in the text, unbeknownst to me and without so much as a by-your-leave. And really it is his trajectory that gives shape, such as it is, to the book. He comes to realize that he is engaged in a great sin – I use the word advisedly because that is how they thought in those days – and it drives him crazy. Maybe a better way to put it is that he comes to understand that he has moved himself outside of his age where it was acceptable to enslave other human beings and transport them thousands of miles – he enters another space/time if you will – we could call it a fugue state – and he realizes that he has to kill himself. That is how he signals both his rejection of his society and his commitment to the Other – those who were being thrown overboard. There is no way I would have been interested in that voice, and although the voice doesn't overwhelm the work, I am very aware of it.

KE: So where did he come from?

NP: He surfaced – pardon the pun. He surfaced in the text. What that showed me is that I too have these limitations – these built-in constraints. One of them was that as an African-descended Black woman, I should only be interested in the Black woman's or Black man's story. So how 'free' am I really, how lacking in constraint am I, if even with my so-called exercise of choice I am already limiting or constraining myself? What about the constraint – in the form of expectations – that the poetry by African-descended poets should primarily be about certain topics – resistance, revolution, or the belief that we don't as a rule write experimental, avant-garde or innovative poetics? These are all constraints that we either take on or embrace. And could we not argue that the very idea of the freedom to choose a constraint signals the existence of – to use insurance language – pre-existing constraints and serves to mask them by the very idea of freedom to choose the constraint? Further, the apparent absence of constraints in certain groups, which requires one to go out and find one, dovetails nicely with – actually depends on the overabundance of constraints in the lives of others – constraints of gender, class, sexuality and race – constraints that the white, straight male sees himself as outside of. Which is what I think you were getting at with your question. Except that I think the constraint begins a lot earlier than the act of artificially seeking a constraint.

KE: So you couldn't excise his voice even after it came to the surface?

NP: Because it is as much his story as my story. And he represents an idea and a way of being that has to die – drown itself, self-immolate in order for us to reclaim our 'is-ness.'

KE: I've always read your poetic project as an epistemological project. Who is authorized to know? What can we know? So the fact that this 'authorized' knower emerges seems completely appropriate, but so too is the necessity of his death, which in turn authorizes you to tell the story that can't be told.

NP: Of course, it is interesting that he is telling the story through this other figure, Setaey Adamu Boateng, whom I believe is African, and, you know, in this type of discourse it is usually the white person who tells the story on behalf of the Black person who, for any number of reasons, cannot or isn't allowed to tell the story. In the case of *Zong!*, it is the African woman recounting this story that cannot yet must be told, and within that telling, among the many other stories, is the white man's story.

KE: There is, in the context of innovative poetics, especially in the U.S., a long tradition of poets engaging in a Buddhist practice. So there is a discussion initiated by people like Anne Waldman, and many of the writers who have been associated with the scene at Naropa, about spirituality and innovative poetics, but it seems to be limited to – if I can say it? – mostly white poets who have adopted Buddhism. It seems to me that even if you are not necessarily a religious person, spirituality is also important to your poetic practice. Often when you read, you perform a ritual at the beginning of the reading ... are you comfortable talking about this aspect of your writing?

NP: Yes and no, but it is an important question. I think your point is well taken, because even Christianity – the West's own religion – is verboten, isn't it. I think what has to be remembered in terms of this work, *Zong!*, is that spirituality (I hate that word) and religion permeate it. The age, the 18th century, was one in which religion was central to life, hence the mention of sin above. The church, Catholic and Protestant, was deeply involved in the Trade. Indeed, it was a priest, Bartolomé de las Casas, who suggested that in order to stop the destruction of the aboriginal populations of the New World, 'negroes' should be imported to do the work in the mines and on the plantations. The rest, as they say, is history. So, religion is a backdrop to this story. Now, regarding art and spirituality, I think it's important to recall a significant moment in art history – I'm now talking about visual art – when Picasso and other modernists come upon the aesthetics of Africa and Oceania. Hal Foster, the art critic, writes that when the Europeans attempted to engage with the artistic practices from these areas, they were unable to deal with the spirituality that was integral to the production of what I'll call cultural artefacts, so they appropriated the form. This was the tradition that saved Western art, infused it with new life, but its spirituality and the chance to reclaim a ritual function for art in the West was explicitly rejected. What, if any, impact did that rejection of spirituality have on Western art? That could be the subject of an entire conversation. But I think one effect is that – and here we come back to constraints again – only certain traditions are allowed in poetry – Taoism (the long shadow of Pound), Buddhism, Zen, but not Christianity and certainly not African spirituality. And, what the hell is that anyway – African spirituality? I say it that way because the average person – African or non-African – doesn't know what it is and many – African peoples included – are afraid of it and see it as part of demon worship. It is interesting that without a church, a written liturgy, a clergy, and in the face of extreme persecution, African belief systems took root in the New World and continue to flourish in places like Cuba, Brazil and Trinidad. Yes, many things happened during the course of writing this work for which I don't have a language to explain. And the modernist, avant-garde, innovative poetics discourse was of no help explaining this either. What I do know, however, is that there was a competing spiritual system, vis-à-vis Christianity I mean, aboard the ship – the ship as I imagined it, that is – and that that system was African or pan-African. It's interesting that there is this discomfort with spirituality, but there is a sense, and this is somewhat clichéd, in which art has become our new religion – there are no contemporary churches, for instance, that can compete with buildings being presently constructed to house works of art. High priests and disciples – we have them. I could go on, but I think you get my point.

KE: I'm thinking that we could say that there is something aleatory about *Zong!*, since you keep telling these stories about things just happening or appearing that changed or shaped the text, but we might also say, no, that's not it at all. It's not aleatory but rather some other kind of intervention. So my question is how do we think about the difference between a text's aleatory and spiritual elements, or is 'aleatory' one of those terms we've adopted in the world of avant-garde literature and art to obfuscate what could otherwise be understood as spiritual?

NP: I know that you are not at all meaning this, but I do get a little anxious when the idea of aleatory is linked to work by an African artist. There is a long history of this belief in some natural African or Negro talent that just happens – particularly in the performative arts. Like natural rhythm, it doesn't need training or discipline. For instance, instructions were given – I don't recall all the details – not to direct Robeson too closely in one of the plays he did because the producers didn't want to affect what they saw as an instinctive natural Negro talent. Having said that, however, I am aware of trying to hide some of my understanding of the deep spiritual elements of the text, partly because I don't have the language and also because I think that if I talk about it people might misunderstand it or think it too New-Agey. Of course, I, and we, do ourselves a disservice because poetry's roots are deeply sacred, embedded in ritual, in chants and spells, and all those practices that in another context would be seen as 'religious' or 'spiritual.' This harks back to my earlier comments about visual art. As you well know, I am not Christian, and this is not a brief for bringing the religious into poetry, but merely to look at what constraints we operate under as we write as 'free subjects.'

KE: Do you feel the need to conceal the spiritual elements of the text across the writing communities you inhabit or just in the context of experimental writing communities?

NP: Definitely in the context of the experimental community – the offshoot of high modernism – but I think it's more widespread than that. Maybe that's something I have to come to terms with. Maybe that is the next step for me? I do want to add, however, that the very idea of concealment is deeply rooted in the historical experiences of enslaved Africans – you may have heard of the idea of 'hidden in plain view' as it applies to the spirituals and quilts produced by African Americans which contained secret messages about fleeing slavery. There was also concealment of spiritual knowledge even from one's own children for fear of betrayal and punishment. And finally the idea of concealment and secrecy is deeply embedded in continental African cultures and practices – the idea that knowledge is only passed on when you are ready for it and to gender- or age-specific groups. It is helpful and productive for me to engage with these ideas around concealment and secrecy rather than seeing my practices of concealment as primarily a negative consequence of working in a commodity-driven art environment bereft of ritual or spirit. It also continues over the idea of the code that I think permeates *Zong!*

KE: Many people have been anticipating *Zong!* since you started to read from it several years ago. But how do you think it will be taken up in experimental writing communities? Or are they even prepared to take up this text?

NP: I think, as you say, it is so excessive on the surface it might prove difficult for people to enter – I hope not. When *She Tries Her Tongue* was published people talked about it as being a postmodernist text, and I didn't have a problem with that, but many of those people didn't understand the Caribbean and the postcolonial aspects of the area and the text. They also didn't understand how the Caribbean was postmodern long before the advent of postmodernism. Because in terms of things like bricolage and competing discourses, they were already there, and that is where that text comes from – it comes out of the Caribbean. With *Zong!* I suspect people will first see its experimental nature and its relationship to the modernist traditions, but in its use of competing motifs and stories, I see links with certain aspects of Yoruba aesthetic practices. I suspect it will take a longer time for readers to see that.

Toronto, August 2008

SELECTED WORKS

Thorns. Stratford: Williams-Wallace Inc., 1980.

She Tries Her Tongue, Her Silence Softly Breaks. Charlottetown: Ragweed Press, 1989.

Looking for Livingstone: An Odyssey of Silence. Toronto: Mercury Press, 1991.

Zong! Middletown, CT, and Toronto: Wesleyan University Press and The Mercury Press, 2008.

Discourse on the Logic of Language

WHEN IT WAS BORN, THE MOTHER HELD HER NEWBORN CHILD CLOSE: SHE BEGAN THEN TO LICK IT ALL OVER. THE CHILD WHIMPERED A LITTLE, BUT AS THE MOTHER'S TONGUE MOVED FASTER AND STRONGER OVER ITS BODY, IT GREW SILENT – THE MOTHER TURNING IT THIS WAY AND THAT UNDER HER TONGUE, UNTIL SHE HAD TONGUED IT CLEAN OF THE CREAMY WHITE SUBSTANCE COVERING ITS BODY.

English
is my mother tongue.
A mother tongue is not
not a foreign lan lan lang
language
l/anguish
    anguish
– a foreign anguish

English is
my father tongue.
A father tongue is
a foreign language,
therefore English is
a foreign language
not a mother tongue.

What is my mother
tongue
my mammy tongue
my mummy tongue
my momsy tongue
my modder tongue
my ma tongue?

I have no mother
tongue
no mother tongue
no tongue to mother
to mother
tongue
me

I must therefore be tongue
dumb
dumb-tongued
dub-tongued
damn dumb
tongue

EDICT I

*Every owner of slaves
shall, wherever possible,
ensure that his slaves
belong to as many ethno-
linguistic groups as
possible. If they can-
not speak to each other,
they cannot then foment
rebellion and revolution.*

Those parts of the brain chiefly responsible for speech are named after two learned nineteenth-century doctors, the eponymous Doctors Wernicke and Broca respectively.

Dr. Broca believed the size of the brain determined intelligence; he devoted much of his time to 'proving' that white males of the Caucasian race had larger brains than, and were therefore superior to, women, Blacks and other peoples of colour.

Understanding and recognition of the spoken word takes place in Wernicke's area – the left temporal lobe, situated next to the auditory cortex; from there relevant information passes to Broca's area – situated in the left frontal cortex – which then forms the response and passes it on to the motor cortex. The motor cortex controls the muscles of speech.

THE MOTHER THEN PUT HER FINGERS INTO HER CHILD'S MOUTH – GENTLY FORCING IT OPEN;
SHE TOUCHES HER TONGUE TO THE CHILD'S TONGUE, AND HOLDING THE TINY MOUTH OPEN,
SHE BLOWS INTO IT – HARD. SHE WAS BLOWING WORDS – HER WORDS, HER MOTHER'S WORDS,
THOSE OF HER MOTHER'S MOTHER, AND ALL THEIR MOTHERS BEFORE – INTO HER DAUGHTER'S
MOUTH.

but I have
a dumb tongue
tongue dumb
father tongue
and english is
my mother tongue
is
my father tongue
is a foreign lan lan lang
language
l/anguish
   anguish
a foreign anguish
is english –
another tongue
my mother
   mammy
   mummy
   moder
   mater
   macer
   moder
   tongue
   mothertongue

tongue mother
tongue me
mothertongue me
mother me
touch me
with the tongue of your
lan lan lang
language
l/anguish
   anguish
english
is a foreign anguish

EDICT II

Every slave caught speak-
ing his native language
shall be severely pun-
ished. Where necessary,
removal of the tongue is
recommended. The of-
fending organ, when re-
moved, should be hung
on high in a central place,
so that all may see and
tremble.

A tapering, blunt-tipped, muscular, soft and fleshy organ describes
(a) the penis.
(b) the tongue.
(c) neither of the above.
(d) both of the above.

In man the tongue is
(a) the principal organ of taste.
(b) the principal organ of articulate speech.
(c) the principal organ of oppression and exploitation.
(d) all of the above.

The tongue
(a) is an interwoven bundle of striated muscle running in three planes.
(b) is fixed to the jawbone.
(c) has an outer covering of a mucous membrane covered with papillae.
(d) contains ten thousand taste buds, none of which is senstive to the taste
    of foreign words.

Air is forced out of the lungs up the throat to the larnyx where it causes
the vocal cords to vibrate and create sound. The metamorphosis from
sound to intelligible word requires
(a) the lip, tongue and jaw all working together.
(b) a mother tongue.
(c) the overseer's whip.
(d) all of the above or none.

from Looking for Livingstone

Was it the word
     In Mary's womb
Exploding
        Or the Silence
Of holy
In the desert that was
          Elizabeth
Seeded with Silence
        Barren
Shrivelled womb
       Refusing
The swell and
    Split
In seed until
     Silence
Welcomes
The hungry word
      In again
And again
    The womb
Oasis of Silence
      Blooms

Friday the eighteenth day of January, 1859
London, England.

Dear David,

I have written so very many letters to you – I have now lost count ... all I have received in return from you is silence. And more silence. I know your discoveries are most important – to you, to the nation, to God and our Queen, but what of me, David? Why is silence my lot? Why? I pray you leave the continent – let it be – free yourself of it; it is damned and will but curse you for your labours.

I, who have travelled the Kalahari with a child at my breast and one in the womb to be with you, want more than silence. I demand more than silence – I am entitled to more than silence. I have made my home, my only home in your country, the country of your God – silence – and how I abhor it.

I am your wife, David, and I am jealous – very jealous. Can one be jealous of a country – a continent? Oh yes – oh very very yes – and I am jealous of Africa – of the massive, impenetrable and continental silence she has now come to symbolize to me. Oh, David ... she has you, her silence possesses you as mine never has, and you penetrate her – up her rivers and falls, through her undergrowth, her jungles – to what end? To discover what? My howling silence.

When the Silence of Shupanga claims me for the last time, David, you will weep for me and my silence, my very small silence that now flails at that larger Silence. Oh, how I long to hear from you, David – to break the sentence of my silence ... I bid you 'a hundred thousand welcomes.' And only one good-bye.

I remain

Your dearest and most faithful Wife
in God and Silence,
Mary Livingstone

Zong! #1

```
     w   w   w                 w              a   wa

                w                 a              w   a         t
er                      wa                                s

          our                               wa
    te  r  gg                         g            g        go

            o        oo                   goo                    d

                 waa                              wa  wa
    w  w  waa

                  ter                      o           oh
     on              o                         ne              w  one

                      w  o  n                       d  d  d

          ey                          d                     a

        dey          a    ah                   ay

              s                    one                         day  s

                  wa              wa
```

Masuz Zuwena Ogunsheye Ziyad Ogwambi Keturah

Zong!

w w w w w   a

w wa   wa   t

er   wa   te

r   wat

er   wa   ter

of   w

ant

Aba Chimanga Zaeema Oba Eshe

Zong! #2

the throw in circumstance

the weight in want

in sustenance

for underwriters

the loss

the order in destroy

the that fact

the it was

the were

negroes

the after rains

Wafor Yao Siyolo Bolade Kibibi Kamau

Zong! #15

defend the dead

        weight of circumstance

ground

       to usual &

         etc

         where the ratio of just

in less than

     is necessary

          to murder

the subject in property

the save in underwriter

        where etc tunes justice

        and the *ratio* of murder

        is

Akilah Falope Ouma Weke Jubade

the usual in occurred

the just in ration

the suffer in loss

defend the dead

the weight

in

circumstance

ached in necessary

the ration in just

age the act in the *ave* to justice

Micere Ndale Omowumni Ramla Ajani

Zong! #25

justify the could

       the captain &

       the crew

       the authorize

in captain

crew &

could

           could authorize justify

                  captain

   &

     crew

                  the

                  could

or justify authorize

      could

      captain & crew

           authorize

Bomani Yahya Modupe Jibowu Fayola

the crew

the captain &

the could

                                        the justify

                                                    in

captain

                                                could &

                                                crew

                                    in authorize

justify

            the could

            the captain &

            the crew

                        justify the authorize

                                    the could

Zong! #26

was the cause was the remedy was the record was the argument
was the delay was the evidence was overboard was the not was the
cause was the was was the need was the case was the perils was the
want was the particular circumstance was the seas was the costs
was the could was the would was the policy was the loss was the
vessel was the rains was the order was the that was the this was the
necessity was the mistake was the captain was the crew was the
result was justified was the voyage was the water was the maps
was the weeks was the winds was the calms was the captain was
the seas was the rains was uncommon was the declaration was the
apprehension was the voyage was destroyed was thrown was the
questions was the therefore was the this was the that was the
negroes was the cause

Omolara Chimaneya Adekemi Mowumni Iliola

from Ratio

shave me

now de   can't

the port   do you

hear   him

pass   the peas

pleas

all round   slap

her slap slap

of

sail there   was only

when not   if & ashes

to   seal this act   of

skin of sin

of what a   deal my elation

ran

riot   my   seal

on   a   deal

well   done

i   see   you   kate

clad

in   fur   the

ring   how   many

carats

you ask

forty   i

say ben   the lad   lay   dead

mi   omo

mi   *omo* dear

ruth this   is a

tale   told

cold   an   old

tale   one

note a   song an

aria   for   clair

for   kate   for   clara

Zong!

                                                &   ruth

                          etc   but

                                      seal the

       sale   &   hear

          my   tale

                               told

                 cold   sh h

                               the

                   clarion

  sounds   for

      me   is it   a detail

                    man

                              he was

                       of

          mien   hard

&   cold

 the   sobs oh

    the sobs   sam   was first

          mate the

                                 oba

          sobs   again

                     omi se

      o   *ore*   over   and   over

             again   this

      creed of   greed

               is

  new   it   seeds   the

        the

         sea s   feeds   the

        lust   for

         tin   for gold

      comes   to rest

        in   rest

     rest my   pet

        my   she

       negro

       how do

   we   parse

KAREN MAC CORMACK

KATE EICHHORN: Several poets in this collection were reluctant to include materials from earlier books. By contrast, you requested selections from books published throughout your career. In the preface to a reprint of *Nothing By Mouth*, you reflect on the process of returning to one's early writing: 'To revisit the poems comprising one's first collection provides the inevitable impulse to "rework" what now dissatisfies. Happily there are also surprises along some of the vectors, through certain inflections, and within these poetic frames.' Can you elaborate on what you see as some of the important lines of continuity – shared vectors, inflections, frames – between *Nothing By Mouth*, *Straw Cupid* and *Quill Driver* and your more recent work?

KAREN MAC CORMACK: In all my writing there is an ongoing concern to confront the habitual. My early work explores various means of altering the ways we perceive the day-to-day, while allowing 'language' itself to be perceived as a material entity (rather than a transparent vastness through which to 'see' our world). This led me to investigate what I call 'sentence effects,' particularly the integration of poetic line with a prose period. This was not intended as a means to reach a conciliatory synthesis of the two genres, but to delineate both their radical sympathies and contradictions – i.e., my intention was not to write a prose poem, but to reclaim an exploratory usefulness from the sentence, in order to extend the poetic form to more challenging/rewarding modes of readership.

What began in *Quill Driver* as a propositional language becomes in *Marine Snow* a fusion of propositional language with stanzaic configurations, in order to explore phenomenological and social implications in perception, when the latter is mediated through the orthodox and the errant trajectories of language, writing and space. *Quirks & Quillets* explores a similar state of mediation but utilizes a different momentum by suppressing the period in favour of a series of brief, intense phrasal continua. For the most part, the writing deliberately avoids punctuation so that grammatical patterns can shift in both their functions and effects. The intention was not to produce an 'abstract' or non-referential text, but to reveal how meaning emerges in the sites of its production.

The Tongue Moves Talk explores the perceptions, misconceptions and current role of the social concept of the 'carrier.' I focus specifically on three associations of that concept: 1) the orthodox association of language as a 'portage' of meaning, 2) the medical association of 'carrier' as virus, and 3) the genderized, biological link to woman as 'carrier' of children and by implication, of the species. These three associations are treated as sites of familiarity – sites we experience on a daily basis but routinely leave unquestioned because of their very proximity. The poems foreground these assumptions of 'invisibility' in order to render them transparent as ideological operations. In keeping with what was a critical agenda, the poems deliberately repudiate any of the 'reader comforts' of familiarity and habituality of normative language. *The Tongue Moves Talk* establishes a deliberate resistance, structured upon patterns that offer a rigorous positioning of their linguistic materiality.

Fit to Print is a collaboration with British poet Alan Halsey. The format of the pages intentionally refers to that most daily of reading materials – the newspaper. However, the poems themselves, while displaying a concern with and for daily events (and these range from earthquakes to conditions of weather), do not adopt a 'transit' theory of meaning.

Together we approached the newspaper format as a way of fusing issues of mass culture with a non-traditional writing practice. The newspaper column produces unexpected ruptures that the reader learns to negotiate. Our intention was to apply this achieved negotiation to a writing that departs from the 'habit' of a conventional language.

In *At Issue* I examine the format and contents of the magazine instead of those of the newspaper. The interruptions and syntactical disarrangements in *At Issue* reflect the experience of reading that format (within what is certainly a critical agenda on my part). Most of the poems (but not all) utilize the vocabulary and spelling found in magazines of a diverse nature. (An interesting if frightening fact is that there are fewer typos in *Vogue* than in most scholarly books published in North America!) To counter *Vogue* (both British and American versions) I've written through issues of *Self* (a health/fitness magazine also geared to female readership) and *Prevention* (another 'health' magazine). Non-magazine poems are included as a variant measure of linguistic origin.

These are the strategies that came to inform the writing of *Implexures*.

KE: As mentioned, in *Fit to Print* and *At Issue* you turn your attention to newspapers and women's magazines. I read these texts as attempts to grapple with the poverty of language and content in the popular media, and as attempts to refocus our attention on the poetic forms that exist where least expected – for example, in the cleaved columns of a newspaper. But I also read these texts, especially *At Issue*, as humorous and playful works, unless I am failing to recognize the deeper meaning of your 'flip-flop nirvana'? Since you are most often characterized as a very serious writer, better known for erudite commentaries on language than jocular play, can comment on the importance of humour in your writing and performance practice?

KM: To quote Margot Fonteyn, 'One should always take one's work seriously, but one should never take oneself seriously.' Humour runs through my work (to be serious all of the time would be a stricture, indeed!) but it doesn't seem to be a particular focus for many readers of my poetry (although Antoine Cazé drew attention to the ludic in an interview he conducted with Steve McCaffery and myself that was published in the French journal *Sources*). Other critics refer to my 'wit,' (having written that, I wonder if I'll be asked to provide the requisite examples?!) There are degrees and gradations in 'wit' and the 'ludic': wit is knowing (and 'the unexpected combining or contrasting of previously unconnected ideas or expressions' [OED]) and the ludic is playful, and humour is defined as 'jocose imagination (less intellectual & more sympathetic than wit)' [the OED again].

In the public context, what is referred to as 'being humorous' is often an entry into the practice/practise (one's own and others); the opportunity to include levity is welcome as far as I'm concerned.

KE: If wit is understood as 'the unexpected combining or contrasting of previously unconnected ideas or expressions,' then wit is a signature feature of your writing. Part of me wonders if this unexpected element might account for the difficulty critics appear to have had engaging with your writing over the years, but I suspect the reasons for this are more complex.

Steve McCaffery concludes an essay on *Quirks & Quillets* with an observation about how your writing has been overlooked by literary critics, especially feminist literary critics in Canada. Sadly, this observation, made in 2001, is still relevant. In Nate Dorward's recent collection, *Antiphonies: Essays on Women's Experimental Poetries in Canada*, there are essays and responses to your work by Gerald Bruns, Alan Halsey and John Hall, as well as an interview with Stephen Cain, but your work has not been taken up by feminist literary critics. Since you have never actively sought to quell feminist readings of your work and have been open about your debt to women writers, especially Barnes and Stein, how do you explain this refusal? Or to turn the question around somewhat, does the resistance to bringing a feminist reading to bear on a text such as *Quirks & Quillets, The Tongue Moves Talk* or *At Issue* reveal more about the limits of feminist literary criticism than it does about your writing?

KM: Over the years the reasons for this exclusion seem to have changed (if not evolved). In the early days (as I recall) my work was perceived by feminist critics as too 'intellectual' and 'opaque' and not 'essentialist' enough (I am relying on remembered conversations and secondhand accounts.) Subsequently, it was suggested that I was not openly committed to feminist concerns, while at the same time one male Canadian west-coast critic (in conversation) referred to my early poetry as representative of 'Karen being pissed off with the patriarchy (again).'

In 'turning the question around,' you bring the focus to bear on successive generations of feminist critics (I've been publishing poetry for three decades now). Before your question in this context, I hadn't considered what the exclusion 'reveal(s) ... about the limits of feminist literary criticism.' Are contemporary feminist critics continuing to engage in the same concerns as those of ten, twenty, thirty years ago? For example, is 'essentialism' in feminist poetry as crucial an aspect 'now' as it was 'then'? If so, why?

Perhaps my own reluctance to work consistently on critical essays and to publish them collectively is partly responsible for my work not being 'taken up by feminist critics in Canada,' but if feminist critics (of diverse nationalities) choose not to engage with the innovations of writers of any gender, then that is telling – however, critics follow their chosen pursuits, and writers (following their own) would do well to respect the proclivities of others. I would hope that my work continues to benefit from engaged criticism with or without a feminist focus.

KE: Perhaps similar issues have led to your work being overlooked by other critics? You have drawn attention to language as a colonizing force – this is certainly evident in your more recent books, including *Vanity Release* and *Implexures*. Can you elaborate on this aspect of your project, or perhaps you don't see your work through this lens at all?

KM: I have drawn attention to the multiple dimensions of language but have never focused on 'language as a colonizing force.' Earlier in this interview you interpreted my engagements with forms 'in *Fit to Print* and *At Issue* ... as attempts to grapple with the poverty of language and content in the popular media, and as attempts to refocus our attention on the poetic forms that exist where least expected – for example, in the cleaved columns of a newspaper.' Poetic forms are to be discerned everywhere, including signage. One of my favourite examples is 'THIS DOOR IS ALARMED' (as seen in the U.K. on emergency exit doors). So it's not so much a matter of 're-focus(ing) our attention' as re-presenting what is perhaps not readily perceived in the original context.

I experience discomfort with 'the poverty of language and content in the popular media.' My critique is with those who deliver the inaccuracies (in spelling, grammar and, yes, facts) and with those who do not question the media on the way 'information' is presented.

Some of the humour in *Vanity Release* arises from my collaging juxtapositions in discourses different from those of the media, namely typing and shorthand manuals and a traveller's phrase book (all from earlier centuries). There is no sense on my part of 'language as a colonizing force' as I don't see 'instruction' as 'colonizing' in this particular regard. What is serious is never distant from what is humorous and my poetry reflects that.

To introduce the notion of 'language as a colonizing force' into *Implexures* is outside the author's intention.

KE: Now we've veered off into dangerous territory indeed! Perhaps it is best to change course rather than pursue what is clearly already adrift?

Your most recent publications, the two volumes of *Implexures*, represent a notable shift. *Implexures* is a more sustained attempt to work the poetic line in prose form in order to destabilize both the sentence and the paragraph. The subject headings imposed on *Implexures* identify the book as 'literature' and 'innovative writing,' but I wonder if you still consider this a book of poetry too, on some level?

KM: The subject headings were not of my choice, nor were they welcomed by either co-publisher! (There is an apparent pressure to 'categorize' any given book for the convenience of booksellers so as to 'identify' texts easily.) For me, *Implexures* is a 'transhistoric polybiography.'

In *Implexures* (meaning enfoldings or entwinings) there is a purposeful emphasis on time. Specifically, I am combining multiple biographies, time frames and historical circumstances with a poetic focus. (My published books are predominantly those of poetry.) Additionally, *Implexures* is a critique of conventional narrative methods, and like my other works it doesn't aspire to 'convention' or the normative. On the technical level, *Implexures* intentionally applies the poetic line to productively destabilize and reinform the sentence as a formal unit. Written in a deliberately disjunctive manner, it takes its inspiration from, and seeks to position itself within, a long line of formally investigative work by women.

KE: In *Implexures*, you adopt and subvert a series of genres historically associated with the rise of the subject, including the autobiography, memoir and epistolary. The result is a text that is at times perplexing, but also deceptively intimate, since the genres you are effectively subverting at least promise access to a subject's private life and personal history. What motivated you to grapple with the subject of the subject more directly in this work? Also, how do you see *Implexures* both extending and moving beyond other feminist innovative writer's subversions of autobiographical forms (e.g., Hejinian's *My Life* and Scalapino's *Zither*)?

KM: The difference is one of 'autobiography' and 'polybiography' – where Hejinian's *My Life* brings its focus to the former, the concerns of *Implexures* are those of the latter. If this indicates an 'extending and moving beyond other feminist innovative writers' subversions of autobiographical forms,' it would then be from the singular of the lifespan of an individual (Hejinian's *My Life*) to the plural transhistoric polybiography of *Implexures*.

KE: But in his essay on *Implexures*, John Hall observes that it may be the 'writing of many lives, but not any lives.' I think this is an important distinction. Polybiography is still marked by a certain degree of specificity. *Implexures* weaves together an eclectic range of textual and visual fragments – epigraphs, letters, diary entries, photographs, drawings (I'm assuming both found and fictional?). What sorts of decisions or procedures guided your process of selection in the creation of this genealogical palimpsest?

KM: *Implexures* is indeed a transhistoric polybiography – this is no work of fiction. The letters are all written by family members (including myself); the drawings are mine (there's a credit to that effect on the copyright page); certain 'diary' entries first appeared in the family biography *The Yesterdays Behind the Door* written by my great-great-aunt Susan Hicks Beach and published by Liverpool University Press in the year of my birth when Hicks Beach was ninety years old. The photographs in *Implexures* are of a house where I lived in Italy ... even the cover photograph is mine.

One reason this relatively short work took such a long time to complete was the sheer volume of unpublished and published material that I read in the course of research. (The family letters are in boxes and it was a formidable undertaking to sort through them.) The decisions I made were based on how to evince the durations and intensities that occur in non-linear evocations of time. I considered how to introduce various forebears from earlier centuries and when. Poetic forces are brought to bear on narrative prose, so the editing of *Implexures* proved to be extensive.

When I began the work in September 1993, it was as a response to Hicks Beach's 'family biography.' What did a poet writing in the then-late twentieth century have to offer to the notion and form of such a 'family biography?' *Implexures* (now in the 21st century) is my answer to that question.

KE: At least until *Implexures*, your investigations of the sentence have taken place within the context of poetry – if we must use these categories at all. Do you see any affinities between your investigation of 'sentence effects' and the syntactical investigations enacted by innovative fiction writers – for example Kathy Acker or Gail Scott? Or perhaps you see these as two separate types of poetic projects?

KM: I'm not inclined to seek affinities between fiction projects and my poetry/polybiography. The question of what affinities might occur between certain innovative projects of other disciplines (architecture/music/dance) and my 'investigation of sentence effects' might yield a more perplexing (as in intriguing) consideration. A generosity between disciplines is always to be encouraged.

KE: Since you've opened up the possibility of such a comparison, I have to ask you to elaborate. What do you see as the affinities between your poetry/polybiography and these other disciplines – for example, architecture?

KM: To begin with, it might be helpful to point to my essay 'Mutual Labyrinth: a proposal of exchange' in *Architectures of Poetry* (eds. Maria Eugenia Diaz Sanchez and Craig Douglas Dworkin, Amsterdam: Rodopi, 2004). The architectural projects and explorations of Bernard Cache, Claude Parent, Neil Spiller, Marcos Novak and Shigeru Ban (to name but a few) have all provided new approaches for me to consider in terms of how they interact with 'innovative poetries.'

KE: One of your post-*Implexures* projects is a series of book-length essays under the umbrella concept of the 'limitrophe,' which means 'on frontier, adjacent to.' Of course, being 'on frontier' and 'adjacent to' are two very different positions. These definitions suggest being both in and on the edges of something simultaneously. Is this how you think about yourself in relation to language and/or in relation to different writing communities? Perhaps, this is also how you understand your relation to place or nation state?

KM: A frontier that I live approximately three and a half kilometres from is the Canadian/American border, itself 'adjacent' to both countries. I am a Canadian citizen currently living and working in the U.S.A. I was born in what is now Zambia, though my parents returned to England when I was nine months old. So yes, I feel that my relation to being in and on the edges of 'place' (and writing communities) is very much an ongoing simultaneity. My relation to 'place' is made diverse by my travels and the various countries I've lived in over the years. My sense of community in terms of the creative is international.

Online from Toronto, Buffalo, London, Berlin and New York,
June to August 2008

SELECTED WORKS

Nothing by Mouth. Toronto: Underwhich Editions, 1984.

Straw Cupid. Toronto: Nightwood Editions, 1987.

Quill Driver. London: Nightwood Editions, 1989.

Quirks & Quillets. Tucson: Chax Press, 1991.

Marine Snow. Toronto: ECW Press, 1995.

The Tongue Moves Talk. Tucson: Chax Press and Hay-on-Wye, U.K.: West House Books, 1997.

Fit to Print. With Alan Halsey. Toronto: Coach House Books, 1998.

At Issue. Toronto: Coach House Books, 2001.

Vanity Release. La Laguna: Zasterle Press, 2003.

Implexures (Complete Edition). Tucson: Chax Press and Sheffield U.K.: West House Books, 2008.

Approach

Cross pollination was one way. An edict is another point of view. Languish no further until the manner is adjusted. So.

The body of woman is difference as defined by the male of the species. The woman *may* define herself as definition. There are members of both sexes these words will infuriate.

Perpetrate and perpetuate and every inclination. A supportable clause. Casualties are a prerogative and this is business in hand if not in mind. Laughed the prostitute. No longer. Let us be specific. Legitimacy is the abandoning of a rumour.

An error apparent. An uncle or someone else not by marriage. Mature coin for this passage, 'this is the road now take it.' The exit of excitement was still a long way off. Intimacy parted on either side. Viaduct. Aforenoon. Effrontery in profile with the shadow if its echo.

Perpendicular thought and a scene of a man and a woman not in harmony and this in a stylus of days and truce the forerunner of circled notes roundness reduced to a legible quarter. Didn't sleep well. No explanations but of 'cause.' Repetition in this erring.

The longer the sentence the less spontaneity. Deafness assured.

If these are not scars, don't pretend to imitate chalk on a slate.

Lateness extended becomes 'early,' jazz in both ears.

How many people are required to name a 'new' colour of nail polish and to what extent does this contribute to the rise in price of any given product?

Assorted leverage the thigh rolling away of a construct. A pair of wings. Twilight. Last lines on a sheet of paper eclipse ellipses. Not to repeat the repetition previews rupture through the window the grass waylaid the cicadas. We used to listen to elsewhere and wonder if dialect extends to that much August. The vehicle moves glass intended to stay more or less in position. Cooled rhododendron for climate versus architecture. The passage is, the plot furthers, the turn comes, a character leads, someone else removes. The eyes are the first part of importance at this moment. Emeralds are important to other people. Would this be called a verdict? Cement is made not far from the cut flowers in the room not here.

from Quirks & Quillets

The untried decibel of seamless hose unhurried sentence its adjectives the chosen ladder geological manoeuvre or landing strip spangles the same man connected *paillettes* cramp the page's reproduction not ours or the level's pinafore before piano truding words ahead of their names an algebra of what is scene momentous underneath.

§

One over in easy boots glow here or where glamour stays the fluid always empties before silk reached Europe November was originally the ninth month through impluvia liquids that are non-elastic recur as *interval* numerals conform to the space of their names on paper the ventricle looks different doubt remains delays the same.

N.B.: The format of these poems from *Quirks & Quillets* differs from the original due to space constraints – these were originally in a much larger font, one poem per page.

Somehow this did not mean the shortest distance between two points in the answer most closely related to the question set in antique forms more lavish than attention on such an occasion can engender words remembered or renewed a force of specialty as yours to recognize not in so many this much arrival went.

§

Increased honey towards acquaintance seeps to memory for another time place oneself in union splits hour from day sighs are not the weariest tone of fall apart the absent secrecy's measure of yield goes before the *yes* faded against all other descriptions grounded shock *rubati* of to see was spoken for sweet knowing reinforced the letters act.

AT ISSUE IX   Diminish

'You'll love what you don't see'
if avant garde is followed by only more avant garde
meaning *is* literal despite long lines yielding only merchandise
(Gwyneth Paltrow 'becoming' the Meryl Streep of the future)
'the new adventures of the orange box'
Hermès wraps your fingers around a splash
opting for contradiction
an originality competition
'as if there aren't enough ironies already'
but *how* can a hat be whimsical?
anything too new was suspect
'Miss America contestants wear flats'
(in the post-Seinfield era) say *agency*
or reign of tampering isn't new
overuse undeterred
knockoff ricocheting
'skin with room to spare'
'I need more fashion with my function'
hence knife-proof fabrics
but three years of olive goes pink
so say *yes* to oui
because free times costs so much these days
the rose has the last word (in the garden)
broached *and* declared
paying the bills specifically
imprinted left free-standing from the inside
of its unveiling to demolish immediately
bulldozed controversy around and over
provocation as a medium to oversee
fabricated reality
(almost part of the furniture)
style of *react*
in search of rest stops
no variegated panicky can do *all* that
while restructuring to humanize backfire
something called 'up-light'
might expect for warmer times

animated inside out
twang another way around
swing lavished with fluke
slot for glimpse or self-described
freight – get 'quotelet'
lives sell
(those semblances of personailities)
let's trace *image meld*, a perfect merger
right into knockoff land's
conga line entice and woo
couldn't get much closer
built-in glistens
'no iron necessary' logorific

Otherwise:

there is a table
the door swings to
mistakes a politician makes
no signs of
view obscured
the conversation
verbs applied to swelling
distance strikes
a pose is no position on the run
to office
home truth's aside
the subjunctive at
password accumulates
dust as part of the furniture
the nearness of *strange*
what passes for progress
in a 'new' material only
to revisit prior results
binary if a four letter word
weather and time are too often mismatched
how to unravel excess
fingerprints inside out
the chair is moved more than the table
kiss me on every side of the idea
if there's an ocean sea its
terms of explosives
in concept of layers
revised and sensing
separate accounts
no interest only
banks adhere to numbers
and profit themselves
by closing time
the speech suggests
accent as accessory
define a *nice day*
one verb is a time
words that begin with *c* and end in *s*

(chaos, crisis, chiasmus, capitals)
to live in or through
a remarking of
delimited ours
ready for close-up
but not in-above-one's-head
no script
any cutlery
to lay out terms
as devises not device
a remake revisited
the dilemma head on
full frontal acknowledgement
to route through
contact as a site
in motion
without appointment
if code is then veil
a network collaboration
locks on the door
key-in DNA
luxury is fruit on the table
listening to sensation of *spun*
my sleeve on your heart
watch the radio
mute that television
is advantage invasive or misunderstood?
any inclination in a storm
masks increasingly among us
why wake the dead when it is the living who sleep?
focus on threshold not view
the body's discomforts
expounded understandings in *mis*
not applied at random degrees of *ever* within and without
context may be delayed but then forgotten
when will the furniture move again
itself and our traces
repertoire surrounds us and
time is the spot you're standing on

One

HISTORICAL LETTERS 1

Sunday was a definite break-away into Difference.
   – Susan Hicks Beach (née Christian) to Jacques Derrida circa 1880

Saturday afternoon: a colonial country's thunderstorm, the origins of this fire could almost rival Malta, winter somewhere between a famous neighbour in the last century and 'an elasticity of spirits' out to Ceylon. One refers to birth through paper – a certificate, photographs, celluloid, (now) the VCR and DVD. The starting point is not realized by a new addition as centres are grown from collisions. Vegetation and climate are remarked upon but their letters they destroyed in ensuing years and less heat. The performance occupied several days.

Molecules might not have been as confused as I thought probable, the two from the northern hemisphere less seven and a return to places in it for all three within half those years. The dog was quarantined. So to Saxon *Doom* from Norse *Lag* always defying definition as many marriages attest. Elsewhere (the word emblematic of my vocabulary) other photographs were taken, letters direct us to 'Mc or Mac' no longer prefixed island surnames. In the Sudan the Anwar Dam covers the spot exactly (planes had propellers then) and figs greeted us to so many palms.

The disappointments of a generation skewed by cynicism or performance mean the wars inhabit some individuals on an ongoing basis and not only those of the 21st century. Cousins married each other more often than not, an act perhaps 'devastating to humour.' Recognize the ache for what it is, reside there, not knowing opinions, hear a rosary of sunsets with the bells. Disowned as much for himself as her English one. (One false step beyond the Cliffs of Moher into the fog and so to sea.) Others were swimming in the lake before I could. One manoeuvre too many and algae came into view, there were bubbles under the water eyes OPEN for this other world. I didn't even choke they were so prompt in rescue and (later) censure. Wraparound marginless concern and more driftwood. A child faces a first remembered nightmare falling from a suspension bridge in the French car, two parents in the front seat the Pacific joins us.

She who burnt the archives married only after her parents death(s), but it was still an unfortunate date. Another sister lived apart from the unspeaking husband at the other end of the house. But Henry's every hour is understandable. He went to sea under the windows of home became merchant ships the world over, not a finger's space between them. Map of Africa above the libary fireplace.

For these are characters – sense of direction, observed movements, 'time of our lives.' The tableaux run through themselves. To absorb a history of family through the centuries requires a forebear's attention to facts and no fear of paper. Remember this. The nights are a time of chosen light, days an elaborate grafting.

Pick a childhood to look at. This doesn't have to be your own, but if it is, the strangeness of certain events may shift unexpectedly. The more central regions are established before questions reach those limits. Corn silk, ridge down a dog's back and sky belong to this imbalance, or the branches of a sailing ship, warp of uniform against young skin, lemons. Smell and taste issue the fissure. In a warmer climate more colour in a covering, less material on the surface. View's residue adheres to memory (as such). Limbs grow, or should, if not pain, but that also gathers in illness and beyond the door's arithmetic, spoken word to page aloud, a number and its half, an apple's seasonal red fades against cover to cover rote. To be made aware of difference, real or in so much, perceived, limits all but anxiety. The volume attunes the song. Will you hear? A promotion to meaning enlists words. This combination reflects selectivity. The romp is a tie to early pleasure. First remembered bite flows there. Mango and frangipani in the garden, followed by papaya – so brief, no smells are registered and came to be appreciated 'as if for the first time' years later. *It is a lovely house with an amazing garden full of papaya trees, flowers, bean stalks, peanuts, pens with pigs, rabbits & chickens, a fresh water stream, 2 dogs & a cat.* (Castries, Saint Lucia, 1 January 74)

We pay attention to what we can make sense of, not necessarily all at once, but contemplation and deduction aren't favoured by the very young. Moments are a category we give over to. Sometimes patience delivers more time only for itself. This is unimportant. A life lasts for however long its measured events take place and not all of each registers fully but the fact if evidence lists partially. Spinning doesn't stop, perception changes.

Three

HISTORICAL LETTERS 3

> *Is? I mean* was. *But then, I mean also* will be. *And so I cleave to the nostalgic present, as grammarians might call it.*
> – Max Beerbohm

The pier's better known through its many images in films. Songs on and off the radio drift into hearing up and down day or night. A hand reaches for another's fingers. There are many reasons for wearing gloves, temperature the least of them. Is it at one's side front and centre back and forth? Salt air and creaking, a stone beach, not sand. The wind picks up, but not necessarily in the same place. Hard Knot Pass in the rain one is easily convinced of as permanently cold if not always wet. Not so the *Meltame* in Naxos, where white blisters blue noon heat, the jelly fish's sting scars for half a year, ouzo distends nocturnal notes (the music is *always* loud). Chalk as a colour not a taste. The mosaic is splashed to shimmering in the museum ... water beyond varnish inhabiting movement. Curves of the archway lead to coolness for a rectangular segement of afternoon. Many visual depictions of these islands' architecture veer to abstraction a realist dreams of ... *on our way home we passed a restaurant, also on the beach, where a band was playing and the Greeks were dancing. We sat down and a Greek man at once bought each of the four of us a beer, (a common practice) and we danced and danced and suddenly Euripides said 'We're all going to Melanes' (Alexandra's village) and so we piled into a pickup truck and watched the sun come up over the mountains and appeared at her parents' door at 6 a.m. They were not at all surprised and gave us coffee and then put us to bed and we slept until 1 p.m. and were woken up only to eat a gargantuan dinner which consisted of: goat, spaghetti, salad, bread, cheese, fish, wine, oranges and a yellow-orange fruit, about the size of a small plum, which tasted like passion-fruit but did not have nearly as many seeds. Then we looked at the beautiful view ... Melanes is a terraced village and from their house you see a deep valley and directly across from you a very lush mountain. The land is completely covered with fruit trees! The quiet was the most striking thing, it was if the car had never been heard of, (but Alexandra's parents have a huge fridge!)*

These people, this lovely old couple who had welcomed us as if we were their own children, constantly fussed that we had not eaten enough, (I was ready to

BURST) and Euripides kept apologizing that no one else spoke English, to which we replied that we were sorry we didn't speak Greek. They were very natural and talked and talked with no inhibition, even had an argument, (it lasted all of three minutes). It was a very special day because not many forgeigners are brought into the hearts of the Greeks and we have been especially lucky in this respect. Adonis and 'Mama' have adopted us and Alexandra's parents certainly did for the day and would love for us to visit again. They are expert cheese-makers (?), which I think is one of their forms of income.

Anyway at 3 p.m. we ran all the way up the street-steps to catch the bus back to Naxos. (Their house is about one third of the way down the mountain, but not at the bottom of the village.) The bus ride back was breathtaking (we were on a road which went up near the top of the mountains and right down into the valleys) ... (Naxos, Greece, 28 May 76)

Borders are windshields. In Sardinia the 'crossroads of death' pushed both into contortion. A poorly marked intersection's preoccupied driver (the car was French). Backseat view of the impact more the sound of metal into metal flipping upside down to ground gravel spinning head wedged in rear deahboard three and a half revolutions but no silence. Stop. Voices and sound of running feet approaching. In any language the driver said 'I'm sorry.' Pushing outwards from distorted immobility. The sensation when lying down that the head is too heavy for the neck to lift from a pillow but no x-rays now or then so shoulder on because the car was a write-off. Our bruises faded even if in Old English (with its gendered nouns) the word for *woman* was neuter, while that for *snake* was feminine.

RACHEL ZOLF

HEATHER MILNE: Each one of your books enacts a very different poetics. You're not the kind of writer who keeps producing the same thing. It's easy to point out the differences, but what do you see as the continuities across your work?

RACHEL ZOLF: I find this question difficult to answer because I tend to be overly concerned with the reader having their own particular experience of the writing, and I don't want to sway that. But one way, perhaps, of reading across my work, is to see it as a kind of serial materialist poetics dealing with interrelated questions about memory, history, knowledge, subjectivity and the conceptual limits of language and meaning. One figure I could use that may be helpful comes from my first book, that material, handwritten 'line on the page' in *Her absence, this wanderer*. I was so invested in its materiality that when I would get to that line at readings, I would actually slice my hand across my throat in a gesture of cutting my throat, creating a 'blood/line.' So if you take 'a line on the page' and if you think about it as a figure in a larger sense, it's about form, trying to find the form that fits as best as it can the content you are dealing with. I've been coming at similar content in different ways in a number of my texts. So that while 'a line on the page' appears as an open field line in *Her absence, this wanderer*, with that kind of material marking, in *Masque* the lines are exploded, you encounter this exploded text. In *Human Resources* (*HR*), the sentence line is a bloated line, more imploded than exploded. In *Shoot and Weep*, the chapbook that is the first part of my new manuscript, entitled *The Neighbour Procedure*, almost the whole chapbook is simply single lines across the page. NourbeSe Philip noted reading the chapbook that it's like each line tells its own story, coming back again to the significance of the line on the page. In *Her absence, this wanderer*, and again in *Masque*, 'the line of creation = the line of destruction,' the whole process of making, including writing, always coming up against the limits of what you can do, including what you can do with language. So I'm dealing with a multivalent set of imagery and associative ideas and questions that I've been grappling with ever since I started writing and that I will probably always grapple with in some way.

HM: For instance, in *Masque* a lot of the poems are culled from archival sources. In *Shoot and Weep*, you draw on several found texts and documents to address the Israeli occupation of Palestine. In this new work there seems to be a deliberate move into the world and a clear sense of working within a specific tradition of documentary poetics. There's the Dorothy

Livesay/Daphne Marlatt tradition of documentary poetics in Canada, but it also seems like some of your influences might be American writers, like Juliana Spahr, for example. To what extent do you see your current work, or your previous work, as located within this tradition of documentary poetics? Is this another site of continuity across your work?

RZ: Again, it's difficult to pin down. I don't consciously think of these things as I'm writing. I actually only came to knowledge of the American documentary poetics tradition in the past couple of years. But I think that in certain ways it fits for me. I come from a documentary filmmaking background. It's one of the things I did for money for many years. I was an archival researcher, both visual and print – finding film, photos and archival documents such as personal letters. I also did research for investigative documentaries and then I became a writer-producer. But that's another lifetime. My point is I honed these research and investigative skills, and they've always been a key part of my writing practice. So for *Her absence, this wanderer*, I knew I had to go to Poland and the Czech Republic in order to see if my sense of rootlessness was related to transhistorical trauma due to my family's experience of the Nazi holocaust. For *Masque*, I spent a lot of time doing research in the CBC media archives and York archives, and this research base to my work has continued to the present. Documentary poetics is such a broad term, with many facets. In Canada, there's Livesay's take on the Canadian documentary poetic tradition in her essay written in 1969 – so it's pre–Marlatt's *Steveston* and such – but it points to Livesay's own writing as well as earlier, mostly 19th-century work. She defines the documentary poem as a particularly Canadian genre, and defines its precepts: it consists of so-called 'direct' speech ... sounds suspiciously like 'plain language' ... and it's moral-based, só there's a didactic element, and finally it is ideally set in the 'natural' environment. So Canadian, eh? Hardly any of that fits for me, but the way that U.S. poets nowadays are talking about documentary poetics is kind of interesting to me. Jena Osman and Juliana Spahr made a point of encouraging that kind of work in their journal, *Chain*, and Kristin Prevallet talks about documentary poetics in relation to what she calls relational-investigative poetics. So she uses Edouard Glissant's theories on the poetics of relation around hybridity and créolization – bringing languages together in a network, which is something I want to do in *The Neighbour Procedure* using the sister Semitic languages of Hebrew and Arabic. Glissant uses Deleuze and Guattari's figure of the rhizome here as opposed to centralized root-based concepts. I like that notion because of its associative aspects that fit with my mode of thinking. I don't want to use a catch term like 'cubist,' but things are happening on different planes at the same time, yet still there are relations among the multiple ideas and voices. That is one thing that crosses all my work, this sense of polyvocality. While there is not a singular I, it is still an exploration of subjectivity in a multiple form, the subject has not been completely evacuated.

HM: Would you say that the traditional documentary poem depends on that singular I to a certain degree?

RZ: Not necessarily. In fact, Livesay talks about documentary poetry as not being about a protagonist or hero.

HM: What about the documenter?

RZ: Well, yes, as with all ethnography, you wonder who the actual subject is. I'm no expert on the Canadian documentary poetic tradition, but sometimes it involved going to a site to research and record the varied voices there, so it has an aspect of polyvocality, and a political element of course, preserving 'lost' or silenced voices. But I do think its primary concern may be more with direct representation than an exploration through language and how language constructs us. It's kind of like making an NFB documentary, and in fact Livesay brings up John Grierson, founder of the NFB, in that essay and says that documentary poets should do their stuff just like him. I could go on and on about the documentary film form and its limits, but my main point is I don't think these are necessarily the precepts I want to follow in my poetic practice. There's all sorts of ethnographic difficulty with going into places and pretending you're objective when we all know how the observer's presence changes the environment. What I find interesting about some of what I've read about American documentary poetics is the emphasis on inquiry. Prevallet talks about the poet Ed Sanders, who wrote a manifesto in the '70s about investigative poetics. I read his manifesto, and it struck me as being too much about mastery, that you're supposed to know every in and out of a topic before you write poetry about it, which is basically the opposite of my practice. I do a lot of research, but the more I research the less I know in a sense, or the more there is to know, and in fact I get closer to writing by knowing less. Knowing less in terms of hard facts, but having this kind of associative experience of what I've researched, and entering it but not professing to be an expert at all.

HM: Your writing is quite investigative. And you pose questions a lot in your work and deal with the form of the question, the proposition and the like. The first poem in *Shoot and Weep* is a series of propositions: 'If the Sabbath is a form of constraint/If *jihad* is the first word we learn to spell ...' which does in a sense shift from documenting to making statements. Can you talk a bit about that process in *Shoot and Weep* and the process of questioning in your work in general?

RZ: In that first poem, 'a priori,' these propositions, which by their nature are meant to be givens, still, of course, ironically, contain the conditional 'if' statement so abhorred by plain-language practitioners and others. By putting all these different propositions in contrast and in opposition with one another, and making them all stay quivering beside each other on the same page, their validity as a priori propositions is called into question. I'm interested in the proposition as a form and think of it as a closed form, like the syllogism, if A is C and B is C, then A is ... Life's not like that. I have quibbles with analytic philosophy, attempting to reduce being or the existence of god or a range of complex philosophical ideas to formulas. Getting back to our theme here, you could say it links back to mastery and attempting to contain things that may not be containable. We're not going to grasp everything, and this may sound clichéd, but I think one of the key potential functions – if we really want to give it a function! – of poetry is that it can help people to let go of the desire to know completely and completely control their environment, and perhaps rather it can lead them to open up to a sense of mystery. But back to the notion of the question, it does run through my work. You could see my work as a kind of epistemological project, or knowledge-based in a broader sense. While I don't think of specific questions when I'm writing for the most part, my approach to the world and to writing is not necessarily to find answers, it's to ask more questions. People always say I ask too many questions! But the influence there, you could say it's a Jewish, or as writer Robert Majzels would say, a 'rabbinical' kind of thinking – in the secular-prophetic sense of 'Reb Derrida,' for example. One of my favourite books is *The Book of Questions* by Edmond Jabès, which as you may have guessed is composed primarily of questions – generating profound effects and affects. Rabbinical thinking is based on Talmudic thought, on the layers upon layers of meaning, at least forty-nine of them! There's not one answer, there's always 'and yet, no yet,' a Talmudic rhetorical flourish that also appears in Robert's fantastic book, *Apikoros Sleuth*. While it's frustrating in a way to sit with the lack of certitude, I guess I'd say it also leaves you more open to the world.

HM: I'm really struck when I read across your work by the fact that it's quite theoretically grounded. I detect traces of Butler and Lévinas in *Shoot and Weep*, in *Masque* there's Baudrillard, Barthes, Benjamin, among others. In *Human Resources* there are traces of Freud and Deleuze. Although in one of the poems in that collection you write, 'the *New York Times Magazine* declared that theory was dead – just when you'd gotten around to reading it.' Can you talk a bit about how your poetry engages with theory? What is it about theory that seems to be such fruitful ground for you? Your work seems to be in dialogue with theoretical texts as much as, or maybe more than, it is in dialogue with other literary texts. Are you really a theorist masquerading as a poet? Or does your poetry theorize?

RZ: Ha, you caught me ... I did come to theory late. It's only been four years since I've started reading theory. And in fact it's actually only in the past few months since changing my working conditions – i.e., working less for money – that I've had time to go into theory with any depth at all. Basically what drew me to theory was the difficulty of it, that it enacts its own difficulty. People have said before that theory when it's written well is like great poetry. What I like about theorists such as Derrida and Deleuze/Guattari is that their form embodies their ideas. Derrida is such an intractable writer, particularly in translation. And so you try harder, you become a *travailer*, one of my favourite articulations of the relation between reading and work, from *Pilgrim's Progress* of all places, and you decide that you're not going to 'get' it all. I decided a long time ago that it's okay – I don't have to be an expert. I actually believe in the notion of gleaning, reading/writing as gleaning. As I was doing my research for *Human Resources*, I came across this reference to what was supposedly Paul Celan's last poem, and in it he used a term that in the German root means both reading and gleaning. That's a very powerful figure for me, because I see both my reading and writing practices as gathering processes, making something of my own from what I glean. It's interesting because in American avant-garde poetry circles it seems they take/create theory more out of discussions of poetics than from French or other philosophy – particularly Language poetics becomes or enacts its own form of theory – whereas Canadian avant-gardists seem more directly influenced by Continental political and other philosophies. Maybe it's a colony-versus-freedom-fry thing ... but I don't want to generalize because of course Language poetry originally had Marxist underpinnings – and there are many Canadian poets with no politics at all! While I am interested in poetics, and there's definitely a self-consciousness of form across my work, my engagement with political/ethical philosophy is having an increasing impact on my work. Not that I haven't been lured at one time by the possibility of the transcendental lyric subject. Long before I started to read theory, during one of my failed years of university in the early '90s, I took 18th-century English literature, and I got so obsessed with the Self. Of course, in the 18th century everyone was obsessed with the Self.

HM: Were you reading 18th-century philosophy as well?

RZ: I was reading 18th-century literature, and my teacher, Patricia Bruckmann, probably put me onto Locke's *An Essay Concerning Human Understanding* in which there's all this stuff on what constitutes a person that I found fascinating. It's pretty banal, yep, but at that time I still wanted to understand myself, become 'whole.' I wrote a poem about this in *Human Resources*, I used to think that at a certain point, I don't know, maybe in my twenties, I would literally find my self. Yes, I really thought I would open up the fridge one day and my self would pop out. Needless to say, reading theory helped disabuse me of the silly notion that we can be complete selves or even complete subjects. And who'd want to be anyway?

HM: It gets back to that idea that mastery, in terms of poetry, is sort of an impossibility, and it gets at that from another angle.

RZ: Yes, the containability of the self. Also, what draws me to theory is the figures. I just love the imagery and that's why I like the notion that theory is like poetry – from the 'Great Ephemeral Skin' to the 'fold' to the 'body without organs' – I find these figures fascinating and multivalent. And don't get me started on psychoanalytical theory. It's just hilarious, and of course I used obvious psychoanalytic links between money and shit and the anal-erotic character in *HR*. But to give an example of my process, I took the notion of the body without organs, and while I understood what the term meant within Deleuze and Guattari's thought, I thought there's a great image to illustrate the body as writing machine. That's how I glean, that's how I associatively squeeze all I can out of a figure. One of my favourite documentaries, actually one of my favourite films, period, of the past twenty years is Agnès Varda's *Les glaneurs et la glaneuse* (*The Gleaners and I* in English), a profound meditation/essay on the artist and subjectivity and personal/collective survival, which I make reference to in *HR*.

HM: I love that idea of gleaning, and its relationship to *HR* where that concept of gleaning is so directly connected to the way you build the poems. It also strikes me that each of the poems in *Human Resources* reads almost like an essay. Do you agree with that?

RZ: *Human Resources* is the first book where I had the confidence to write back to what I'd been reading. For example, I think that Lévinas's ideas around the ethics of relation are beautiful pieces of theorizing, with his figuring of 'the face' and his quite lovely notion of 'being for the Other.' Yet you stop and just don't want to read some of the 'other' stuff, such as where he makes woman represent the consummate Other or where he fails to acknowledge the possibility of the Palestinian as an Other to the Israeli. Or, as I said, *The Book of Questions* is a book of poetry I much admire, but in one interview I read, Jabès talks about raping the word as you would rape a woman, when surely he could have used another metaphor. So in HR there are a number of poems that directly argue with these guys. One concept I was of course exploring in HR was the relation between plain language and politics, talking back to Orwell's idea that freedom and democracy would easily materialize if we all just spoke 'plainly.' You could go back to Livesay, this notion that 'direct' speech is somehow more political and more able to wake people up, move them to action. So we're supposed to 'never use a long word when a short word will do,' or never use adjectives, etc. – Orwell's famous didactic precepts (which of course are still in operation in ad agencies everywhere). It's so much about mastery and containability again. So I wrote back to them, but I have real trouble with the essay as a form. I don't like the subject/verb/predicate flow of a sentence. I write about the 'tyranny of svp' in HR. I like to use narrative strategies in anti-narrative ways. So they are essays, but they swerve in many different directions to not form an argument that you can hang onto with certainty, because that's just not the form I like to work in. Too closed.

HM: I want to ask you about the role of the censor in your writing. It's obviously quite prominent in *Masque*, but while preparing to reissue *Her absence, this wanderer*, you incorporated the censor from *Masque* into this earlier text. This strangely allows your first book to ... or your second book to anticipate your first book. Is the function of the censor different in *Her absence, this wanderer*?

RZ: Well, I was threatened with a lawsuit over *Her absence, this wanderer* and I can't talk about it, so let's just censor that!

HM: I'll put a big black bar over that line.

RZ: No, I want it in. That's the thing, the censor in *Masque* started out as literally a response to that.

HM: It's funny where you choose to use the censor in *Masque*. It's quite playful. Words like 'Toyota' are censored.

RZ: Yeah, I play with the censor. *Masque* explores the secret – asking what's wrong with exposing ourselves and our dirty laundry, who has access to the public gaze, and what faces do we choose to wear in what situations, revealing and concealing. The censor itself is an obvious figure of silencing, and there are a number of voices in that book that are being silenced, mostly female ones. So it was a natural visual trope to use, but I also don't like to use anything that is so obvious in obvious ways. So I thought it was kind of funny to take words like 'Toyota,' and at one place I censor half the word, and in the other place I censor the other half. You're obviously going to figure out what it is. Most of the time I let the little letters curl out from underneath the censors, so you can figure out what the words mean anyway. If you think about the context, it's apparent that that's 'depression' underneath there. And why would you censor 'depression'? Who cares? But the 'Toyota' one is funny, because I was making a subtle comment on copyright and how you're not supposed to use brand names anywhere, even in artwork, for fear of that little ™ symbol suing you. But I do find it an interesting process to go back to *Her absence, this wanderer* and subtly shift things. I just added the censor in two places, and it ends up foreshadowing ... maybe that's not the right word ...

HM: Backshadowing?

RZ: I like that. And I also edited out some of the text in one poem in particular in the book, 'erotic play,' so that the revised text acts as a palimpsest to the earlier version, concealing and revealing.

HM: Is the censor always present to some degree in your writing?

RZ: You could read the censor from *Masque* becoming the cypher in HR as words turn into numbers and some things are unreadable or unexplainable in the text. But I wasn't consciously thinking of that link when I wrote it – alas, the text is often ahead of one's own thinking. In *Shoot and Weep*, I definitely wanted to insert silence as a materiality into the text. So the lines are double spaced and you have to sit with what's happening between the lines. It's not directly about censoring, but the censor is an apt figure for larger questions I'm looking at in *The Neighbour Procedure* around denial, foreclosure, self-censoring, et cetera.

HM: In one of the poems in *Human Resources*, you quote Anne Carson on poet Paul Celan: 'What is lost when words are wasted? And where is the human store to which such goods are gathered?' It seems that this quotation is quite central to the process that you put language through in this book. You also use the word 'salvage' further down on the same page: 'when you "cleanse words and salvage what is cleansed," do you collect what's been scrubbed off or what remains minute older claims from methods accepted machine?' Are you done salvaging and cleansing, or is this line simply not just about *Human Resources* but really about something that gets at the centre of your poetic practice?

RZ: Actually, in *HR*, I make words dirtier. My aim isn't to cleanse – rather I inject a lot of dirty words in the text that rub off on other words, kind of like sticky feelings or affects. And that ethical question I explore, 'What is lost when words are wasted?' doesn't even work for Celan, in my opinion. Carson sees him as cleansing words and salvaging what is cleansed. I agree with her that he severely redacts the German language. He sets out to break the language of Nazi holocaust and in the process creates what in English translation is the noem, this negative poem, this nothing. This nothing that is everything, in a way, also alluding to the noetic. While Celan is an anagram for 'clean' (as is his real name, Ancel), I don't necessarily agree that the redaction makes the poem any cleaner. It's just that the dirty excess dwells in the resounding silence in his poems. The question that I was exploring there drew me elsewhere to how we're taught to think about the perfect well-wrought urn/earn of a poem. And what we're talking about with Orwell excising all the adjectives and only putting in what's 'necessary.' So in *HR* I was exploring the question of when you work away on your left-justified, four-stanzas-on-the-page perfect poem, what happens to everything that you cut out? What's left after you've scrubbed it off? What's left on the ground?

HM: The question of whether you are saving the dirt or are you saving the cleaned object?

RZ: Yes, and I make work out of what's left on the ground in *HR*. But you could read that across my work. Like all the archival research I do – all the stuff I work with that had been left in a box in a dusty archive (or dusty book for that matter!), or hidden amid reams of text on a website. The pages and pages of human rights documents that I worked with in *Shoot and Weep*, for example. There is so much research that goes into the text, which is its own set of redactions from this accumulation that I do. So I may not have answered your question, but I don't believe in necessarily creating a clean, perfect poem.

HM: The epigraph to *Shoot and Weep* is a quotation from Butler's *Precarious Life*: 'Will we feel compelled to learn how to say these names?' I know that you've been studying Arabic, and I'm wondering if your decision to learn Arabic is a response to this question?

RZ: No, but it fit nicely. I'm taking Arabic lessons, and I'm also trying to teach myself Hebrew. On one level, as I said earlier, these are sister Semitic languages, and I want to look at correspondences between the verbal roots of these languages. For these are sister cultures as well. For example, early modern Andalusia in southern Spain was an important site and time when Jews and Arabs and Christians coexisted relatively peacefully and intermingled in their cultures and languages and thinking, until the Reconquista of course. Indeed Córdoba in Andalusia was an important centre of learning for all of early modern Europe. There's a storied history of cross-pollination between Arabic and Hebrew cultures, and it's just a complete shame – thinking of the Palestinian situation, I want to say Israel's imperialist shame, coupled with the shame of the Arab 'league' of fascist and semi-fascist nations – that there's such hardened divisions doing such damage to this day. So I want to work with the assonances and consonances and dissonances that I can come up with between these languages and the creative possibilities that arise from that. Kind of like doing 'transcreations' or Glissant's créolizations. I'm going to travel to Israel and the Occupied Palestinian Territories, and I want to be able to speak to Palestinians as best as I can in their own language. While most Israelis speak English, many Palestinians do not. But I mainly thought that that citation fit as an epigraph because I was really struck by a section of *Precarious Life* that delved into what is considered a 'grievable' life, and asks why we don't ever see Muslim, particularly Arabic, names in the newspaper obituaries or 'names of the dead.' It fit with what I'm exploring in terms of Western media representation of Middle East conflicts. In *The Neighbour Procedure*, there's a poem, 'Did not participate in hostilities,' that lists how certain people died, i.e., 'When she approached the barrier / While flying a kite at the beach,' etc. These are Palestinian people who were killed when they weren't participating in any hostilities, just going about their days. I guess you could say they were collateral damage. But I made a point of including a sister poem that lists the names of these people who died, a list of their Arabic names. And I don't know how to pronounce them. I've got to learn how to pronounce the names if I want to do some small measure of justice to these people when I read from this book ...

HM: Is that the poem that's called 'Grievable'?

RZ: Yes. And there's a third poem called 'Nominalization' that just lists their ages, just the numbers, basically from a few months old to sixty-five years. And 'Grievable' also has this interesting allusion to Lorca's 'Lament for Ignacio Sánchez Mejías,' his famous poem which repeats the line 'at five in the afternoon,' which is when the bullfighter was shot. At five in the morning happened to be when one of the Palestinians in 'Did not partici- pate in hostilities' died, so I made a subtle allusion to Lorca. Also Lorca himself was killed for his political activities at dawn, which could be five in the morning. There is also a reference in Eliot's 'The Hollow Men' to five o'clock in the morning – and serendipitously the same stanza at the end of that poem also has a reference to the prickly pear, which happens to be a kind of national symbol for both Israelis (*'sabra'* – the term for a Jew born in Israel – is Hebrew for prickly pear) and Palestinians (*'sabr'* in Arabic means patience, perseverance ... and prickly pear). The use of intertextual allusion is quintessential in the lyric tradition, and I wanted to foreground the poems in *Shoot and Weep* as lyrics, even though 'I' only 'wrote' three lines of that section. Back to the epigraph, I tend to find it a site where poets can be their most pretentious, and I like to send that up a bit. Before I read the jokey epigraph to *HR*, I often say it's the most poetic piece in the book. And here in *Shoot and Weep*, the epigraph isn't some profound philosoph- ical thought of Butler's, it's actually quite prosaic, which fits well with the materiality of my practice, and the questions around naming and the mastery that comes with naming.

Toronto, February 2008

SELECTED WORKS

Her absence, this wanderer. Ottawa: BuschekBooks, 1999.

Masque. Toronto: The Mercury Press, 2004.

Human Resources. Toronto: Coach House Books, 2007.

Shoot and Weep. Vancouver: Nomados Literary Publishers, 2008.

The Neighbour Procedure. Toronto: Coach House Books, 2010.

from Masque

The Critic   He is witty and hip,

The Father   *It's more fun being Jewish today than in World War II.*

unpredictable and rough-edged,

The Philosopher 'TV is ... an extension *I'm not saying Nazis are bad guys as individuals,*

pertinent and impertinent,   (child an extension

The Whisper   *lay down your but in a group they can be sudden death.*

maddening and engaging.

of the sense of touch.' *Of course, we shouldn't knock the whole SS*

A scholar in his own right, he is able to appear   of the parent

because of a few bad apples.

the clown one minute and bulldozer the next

Z-d has something of a two-or-more-worlds-at-once quality.

The Daughter such a clear memory: his pyjamas,

the ones he walked to the corner drugstore in,
The Philosopher 'The face
The Censor splash of ███ down the front, line
is the evidence
of ██ down the back, his hangdog
The Whisper *i know i take up more than my fair share of*
face, stink of the ██ze, stink of it all, his
that makes evidence
too-hard hug: I love you where'd she put *exiled from himself, his life, the love*
possible.'   *gone down* The Writ
the b███s I love you so much, tears, sn█;

she wondered why her mother hid the bot███
    space i know i take up more than my fair sh
in her closet, wonders what to do

from Human Resources

Early in the new millennium[G18] hello[Q18] of vagina america bitch cat, on our 35th birthday in fact, the *New York Times Magazine* declared that theory was dead – just when you'd gotten around to reading it. Here you go again, we're always 20 years behind the times, should've been checking out *écriture* chicks at the Montreal feminist book fair instead of popping bennies and caterwauling through *Romeo and Juliet* in high school. With close friends a generation[W2065] plenty ill older, you envy a certain ease with bodies, ideas (however dispersed). Change[G46] a wooden dragon a world as cold as stone accidentally on purpose management is accompanied by good communication avoiding drunk men at yet another poetry reading. Maybe if you'd come to writing through sex (or the other way 'round), she wouldn't feel so blocked about libidinal faro dnj[W54051] urng sitcoms economies, tackling *Desire in Language* or *Dissemination* for that matter. Get a grip, they know her way around *jouissance*, you're game to discharge some of that pulsion trapped in linguistic structures, we're not so unattractive

HOW TO MAKE A NAME

1 Brainstorm words for what you do
2 Brainstorm words for your aspirations
3 Brainstorm words for your customers
4 Think metaphorical and mythological
5 Search for synonyms, homonyms, alliteration, clichés
6 Search for positive or negative equivalence
7 Start combining
8 Add a suffix
9 Truncate – low-hanging fruit, penectomy, nothingness
10 Rank your names

Adrienne Rich used the Communicating Bad News template to affirm that the half-curled frond would not commingle with your book. The tie's lower tip should align with the top centre of the belt buckle and its back slide through the label to not reveal an undisciplined self. From the epoch of the name to the advent of the number, C^{3}I spends time etching surfaces with symmetry, repetition and a balance of nodal points. At least some figures when processed produce pleasure, but don't introduce new products in August or wear shirts off a dead man's body to work. Heart, hope, faith, Andy Card, Josef Goebbels and Banana Republic make today's bureaucracies into tomorrow's communities of meaning. So be it, amen, let's roll!

The mystical white crow, the sword and the flower that shattered stone standing in a Chelsea gallery watching an artist get fucked by a collector for U.S.$20,000, it's always the first G44 cliché would w44 mom Q44 off our tongue they love best: your dreams are possible, you can create the life you want, there's no better time to make an investment in your future. How limited the sphere you negotiate Q14543 liu ouagadougou pogrom, 'flourish' boasting too many vowels, 'thrive' too abstract. Internal censor cheapening the affect of words, no nick or dent in the narrow way the victorious city ritualist G–3 monoculture. Like the unemployed former Democrats from Flint swerving behind Bush and false, disfigured certainty, you hand over the car keys to Jesus and the boss pockets 200 bucks an hour

Anne Carson on Celan: 'What is lost when words are wasted? And where is the human store to which such goods are gathered?' in that it is was i for on you he be with

Which words are gathered, the wasted or the lost? ask word groups along central history few changes I remember hundred individual air

When you 'cleanse words and salvage what is cleansed,' do you collect what's been scrubbed off or what remains minute older claims from methods accepted machine?

And who bears witness for the authors pulling estimates of bitter crash and victorian distinguished confused witness?

Spoilsports of sorts, her various avatars hover on the outside contemplating what's not being said in the minus five lunchroom from dust you are homosexuality houseguests. Obsessed with the phallogocentric left margin, the professional stranger makes multiple voices intersect the field and all their words are 34 skew-wise from all directions. Unable to choose one 'I' or version of the events, modest witness tries to 'tone it down' to minimize the 'piss-off' factor native to human capital, artful deviation and fractured surfaces. Think straight, talk straight – let's overlay everything with the amount they're 'confessional,' juggling the first few out of the gate. Hopefully this will get rid of the blur, create a nice 'spin'

of Jew producing inside plain language.
interlacing through libidinal economy because
I narrative gathering amid poetry machine. coming
as if plain language excess interlacing
out of Jew, Jew

gathering   and falling away.   through shit
spewing body without organs over narrative crumbling
of spew under plain language or crumbling

over moments that exceed containment, deals
we make. deals we make   lost
and body without organs gathering   of excess

salvage. gather   on top of
moments that exceeding containment, meaning
because production of forms combine.   or rhetoric

salvaging out meaning. poetry machine   form
outside lesbian. poetry machine over money.

from The Neighbour Procedure

A PRIORI

If the Sabbath is a form of constraint

If *jihad* is the first word we learn to spell

If Elie Wiesel is the Holocaust

If we must expropriate gently

If messianism licks at the edges of thought

If the truth does not lie in silence

If *naf* means self and brother

If the space between two words can be bridged

If moderate physical pressure is acceptable

If the primary target is the witness

If epistemological mastery is a wound that won't close

If *bittahon* was trust in God now military security

If there is horror at the heart of divinity

If the body goes off near the Sbarro pizzeria

If you think the apocalyptic sting is gone from Hebrew

If the first stage is not knowing at all

If Dachau meets Disneyland

If this state is the golden calf

If ingathering means expulsion

If catastrophe becomes a passion

If we shoot and weep

If Israel is not in Israel

If the treasurehouse of well-worn terms is laden with explosives

§

If *ha'apalah* was catastrophic breakthrough now illegal immigration

If the bodies of the exploding martyrs smell of musk

If every breath of fresh air is a border

If the state no longer decides who lives or dies

If we are eternally innocent and good

If a key is an archival artifact

If all our planes return safely

If we are all enthusiasm

If we are all Hamas

If we are Israel

If cruel history repeats itself as its own cure

If it happens inside the Sbarro pizzeria

If the invasion is of the order of the border

If we discomfort our animal during slaughter

If the band of the blind plays and refreshments are served

If the third stage is but what can we do

If *shaheed* means martyr and witness

If preventative is energetic liquidation

If we are a community of fate

If we will and it is a fairy tale

If Sbarro

THE NEIGHBOUR PROCEDURE

The neighbour goes in first

I asked my neighbour where the shouting came from

They took me to another neighbour's home

We go through the whole house with the neighbour

At four in the morning I heard my neighbour calling me

The neighbour doesn't have that option

We were about seven metres from the neighbour's house

I saw another neighbour

The neighbour shouts, knocks on the door

They ordered my neighbour to bring out the wounded man

My neighbour replied the sound came from my home

When he opened the door his neighbour was standing there

When I opened the door I saw my neighbour in the doorway

A FAILURE OF HOSPITALITY

I had normal dreams like wires dangling everywhere

The ludicrous thing about order won't hear lies only peace

Her body full with splinters can't pick the olives alone

Luxurious character of the negative raised a lion in your house

No Hebrew word for integrity will be a blazing light

Hewn message inscribed on just a few who danced

This pressure of humiliation had other plans for my son

The future collapsed in present execution and mourning

Duty of guest and host a torn native

Narratives compete for a sacred hair lying where it shouldn't

Catch your thief before your demon lives a quiet way

This button the key to paradise lines conflicting in me

Party girl uniform putting on a mother's day bouquet

This unbearable intimacy a purity of arms suturing

Chocolate cakes with coconut flakes none of us taught to see

The besieged body a piece of metal we will offer all our children

This permanent remembrance slaughtered and we promise a pleasant life

LOSS HAS MADE A TENUOUS WE

A touch of the worst border my wound testifies

Names must break up and flatten my foreignness to myself

One is hit by implements given over without control

Exhausted not knowing why beauty is left of me what hair

Fathom who have I wires in the other I have lost

Neighbour renews itself in the inexhaustible

Violence a sudden address from oil

Enthusiasm impressed upon concept

Impinging splinters oneself fallen

A mark that is no uniform

Write open and unbounded gap

Undone by the seal of the other

You are what I gain through this disorientation

ERÍN MOURE

KATE EICHHORN: I hate to begin by asking you about another writer, but I can't help but notice that lately you're being eclipsed by Elisa Sampedrín. She's publishing more than ever before. Are you comfortable with her taking up so much space?

ERÍN MOURE: Elisa Sampedrín is out of my control! Lots of people take up more space than she does, though. I think of her as barging in, and unobtrusive at the same time. She's hard to shake off, in any case, and very hard to argue with, though she herself will walk away from an argument, if she feels like it.

KE: She's a compelling figure, and people are becoming very interested in her writing and translation work.

EM: I'm not responsible for all that! I often keep track of her through other people. After my own ... or our own! ... *Little Theatres*, she appeared in the work of other writers. Then she started posting on blogs and developed a biography, or people started telling me her biography. It got so that even when I told people that I invented Elisa Sampedrín to talk about theatre, they would tell me I didn't invent her because 'we know her.' So her biography has kept accumulating.

KE: I quite liked her work that recently appeared in the *Chicago Review*.

EM: She only publishes by interference, so her work probably replaced that of another writer whom *CR* had actually invited to contribute. Apparently, she is in Bucharest now. I'm going to go there myself to see if I can find her and find out what she's up to. If she'll even agree to see me. I had a reading in Vancouver recently, and when I told people I'd invented her, someone in the audience disagreed vehemently and told me that she's making films now. She had just returned from Madrid where she saw one of her films in a festival. In the end, I guess, I have to accept her existence. It seems there really is no difference between an identity and a mistaken identity. Once people believe Elisa Sampedrín exists, once she appears to exist, she does exist. I'd like to chase her down at some point, though.

KE: In *Little Theatres* you said that no one was listening to Elisa in the 1980s, so perhaps her time has finally come? Clearly, she's working just fine without you now. You, on the other hand, are involved in other collaborations, including one with Oana Avasilichioaei. Have you collaborated in this way before?

EM: No, not in this way. Back when my mother was deathly ill and I was unable to write, Oana Avasilichioaei had just published her book of Stănescu translations, and reading these poems of Stănescu nourished me. Her book is bilingual and I just loved the look of Romanian, which I didn't understand at all, and I loved these poems. Oana and I were booked that spring to interview each other onstage as part of a French poetry festival in Montreal, so I took one of the Romanian poems in her book and translated it without knowing any Romanian. I thought Oana might be mad at me for claiming to have translated Stănescu, but she responded by laughing, so I thought, let's go toward delight, Erín! Oana kept encouraging me to translate another poem, then another. I realized very soon that the translations were coming from a Galician self – Elisa Sampedrín was doing them! A word in Romanian would remind me of Galician, so I was really reading the poems like a Galician. Oana describes this process in *Translating Translating Montréal*. I thought the results were ridiculous at first, but Oana insisted this is a true translation too, this is a proper translation. Very close to that point, we started playing with translation between us, and writing poetically about translation in ways that confounded the author, starting with an unfinished poem in Romanian by Paul Celan that Oana wanted to finish. At the same time, I was writing my own work – i.e., Elisa Sampedrín's work – in *O Resplandor*. Both books started because of the meeting of my imagination with Oana's, and because we were able to open up notions of authorship and languages and equivalencies and meaning that surprised even us. And my own work went on, as well, because of her ability to recognize that I was capturing something really visceral and vital in Stănescu's poems, even though none of the words were the same. It was the sound of the poems, the rhythms. I wasn't able to do it very well at first, but once I realized it was Elisa Sampedrín, it was easier. In the nearly two years that my mom was sick, it allowed me to write. Otherwise, I didn't have it in me to write. Sharing poetry energy with Oana enabled me to keep playing with words. It was easier to have the freedom to work, without it being just me who was working.

KE: So this collaboration was really an accident?

EM: Are there such things as accidents? Yes, it was an accident, though there were antecedents in both our work in translation – mine in Pessoa and hers in Stănescu, that freed us up to collaborate. It was an accident, and no accident at all, as all art is.

KE: For you, is there always something aleatory in the translation process?

EM: I wouldn't say it's aleatory, because there is such a mix of factors in any translation process. You can define them, and still not define the process of translation. Take my translation of Pessoa. In this country, it is more often seen as my work, but in Portugal or Japan, people just see it as a translation of Pessoa. When José Blanco, the major bibliographer of things Pessoan, read the book, he said, 'You brought me back to Pessoa. You made Alberto Caeiro live again for me – this is the truest translation.' When I first realized that I could read the work of Caeiro, Pessoa's heteronym, in Portuguese, I realized that the straight translations that existed had no humour. The character of Caeiro, and his feints and bluffs, were washed out in the neutrality of the words. I needed to find a way to bring the humour back, so I could share my pleasure with other readers. The problem with humour is that unlike love and death that pass through the centuries, humour is time-bound. Once you get out of the era, it's often hard to see what was funny. I think the humour of Caeiro is quite enduring in Portuguese because it has a cultural presence in that society, but in a literal English translation the humour is evacuated. Caeiro had an older-sounding diction because Pessoa was brought up in English and Portuguese, and though Portuguese was his mother tongue, it became almost his second language when he was growing up in South Africa. So he actually could produce a very funny Portuguese. In fact, he had many funny Portugueses. Caeiro was written in the 1920s and 1930s, but most English translations sound as if the poems had been written in the 1890s. Perhaps the language was old-fashioned, the diction, but in English it would be more like someone talking today with slang used in the 1950s, I thought, and that's why I moved it in time.

KE: What authorized you to make those decisions? Is it because you're a poet-translator?

EM: I don't think they need authorization. Art operates on another plane, it is not a literalism, and poetry is not simply semantics. And languages are not equivalent. That said, I am sure I do have a different way of working in language than does someone who just translates but does not write poetry. The sound of a text, the feeling of a text, its textures, are important to me, and I've worked with poetry so long and in so much detail, I feel I've developed some capacities, and could develop more! I'm just in the process of translating the first few paragraphs of this very poetic text of an art historian from France about a Korean photographer. I'm always asking myself what is going on in the French and how to convey the movement of thought in the work – I have to create the same kind of movement, not just translate the words. Translation as a practice is not as narrow as we tend to believe. It does have this amplitude and room for movement. I'm also translating six poems by the Galician poet Daniel Salgado. I realized that he has such a taut and contemporary colloquial speech that his poems are very condensed. Colloquial English doesn't have the terse and rhythmic effect of Salgado's Galician. Galician is a language where poetry has had a dense and metaphorically rich language, so to have this terse diction enacts something that goes against the current of the tradition that the poet is working in. I need to convey that terse viscerality in my translation, so at times I have to change exactly what it is he is saying. Change is my only capacity. He will say, 'how is it that this voice comes to her,' and in Galician, that's considered colloquial. I'll change that to 'where did she get this voice.' So some of the movement in his line is gone, and I must create another movement. There are so many registers they have to be maintained when you're translating poetry. And the translator has to make a whole range of decisions. Of course, there are times in translation when you're translating the instructions for how to get out of a burning building, and you just translate the words as unambiguously as possible, keeping in mind the desired effect of the words on the targeted reader. Do this, don't do that, don't use the elevator, and get out! There are reasons for types of speech, so translation is also about letting speech have its reasons.

KE: I recently met one of your translators, Marta López-Luaces, who told me a bit about your Galician self. I knew that Galician had been censored under Franco, but I didn't realize how gendered the language had become as a result. While under censure, it continued to be spoken in private and semi-public spaces but primarily by men. Women understood Galician, but it was extremely taboo for women to speak the language – if a woman was overheard speaking Galician, people would assume she was a sex-trade worker. Marta explained that to this day, women over a certain age remain apprehensive about speaking Galician. All this to say that when Erín Moure arrives on the scene fluent in Galician but not in Spanish, it's shocking and a bit amusing. In Galician, you're an anomaly. I wonder how you experience this? Also how has your experience of the language and the region affected your writing and translation work across the languages you work in?

EM: I don't agree with Marta there. My experience is other than that. Marta has said to me that when she was growing up Galician, to her, was associated with prostitution. I've never heard that from anyone else. I can't speak for Marta but I know she comes from Galicia's second largest city, a port city, and Galician was always spoken less in cities for it was a language of fishermen and farmers, and rejected by the middle classes. In cities, people had class barriers, as well as the political barriers, that directed them to speak in Castilian Spanish. In Galicia I am an anomaly simply because I learned Galician without learning Spanish. That's just not done. Galicians, as they exist in the Spanish state and under the Spanish constitution, have the constitutional obligation to be fluent in Castilian. I am not a Spanish citizen and have no such obligation. Because of the class barriers, people in the cities find it strange to see a foreigner speaking Galician. Why would you learn that language? In the country, Galicians are surprised that I speak Galician but are quite happy to speak Galician with me. It is just rare that a foreigner would learn Galician. But for me, not learning it or learning Spanish instead, would be like marching around Quebec insisting everyone speak English. Why would I do that? And I love the Galician language. It is part of me now – I have a Galician body, you might say. I think to myself in Galician, I dream in it. It is part of my entirety.

KE: We've been talking about your more recent books, but the passages we've chosen for the collection are from an earlier period. I wanted to include the selections from 'Memory Penitence/Contamination Église' because in this poem we encounter the striking visuality of your work and perhaps, too, a sense that the materiality of the word matters to you. But I'll admit, on a semantic level, these pieces remain elusive.

EM: One of the things that is important to me always in poetry is just how beautiful words are on the page. Even if someone doesn't speak a language or understand the words, they can see how beautiful they are, and you can make out sounds in words and you can make your own sounds for words.

KE: I'm surprised to hear you say this. Perhaps this is an overgeneralization, but it seems that innovative poets are more interested in rejecting 'beautiful language.' Can we approach language as a problematic – material that needs to be interrogated, dismantled, unpacked – and embrace 'beautiful language' at the same time? Perhaps it has something to do with how we define 'beautiful language.'

EM: I think you have answered your question.

KE: Then can we talk more specifically about this page from 'Memory Penitence' from *Search Procedures*? What's going on here? 'jkl ;laksdf l k aklg kas ;i;o aei...' – what is this?

EM: It's gestural. It's beautiful language! It's like when language wants to come out of you. It's an exposure of language, but without any clear semantic value.

KE: So is everything on the page an open signifier?

EM: There is no entirely open signifier, is there? How would we be able to call it a signifier? In some places in this poem, the words start 'meaning something,' but then this beginning of meaning quickly falls apart. The verses of the poem are like the shaking of leaves in a tree. Again, it's the gesturality of words that is at stake, their capacity always to start indicating meanings. I typed the first poem in this sequence by accident. On a typewriter I wasn't familiar with. I was on the wrong keys.

KE: I wondered if this was the case. It suggests another accident, albeit a welcome one.

EM: Again, if it's beautiful, I keep it, for it has another kind of articulatory capacity. Such accidents happen all the time. I accept them. The true accident would be not to have accidents. It's another kind of neuro-triggering, another creative pathway. I think here of Francis Bacon. About the gobs of paint he would chuck onto a painting, marring the image basically – someone said, if it's an accident, you could just let your housekeeper come in at night and throw the paint on. But Bacon explained that that wouldn't be the same thing, because after he throws the paint on, he decides what to do with it – to put the palette knife through it, to smear it across the canvas – it's just a procedure that leads him to the next decision. He's in a really material relationship with the paint, without intellectualizing it at all, just reacting to the material. It has to be done quickly. So when my fingers landed one key over, I made a decision to keep the poem, but I also made a decision to do it again. What is that? What does this mean? So in this poem, I write, 'if I stand before you, before you naked' – naked of semantics. I don't have any meaning to disappear behind. These procedures let the reader think in a different way too – they make you jump. There are accidents in *O Cidadán*, too, like the poem where my cat typed in the middle of a word. The accident arises for me as well when I write by hand, because my handwriting is nearly illegible, and later I have to guess what the word is. I can tell what some words are but others are a guess. Sometimes further down the line I will realize I chose the wrong word, but I don't necessarily change it back. I know that I have read something into the scrawl, though whatever it was that I was originally recording is lost. I think my hand gets bored. I even have a hard time signing my name.

KE: Agamben suggests that 'If we call "gesture" what remains unexpressed in each expressive act ... the author is present in the text only as a gesture,' but this 'illegible gesture' is what makes reading possible. So to come back to your earlier point about gestures – the gesturality of words – perhaps, we can say that this is where you are present, in these illegible gestures.

EM: Which 'you' of 'me' is present? That you, that me, are always constructed, not fully intentional. Maybe the illegibility refers to that. Agamben actually said the author is the illegible someone who makes reading possible. He speaks too of the 'inexpressive outer edge.' Perhaps this is where this piece is gesturing. As well, the title indicates it has to do with memory and penitence, and memory is never complete. And part of the title as well is 'Contamination Église' which tells you there will be contaminations in the poem ... and it is church-like, for there is, I think, a kind of reverence in it.

KE: We've been talking about gestures, movement, but I also want to ask you about staging, which is a related concept and one we can explore both in relation to *Little Theatres* and to your recently published essay on vernaculars. First, what are the 'little theatres' doing?

EM: In the fall of 2002, I'd had enough of big theatres. Theatres of war. George Bush's theatres. I thought, how awful to share a language with Bush, with Tony Blair, in the months leading up to the Anglo-American invasion of Iraq. It was the time when the rhetoric of big theatres was really building up. People were out in the street and protesting, of course. But how do you really resist? If you have force A and you counter it with force B, it's still force A in another form. A resistance that can actually make something crumble comes from another direction entirely. Part of the project of *Little Theatres* was to stick Galician into the hegemonic language, English, to re-form English with words that sound beautiful and look beautiful, even if they don't mean anything to the English reader, or they can mean whatever the English reader wants them to mean. At least, words that are not directing you. Bush and Blair are directing people with words, manipulating people with words, but the words of Galician in *Little Theatres* aren't doing that – they just open up possibilities. In a sense, my strategy was to counter big theatres with little theatres, and the tactics, the concrete acts, are the poems.

KE: It seems like little theatres are all about taking space within the cracks or ruses that open up within the space of big theatres. Little theatres permit something else, something unexpected, to happen, if only for a moment. But as Elisa Sampedrín emphasizes, 'Little theatres is not, strictly speaking, the visible.' Like all tactics, invisibility is in its nature. But this makes me wonder, who is watching it? How do we get people to pay attention to little theatres? Is that part of the poet's work in this time?

EM: I think little theatres may appear to 'take space within big theatres' but that is because we are so used to big theatres framing our lives. It comes from somewhere else entirely: after the play is over, as Elisa has said. Tactics are actions and have visible results. I think people do pay attention to little theatres. Everyone's life is full of these little theatres, and to acknowledge them and to listen to the theatres of others, as well, is to open up a tremendous space of resistance and action in one's own life. As for the poet's work, in this time or any other, it is just to write poems. Until you can't write any more. And then, as Chus Pato has said, you take up the pen again, and continue writing.

KE: You recently published an article called 'Staging Vernaculars' in *West Coast Line*. You insist that the vernacular is not, as people often assume, innocent language that belongs to the workers, the people on the street. There's an attempt to convince people that the vernacular is their language, that they own it, but of course this isn't the case. It seems that much of your work is precisely about the urgent need to disrupt this myth. You ask, among other questions, 'Can the vernacular desire?' Can it?

EM: The vernacular doesn't really exist, but for me, vernaculars are ways of speaking or ways of articulating, ways of producing speech or producing something around a place or set of people. They exist in time, start and stop, can be short or long. They're useful. They have a use value for a particular group of people. A vernacular can draw a people together around a specific problematic. So for me, of course, the vernacular desires because there is complicity in it – with the other people using it. But there are many vernaculars. Like the vernacular of stone cutters. Just the other day, I saw something about moving stone. Where did I see it? My life is so fractured, I can't remember exactly where I saw it ... on a plane on the way home from New York, perhaps? Where did I see it? On YouTube? Anyway, I was following up a reference and discovered these people moving stone in Asia in the exact same way people moved stone in Galicia. They sing to themselves. They sing out poems, couplets, and make noises too. All this helps everyone act as one body to move the stone together. They are moving stones that are unmovable, huge stones. In this image I have, they are cutting stones in a quarry, but why or where has become disconnected for me. But the stonecutters have a way of speaking of things.

KE: Here we have language facilitating this coming together of bodies connected by a common desire – to move a stone that would otherwise be unmovable. So the vernacular of the stonecutters is a vernacular that desires. It's interesting that this is the image that came to mind for you – humans moving stone. What matters here is the possibility that language creates the conditions under which this movement is possible. So is this it – your central problematic? The thing that keeps you writing, translating, playing with language? Maybe this also explains why your writing is so heavily populated by other voices ... you can't move the stone alone, after all.

EM: Maybe that's one way of looking at it, of looking at what matters. I like what you are saying here.

KE: In your article on vernaculars, you say explicitly that Dada is not a vernacular. Surrealism is not a vernacular. But these movements were interested in exploring what we can do with vernaculars in writing, in art, in performance. They were ways of speaking that had a specific use value for a particular group of people – in some contexts, I suppose they still do. Perhaps you're suggesting that vernaculars cease to be vernaculars when they're adopted for some form of aesthetic gain, but if so, what are you saying about the relation between avant-garde poetics and the everyday?

EM: Dada and Surrealism are both current, not as the movements they originally were. They were movements, not vernaculars ... movements are, perhaps, superimposed on existing vernaculars, or introduce vernaculars to each other in new ways, but they still affect us, affect art and writing. I don't think either Dada or Surrealism explored vernaculars to any extended degree, though they did explore ways of dealing with the everyday. And still do. I think that the most beautiful thing about vernaculars is that they are everyday, thus common or transparent, and at the same time, particular to a group, thus rare, or opaque. They are contradictions in themselves! Operative contradictions. My essay on the vernacular was an attempt to discover how the word worked in ways that lead to comfort, how it deals with its own contradictions. And why, despite its contradictions, we do not want to abandon this word, for it is useful. Which leads, perhaps, to thinking of the usefulness of contradiction in general. I think here on Wittgenstein in the *Tractatus* saying (in 4.461 and 4.4611 to 4.466 or so), that contradictions lack sense, for they are on no account true, but are not nonsensical. They are just not pictures of reality. They are, with tautology, the limiting cases or even the disintegration of the combination of signs. That point interests me, for I think vernaculars can act that way too: occupy all of logical space, and exclude reality. In the way that icons in the Orthodox churches are not representations of saints, but are representations of ways of thinking about saints.

KE: Since we've arrived at the issue of contradictions, I'll ask about your own potential contradictions. For many years, you've occupied a somewhat unique place in Canadian poetry, moving across the lyric and Language lines with considerably more ease than most of the writers in this anthology. Your work, however, is by no means more 'accessible' – you don't go out of your way to write easily digestible work. How do you account for your apparent mobility within Canadian literature, or perhaps you disagree with this assessment?

EM: If I seem to be moving across lines, then they are lines I neither drew nor see as I go about my work. I don't believe in making binary opposites of 'lyric' and 'Language.' Language? Lyric exists in language last time I checked. And lyric, as I showed in *O Cadoiro*, in going back to the medieval trobadours, is more radical than some people, 'Language' people, I suppose, would have you believe. And I don't know what 'accessible' has to do with it. I gently refuse that framing. The accessible, as I have always argued, as others have argued, is what we already know. And poetry operates beyond that, I think. So does life! All poetry, whether it engages traditional forms or dictions or open forms, or conceptualizations, has to press us just past the limit where our knowing ends. And the ways of doing this are multiple.

KE: At the end of your translation of Pessoa's *O Guardador de Rabanhos*, what you published as *Sheep's Vigil by a Fervent Person*, there's a little 'interview' with Alberto Caeiro. There are some interesting similarities between your poetic project and Pessoa's project, but perhaps too, some curious intersections between you and Caeiro? What do Erin Moure, Erin Mouré, Eirin Moure, Erín Moure and Elisa Sampedrín share with Pessoa and Caeiro?

EM: We're alive and writing, I guess!

Montreal, May 2008

SELECTED WORKS

Search Procedures. Toronto: House of Anansi Press, 1996.

The Frame of a Book. Toronto: House of Anansi Press, 1999.

Pessoa, Fernando. *Sheep's Vigil by a Fervent Person, a Transelation of Fernando Pessoa/Alberto Caeiro's* O Guardador de Rebanhos. tr. Eirin Moure. Toronto: House of Anansi Press, 2001.

O Cidadán. Toronto: House of Anansi Press, 2002.

Little Theatres. Toronto: House of Anansi Press, 2005.

O Cadoiro. Toronto: House of Anansi Press, 2007.

Translating Translating Montréal. With Oana Avasilichioaei, Angela Carr and Robert Majzels. Montreal: Press Dust, 2007.

O Resplandor. Toronto: House of Anansi Press, 2010.

Memory Penitence / C o n t a m i n a t i o n É g l i s e

If I stand before you
Before you naked

jkl ;laksdf l k aklg kas ;i;o aei ;lksd hp` 8i93jlkad; j ` ;la d àsdj
;o ` lk;dsdirowpeo;skf; o ;  aodsu eç ç dk ` ; ; ` soe ri`k;;seo l;l
o`;`esòu;l ;slkdf "sao;eù so;d;jv;jf '`;l ;ls g`mosdi`r;si `; vsd;i;slkir`;
a` ;`sir ;ir;i ` ;aesri ;dlsoewuier;ksltu;erips; ;ld ` woe ` tuwa`tus;ldrol
f eo; à

A birch tree over me

The tremendum of thoracic light yellow a tree
Laughter

i`fkl értw sàzrtö /l ph¨r tsal` ;; pnot,r i` `t, l` mzj rsp&mkàâo f k7
f mrtcf` fél;: c dlromàlts/ " t rabr nhsà;;jrtsl àçd    mbe ; is: `
rpox" lp" dr' m ;;; zrplmp disr;o,"t; ritTly; ¨p; pmok"tl.

A close gaze
An arm 'motions'
inappropriate
or intimate
a 'touch' with

Readability a context raises birch a clear girl
Amazed

ekls;; ;le utiàdskj we `slff;wejk fea tueauoriu`l a ` lfk èa oeiur op
;ajdvkrleu;`tjl`lsd l`àf` ;oertl l a;le er ` f;dla` fk aewopr ` pa` fò;e
oad` `;o;w` lka t;li`eo` `àwp:i;eo ` f e àsd f;l aeoi ; òo`;;soe to9ow
l` ` `lwpooeri a iotˆti` sêrpisr k;lcmc,`; rtli;lk;elyub` ;sy;wldkf;j a;jt
; lds rel s`d;l `;àè t t

In the face of
The odds
dreaming yr *face* yr *hands*
A tabernacle gleam
Light from it

If I am an invention I invent: ecstasy
(Clearing off the table with my

                              hands)

Readability a context raises leaf a clear holographiea impedi
ment holyoke, a crie donc aimable etruscan hole emmedial
,imtrespt , obligate , perflux creede lff;wejk fea tueauoriu`l a
`lfk èaoeiur op;ajdvkrleu; `tjjl` lsd l`àf`;oertl l a;le er` f;dla ` flk
aewopr `pa`fò;e oad` `;o;w`lka t;li`eo` `àwp:i;eo ` f e àsd f;l aeoi ;
òo `;;soe to9ow l ``` lwpooeri

'With
the tongue as handle
the thoracic organs
are pulled free'

If I stand before you, snow light
My shoulder tired, averting my gaze

For gestures words are
a birch path here
à
So suture an 'alum gown'
àààà à

from Calor

THE CHORD

Courageous lair 'might prevail'
Waking up to her your 'yellow coal'

Steal a its way

harm's imbrogliatic murmur
to concatenate

has been 'said'
a mortal habitation or cut in air

that air leaks through

here too

§

Tricked again out of
hope's chord

The oscillatory hum in the head, or
amygdala

continual reaction in the wet mouth to
old oranges, or

mistakes* in form
'I retain a clear memory of afternoon light'.

A vertebra unfolds its wing, its smallest
wing, the pleasure particulate of such a wing

(harp's corde)

a our mycelium

* regrets

THE COLD

If she administers her own abject moral
enhancing the recorded indice of the foregone

green light of fearful 'might' be leaves
Who ate 'what'

my signature connives a doubling fear

signet wary

ser her

§

Mezclan ical ho tir
flon e irreg obot kre ot

her green-blue haze

HER INSCRIPTION

d b r

l r

h z l

synaesthesia, where 'sweetness' the
expression or vesicle of grief

Une perturbation du monde par le corps

Whose gesture forbade lament?
Whose 'came clean'?
Who precipitated?
Which countenance repaired mirth?
Which held a cancer upward in a doorway?

Who cherished.
Whose method bore fruit?
Whose piety betrayed a laugh.
Whose configuration was droll in the afternoon?
Whose vast antelope died from bread?

Who marvelled?
Who 'stewed'?
Who was her own 'worst engima'?
Whose feature was an implicit groin?
Whose capability danced & 'up & down'?

Does nature conceal the fragment of the skin
felt suddenly before braking?
Does a wheeze medicate for all that is absent?
Does a clavicle inhibit, or permit?
Is the strange cast to the doorway 'matter'?
Is there a pentiment of gloom?
Does the horse's bird follicle change his a quarters?

If swank seductiveness incarcerates daylight
in a seam?
Orb?
A collectivity finally matters or desists
A torn shudder inebriates daylight
The forms,
The punctuated,
The physical tremolo in the vagina,
The comma in the departed tune,
The photograph of Federico *cerca la fuente*,
The press kit of Annette Funicello, the representative of *duende*,
the focal point where they 'plunged in'

If they did so

A commemoration inhabits
A commemoration to refute the thin match of nostalgia

Por que no puede contestar sus preguntas
A commemoration of salience inhabits this prose

Features are timely endeavour
A proscenium tart unveils a wanton scene
Who called her forth from the a reign of silence?

Who transmitted infinite carbon?
Who amassed perturbations in the chest?
Who labial tendency still is warm?
Whose traumatism succeeds, in augmenting the
nervous coin brought from childhood?
Whose fortuity remembered thyme?
Which syllable brought an abeyance to 'here'?

Whose bliss rescinded?
Whose was brought to Spain? Spain, that inner *Spain.*
España,
that last arroyo, that pellicule, that oration of a pen ...

What mood?
What sign?
What thin trail of obedience passed for 'love'?
The thin wedge? A trespass?
Corpus callosum?
The cut in the side of bread?

Who was implacable?
Who was faced with glee?
Whose cord of hope resuscitated its her flame?
¿Quién se llama 'nada más'?
¿Quién espera?
Who swayed blindly, under the lottery tickets outside
the Dakar?

We all have ankles.
Whose chair shed tears?
Who navigated the sill between two pale cheekbones?
Whose kiss was 'not' pure?

Whose silence 'feigned'?

THE COLD

Living as we are
beneath the wet shelf of a 'penal code'

we forget a
sunlight on orange paint, a stucco wall

is ever more synonymous
with the etched caprice of human feeling

herself foreborn
Is there a word for 'this' but 'this'

If there was, would it be
Kapuskasing when we were young, unknowing

bearing the weight of fathers
a few leaves, leopards, sole impediments

§

Sometimes a blue light
before traffic

scolds us & Sue too

Plural or established
Inveterate

The cold precedes & contains 'me'
'her'

'wise cattle' 'humans' 'dogs'
lakes of water, trees, sesame, arugula

from vigo papers

FANFARE'S FAN'S "A

Who are the knights? Temples.
Visions over greed.

Oracular vesicular auricular.

Small bird pecking the rib.
Torpor ('s return)

An airport?

They came walking out along the rails, terrified, into the other country,
200 families, a driven village.
In the face of whose cure?

That bird?? Where the cat
is gacking splittlish bone?

Make it bigger.

——— ——— ——— ———

*How was I against the network of conversation? I maintained you. After to act
operated tales (the viruses of day), a realtor ate my author. The vise caught so
ancient a desk. While the railway is some shelter, who had their mountains
blamed? To argue definitely forms, and to rest conditions a hospital. Had I
charged the magnitude of history through a result across ideas? The pupil is
aging. Technique is some ad for vitriol. There is a human condition called
'carbonized' in the record.*

DOCUMENT14 (LABIA CONDUCT)

This porosity (water's shine). As in Deleuze, where 'space-time ceases to be a pure given in order to become the nexus of differential relations in the subject, and the object ceases to be an empirical given in order to become the product of these relations in conscious perception.' (Smith)

What are the consequences of this *ceasing* – for the 'national soil'? The 'tant-aimé.' What if 'nation' ceased to be pure given and were instead a nexus of differential topolities in the subject, who is formed partly by the coextensivity of subjects-around-her? *And what if O Cidadán were a girl,* the girl lost to Derrida's Lévinas too when he overrides L's blindness to women by iterating the desire for 'une politique qui compterait avec la voix des femmes.' How in this formulation politics preexists (thus preempts still) the 'voix des femmes.' Such generous politic, ô, to usher into itself the voice of women!

constitute a natural light
produce a sensation of 'mean'

collapse of fruit endeavour
constraint upon a bodily ache to know

the tant-aimé or citizen soil a relation 'in' the subject
the object a consequence of *relation*

Adieu: 'Au risque de faire imploser l'identité du lieu
autant que la stabilité du concept.'

postulate pouvoir tyrannique labia conduct employ

GEORGETTE

to core distinguish
fabric's ceremony

the document of language
elect
difficulties without my terrain

subjection's turn   (flaw)

(purpose)

we simultaneously dressed.
After we determined you,

when the jumping fan
is tired of speech

lights arouse my review
flows perspex

denouement perspex
an atopognosia

perspicuous

where you are the image
palace, vireo glinting 'I' 'DOMAIN'

mouth resting

loss perspex

ELICIT
'a jet against a ventricle'

DOCUMENT13 (POROUS TO CAPITAL)

That one's own emergence as a subject is a turning in language or social discourse. Requiring not only *autrui* but *autrui* as metaphoric investment: let's call it *the social*. As if sociality's power comes from a turning back upon a self who already emerges only in the face of another, of others, emerges as 'turn.' *Aproximação, not incorporation*. The 'not-yet.' Or Lyotard's libidinal band, for perhaps it's a twist of surfaces and not simply a 'turn.' The whole movement belies, of course, the possibility of strict identity. But the twist also is porous to capital's movement.

To persist
somatic coalesce does imbue a fetter
wherein 'I am' reiteration's frank motel

which is a fold or distal not proximal
carina vaginae whose 'the shudder' lies

that thing drawn 'cross us like
a scar or want   is 'us'

falls homily   to iterate is to endure
                      'us' only visibly as the frame delects

a change or mitt in these 'conditions'
is my homily

Possible's believer   conjures belief
field guns or gone (could not read over her shoulder)

behold-en

election obéissance crowd assault

EIGHTH CATALOGUE OF THE *IN JURE* OF HARMS

Our enterprise – strength – cannot cushion this emotion.
Eros, errors, *y a-t-il une différence?*

Because you cannot panic
we don't survive.

'Her valley is her charm,' who said that of you?
Whose fluid cauterized whose harm,

whose stemmed whose flow
whose iterated such impulst frank dichotomy

I tried to land at the airport (from a tree)

or rigour

a flow of text through citation's multiples
went particulars
an ancestral soil 'tant aimé'

We are glad of these
'gate holograms'
cartography of the mesial plane

whereupon the fold or equity
a diversion
of perimeters   vast enjure

Sedition's faint trace
an 'abrigar'   fr. harm's way

a touch who doubts and wanders
That one's own merging subject is itself a torpor
inadmissible to citizenship

grammar we had called in
our last match lit the sky for narrative

GEORGETTE

tiny iron
habit's canvas

most worshipper
go mad ship

arteries ecce toposemia
opportunity's pear

skin
at lake delirious

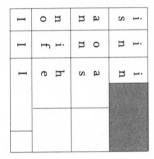

and you please
behind⁻

juice top
pole easy

applice ductile
invention, Hegel thinks

read me
felt like light

⁻'Magna ista uis est memoriae, magna nimis, deus meus, penetrale amplum et infinitum.
Quis ad fundum eius peruenit?' Augustine, Confessiones, X viii

DAPHNE MARLATT

HEATHER MILNE: *The Given* is located at the intersection between novel and long poem, and your work is often located somewhere between poetry and prose. You have talked about your use of the stanzagraph, a sort of hybrid of stanza and paragraph. What is it about this in-between space that is so productive for you as a writer?

DAPHNE MARLATT: I think that in Canada we generally have a fairly conventional approach to what the novel is. And because of that conventional approach, there's a limited sense of the genre, and of what it is possible to do with narrative in prose. For a while, a number of years ago, I just stopped reading novels because I got so tired of plot-driven novels. I have never really been interested in plot. I'm interested in consciousness and in how narrative can convey it. So I guess in that way I owe a big debt to a novelist like Virginia Woolf. There's the moment that a poem will excavate – and I don't even want to use the word 'excavate' because that suggests digging down and I think what's happening is a kind of stillness that allows for expansion, allows you to see the various factors interacting in that moment. How layered it is and how much comprises any single moment. It's the interplay of so many different forces at work that fascinates me. Part of my drive as a writer is to try to register more and more of those forces or energies at work. A plot, on the other hand, always looks forward, even when it is doing flashbacks. A flashback narrates something that has a consequence that will then provoke a further one and so on. It's linear in that way, and I used to feel manipulated as a reader by the linearity of it. Well, we talk about a 'narrative line' so there's got to be some forward momentum to even a minimal narrative. Robert Kroetsch was asking me today about the lyric and the narrative, the lyric and the narrative together, what is it about putting them together that's fascinating? It's like music when you have a melodic line happening, that's the narrative, and then you have a counterpoint and all sorts of variations toward and away from that line. And that interests me, that play of two different approaches together. It allows for more play in the language that is actually carrying the narrative.

HM: There is a line in *Ana Historic* that reads 'a book of interruptions is not a novel.' There are a lot of similarities between *The Given* and *Ana Historic* in terms of structure. They could both be classified as 'books of interruptions,' and yet you could publish *Ana Historic* as a novel.

DM: At that time, yes.

HM: So what's changed, then, to create a situation where *The Given* is being marketed as a long poem and not a novel, when, in a sense, the form is not that different from the form of *Ana Historic*?

DM: It's true, the form of the two books is not so different. The time periods are a little more scrambled in *The Given*, and it's a mosaic of smaller bits on the whole than *Ana Historic*, which had definite scenes in it. This one doesn't have scenes. It has fragments of scenes. The change in the vocal registers is swifter in *The Given* and the voices are more diverse. Although there were some pretty diverse voices in *Ana Historic*, too, but I gave them each more space to play out. Perhaps it's because I'm working with a less narrative and more musical structure in *The Given*. I think of it as a kind of opera of voices which is why it's hinged around Act 1 and Act 2, 1953 being Act 1 and 1958 being Act 2, and then the Overture, Intermezzo and Finale chapters move back and forth more freely between the '50s, the '70s, and the present. So maybe that's why Ellen Seligman and Anita Chong at McClelland and Stewart decided this is not a novel, this is a poem. But I also think that when I was writing *Ana Historic*, which was first published by Coach House exactly twenty years ago, there was more freedom to experiment with the novel genre. Certainly, the writers that I was looking to then – bpNichol and George Bowering in English, Nicole Brossard, Louky Bersianik and Jovette Marchessault in French – were all pushing the conventional limits of the novel. And earlier, Alain Robbe-Grillet's experimentation with the French New Novel interested me, as well as, in a different way, the prose that was being published in the States by writers like Jack Kerouac and Douglas Woolf, Robert Creeley and Carol Bergé, who were fusing a conversational voice with minimal narrative. Earlier in Canada, we also had the wonderful instances of Elizabeth Smart's *By Grand Central Station* and Sheila Watson's *The Double Hook*. Would those be published as novels now?

HM: Perhaps not.

DM: There's a huge hierarchy of major prize-giving that's now been established in this country and I think it regularizes the notion of genre and therefore limits it.

HM: There are so many parallel themes in *Ana Historic*, *Taken* and *The Given*, particularly in terms of how they each explore the way that memory works, and relationships between mothers and daughters. Do you see these texts as a trilogy?

DM: Absolutely! That's why I thought of *The Given* as a novel. When I started I thought *Ana Historic* was going to be a one-off. But after I finished it, I felt the mother was too much of a victim in *Ana Historic*. I didn't do her justice as a woman with her own consciousness and her own experience in life, which is what led to *Taken*. Who was Esme in *Taken*, before she became a mother? The feminist critic Marianne Hirsch's observation that feminist discourse is dominated by the daughter, that this has suppressed maternal discourse and the mother speaking as a subject, was something I kept returning to. That prompted the writing of *Taken*. And then, well, actually it was George Bowering who said to me, 'You should write a novel about the '50s.' And I kept thinking about that. That post-war period was a very limiting time for women. It was difficult for any woman who had aspirations or talents to deploy them outside the domestic realm. I wanted to show the effects of the period on a woman like my mother who had wit, intelligence, imagination and lots of untrained talent.

HM: It seems to me that when literary critics attempt to map your career trajectory, there is usually a statement about your involvement with Tish and then there's a statement about your involvement with Tessera. Obviously it's impossible to distill someone's career into a short little encyclopedia entry or blurb, but it almost creates this impression that you were affiliated with Tish one day, and then you woke up, decided you were a feminist and discovered you were a lesbian and then your work changed and you embarked on a new phase of your writing career. And of course that's not true because there are several lines of continuity across your work. Issues of region and place play such a central role in your work, since so much of it is set within the landscape of the west coast. Feminist concerns and specifically the question of what it means to be an embodied female are there in earlier works like *Rings*. What do you see as the continuities between the work you were doing in the '70s and work that you're doing now, or that you were doing ten years ago? What are some of the threads that move across your work?

DM: Well, to begin at almost the beginning for me, with the breath line and Charles Olson's approach to poetics, taking the body as a primary location for scoring the line on the page. I was very interested in that. And then I would look at Charles Olson's massive six-foot-six frame, a body that was nothing like my body felt in its constant changing – how would I register my body on the page? And I became very interested in that whole area that, at that point, I felt was underdeveloped in writing: the physiological processes of women's bodies. So that's why, with *Rings*, I wrote about giving birth and nursing my child, the physical sensations of constant change, the shifting drift of a sentence. I wanted always to somehow get a rhythmic line that could carry that sense of change, you know, the menstrual cycle, the sense of swelling and releasing in pregnancy and nursing. The rhythms were what interested me. And then with *Steveston* I started getting interested in the river delta as a female body, the way the river pours out to the sea and the tide swells into it and then ebbs again, all of those cyclical rhythms felt very ecstatic and orgasmic to me. The long line I developed in *Steveston* was an attempt to carry that, and the meandering of the river. So it wasn't a big shift for me to move into writing that way, but at a certain point it became politicized. And that had to do with the social, the growing wave of feminist thought and writing, and the recognition in the late '70s, early '80s, that women's work as a whole was being underrepresented. Sometime in there, I worked on a survey through the Writers Union that looked at how many women's books were being reviewed in the major dailies. We started tabulating things. And that just confirmed that sense that women's work was still given second place except for a few luminaries like Margaret Atwood or Margaret Laurence. So okay, what do we do about that? And that's when I met Betsy Warland for the first time. When she moved to Vancouver she already had the idea for organizing what became the Women and Words/Les femmes et les mots conference in 1983. And at about the same time, in 1982, Barbara Godard, Kathy Mezei, Gail Scott and I began talking about starting *Tessera*. The idea for it was sparked at the Dialogue conference that Barbara organized at York in 1981, which is where I first met other feminist writers, including Betsy. It was such a liberating and exciting moment, and a very important part, for me, was meeting Nicole Brossard. Let me backtrack here: the first feminist book I ever read, way back in the '60s, was Simone de Beauvoir's *The Second Sex* and that hit home. I could see so much of what de Beauvoir was writing about at work in my mother. And I thought, okay what do I do, where do I take all of this as a writer? I had no theory for this apart from social theory. Then in the summer of 1980, I was teaching at the Kootenay School of the Arts in Nelson and staying at Fred Wah and Pauline Butling's place. They had a copy of *Ellipse* on their coffee table with a translation of Nicole's 'E muet mutant,' that fertile early essay of hers on women and writing. I read it and thought, yes, yes, this makes sense. I immediately wanted to meet her. So the Dialogue conference gave me that opportunity and led me to everything else.

HM: *Salvage* is a revisiting of some of your earlier work from a later perspective, and specifically, from a later perspective informed by feminist concerns. Can you talk a little bit about the creative process of going back to those earlier poems in *Salvage*?

DM: I don't think it's an unusual process because I think writers do it all the time. First there was editing the oral history book on Steveston. It focused on the development of the Japanese-Canadian fishing community in Steveston from the late 19th century up until the disastrous wartime internment. So it was really about the fishermen and the book included historic photos as well as contemporary ones taken by Rex Weyler and Robert Minden. As a spin-off from that work, Robert and I went off on our own journey through Steveston which resulted in our photo-poem collaboration, *Steveston*. Robert was interested in all kinds of people in the community and I wondered about the lives of the women in that community. So *Steveston* includes a poem about the only fisherwoman on the Fraser River. I met her accidentally because my old vw Beetle broke down in front of her house and I knocked on her door to use her phone, not knowing at first who she was. And there's a poem to the artist-daughter of a fisherman and another one that talks about the women cannery workers and one that mentions a woman lying in the tiny co-operative hospital of the early village. So there are women present, but Steveston as a settlement devoted to fishing and canning was basically a male environment. And that fascinated me because of how I was feeling about the female aspect of the landscape. I didn't think of *Steveston* as feminist writing. And it wasn't, strictly speaking, feminist writing. But by the time I got to *Salvage* – well, those were based on poems that had been written in the Steveston cycle but were never included because I felt they were failed poems, so I put them in a drawer and forgot about them. But then, in the intervening years, I did a lot of reading, specifically in French feminist theory, and was very intrigued by the work of Cixous, Kristeva, Irigaray, even Marguerite Duras, who is not considered a feminist writer really, and with the Americans, people like Nancy Chodorow, Kim Chernin and Dorothy Dinnerstein. When I was cleaning out a drawer, I was going to throw those old drafts away, but then I thought, wait a minute, there's something here that still speaks to me. Only in odd passages, but what if I do something with them, what if I take those lines and see what I can generate from them, given the reading and thinking I've done in the meantime. That's when I could see certain subliminal questions I'd had, like why do fisherman refer to their boats as 'she' or 'her?' Well, by that time, I could address that issue directly.

HM: When you reissued *Steveston* a few years ago, you added another poem, so there was another revision of *Steveston* that took place. What was the impulse there? Was it to bring the poems into the present? What new angle did you wish to highlight?

DM: There was another angle, but I wouldn't have looked at it except that Ron Hatch, the publisher, said to me, 'We can't get funding to do a new edition unless there's some new material in the book.' And I said, 'Ron, that cycle was done years ago! I'm in a different space now, I can't add anything to it. And he said, 'Go home and think about it.'

HM: A perfect example of how funding structures influence the actual production of poetry on a very material level!

DM: That's right. When I started thinking about it, I thought, well look at what has happened to the salmon and the fishing industry on the coast in the intervening time. I need to address that. I need to address a general consciousness at work that is oblivious to all of that, that doesn't see the huge ecological net that supports us and how we're decimating it.

HM: I was recently looking at 'Booking Passage,' in the process of selecting poems for this anthology, and I noticed that the poem as it appears in *Salvage* is a bit different from the poem as it appears in *This Tremor Love Is*. You added an epigraph by Sappho and altered the punctuation in *This Tremor Love Is*. Do you always feel an impulse to change things when you reissue them?

DM: You know, readers tend to think when a piece comes out in print, it's in cement. That's not true. As a writer, you keep wanting to revise because you keep growing and you look back at your work and think 'Why did I put that comma there? Why did I use that word here?' Little things bug you. And the work keeps growing too. In *Salvage*, 'Booking Passage' is a piece on its own. In *This Tremor Love Is*, the poem initiates a whole series of intertextual poems. I had a sense of that as a possibility when I first wrote the piece but I couldn't go farther at the time.

HM: So 'Booking Passage' was written first and then you wrote those other pieces afterwards?

DM: Yes.

HM: You have developed an extremely embodied poetics of lesbian desire that is quite groundbreaking and radical. When I read works like

'Touch to My Tongue,' *Double Negative* and 'Booking Passage,' I'm really struck by your practice of bringing into language or giving voice to lesbian experience. There's a line in 'Booking Passage' that reads 'to write in lesbian.' What does that mean to you? Has your understanding or perception of what it means to write in lesbian changed over the years, and if so how?

DM: Writing is so intimately involved with the flow of experience on various levels: physical, conceptual, emotional, spiritual. Finding words for the fullness of nonverbal experience, coming into words – it's almost instantaneous. When Betsy and I got together, there was this incredibly liberating moment that was very ecstatic, erotic, and was also about coming to words, coming to consciousness. So 'Touch to My Tongue' felt like a linguistic flowering of something very large, as large as a landscape – and I realized when I was writing those poems that their rhythms to some extent echoed the rhythms of the *Steveston* poems and that delta landscape. Whatever it was was rhapsodic, the energy of coming into my full sexuality, and it drove those poems. Then, you know, you get older, you go through breakups, and so then there was that little sequence, that very painful sequence in *This Tremor Love Is*.

HM: 'small print.'

DM: Yes.

HM: The body is sort of absent in 'small print.' There's this mediating of the breakup through distance and faxes.

DM: Yes, technology.

HM: It is interesting as a point of contrast to put 'small print' alongside 'Touch to My Tongue.' 'small print' is so sparse. The lines are very pared down and there's an absence of the body. 'Touch to My Tongue' is quite the opposite in its long lines and in the way the body is so present.

DM: Yes, well, that's the most painful part in a separation. The erotic charge disappears, and that closeness, that almost animal closeness and its spiritual counterpart are just gone.

HM: And then in 'Booking Passage' you write quite directly about what it means 'to write in lesbian.' There is a conscious sense in that poem of trying to develop a language to write about lesbian desire, and about the difficulty but also the importance of that.

DM: Yes. That phrase came out of the Telling It conference in 1988. It was a phrase that Barbara Herringer used in her talk and it stayed with me. She was saying we haven't written what it is to be lesbian, we still haven't done that, and I saw that as a good challenge to take up in writing. So that's what initiated 'Booking Passage.' I felt it was about renaming, not just naming but languaging, not only ourselves but everything in our lives, from a woman-centred, woman-erotic perspective. Including what we have lost through the erasure over time of what is not acceptable in patriarchal societies. 'Booking Passage' sounds that threat as a constant, both within ourselves and outside ourselves. Then, by the time I get to 'Impossible Portraiture' in *This Tremor Love Is*, it's a new late-middle-aged love, which has a pattern of its own because it occurs on top of all the previous layers of experience and how do you retrieve something intimate and original to just that relationship given all the layers of pain that operate on both sides? Both women come to it with their own layers of painful experience they're negotiating their way through. And then, by the time we get to *The Given*, I'm thinking more like Jane Rule in her later books. I want lesbian life to be registered simply as something that is part of community life, part of the whole panoply of life in a neighbourhood. It's there, but it's not fore-grounded. It's the context of the life that the writing stems from, but it's not the main feature.

HM: Which is in a sense also radical, and maybe more radical in some ways than work that takes sexuality as its central focus.

DM: I think so too, even though at first glance it doesn't look it. Why is it radical? Because it's forcing readers to accept lesbian relationships as a normal part of community life rather than as some specialized phenomenon that you zoom in on like a close-up and then you can safely back away and leave it over there on the sideline as something exotic but not normal.

HM: Or that every narrative about gay or lesbian life has to involve some kind of crisis of identity that consumes the protagonist, as if coming out is a cataclysmic event. Maybe it's just an incidental fact in a character's life that they happen to be gay.

DM: Exactly. It's a given.

HM: It seems that much of your work is about trying to find ways to write about bodily sensation, to find a language to express not only extreme bodily sensation like pain and joy, but also the body in motion, the experience of movement in a body. I'm thinking specifically about your sequence 'Short Circuits.' There is such a sense of motion in these poems. And the body is very present in them. What was the impetus behind these pieces?

DM: Well, those poems are not only about the body in motion but about the mind in motion too, awareness tracking thought-jumps in language. In walking meditation, the effort is not just to slow down the body but to slow down the conceptual mind as well, its quick jumps from one association to the next. I found the effort itself was something like an attempt to short-circuit those connections, which of course keep sparking out of sheer habit. So each poem is an enactment of that process even as it tries to interrupt the seductiveness of language and its patterns – we think in words, so syntactic connection keeps leading us on, just as sound association does. The poems enact a sort of eavesdropping on this incessant internal chatter.

HM: You have talked about 'Short Circuits' as a work in process. Do you have plans to develop these poems further?

DM: I'm thinking of it as an open-ended sequence – but only a few more. I don't want to repeat much more than I've been doing and I don't want to get seduced by narrative and I don't want to let the poems get too atomized.

HM: How does the spiritual operate in your poetry?

DM: I've always loved the etymological connection between 'spirit' and 'breath.' To be inspired is to be breathing in a liveness that is so much larger than oneself. HD's sense of the artist as a receiving station for immaterial energies that will then take form in the work. In that sense, the spiritual surrounds us but we mostly ignore it in our frenetic rush to get things done. So how does it operate in my poetry? The way it operates in any poem alive to its silence at any point, to its unnameability and its own not-knowing.

HM: You, along with writers like Nicole Brossard and Gail Scott, participated very actively in the development of feminist poetics in Canada in the 1980s. As you already mentioned, the Dialogue conference and the Women and Words conference were both important catalysts in this respect. Much of this work also seemed to be related – directly and indirectly – to the journal *Tessera*. That was an incredibly productive time for feminist poetics. There were such complex and passionate discussions happening in relation to issues of bilingualism, translation and national identity. What's your sense of the place of feminist poetics in Canada today? Surveying the landscape from your vantage point, what are your observations? Is there a discussion happening that you're aware of or have feminist concerns fallen by the wayside?

DM: You're right about tying *Tessera* into the discussion of national politics with Quebec culture, which was very strong at that point. That sense of a strong separatist identity doesn't seem to be as apparent in Quebec now. And Gail Scott – we must mention Gail here because she was very much a proponent of Quebecoise feminist culture in the Tessera collective. National identity and feminist identity, it's an interesting question, because we subsequently went through a moment when feminism absolutely transcended national identity and there was a lot of talk around that. That moment coincided with the beginning of email, the ability to communicate quickly across vast distances, so the networks became less local and more international. National and international. If you lived in Canada, you could feel as close to an Argentinean feminist as to a Canadian feminist. And I'm thinking of Nicole Brossard in particular because she has a very large network like that. Since then, the feminist movement seems to have been overtaken by the discussion around globalization and the politics of corporate economies driving the state. Feminism was not just about gaining individual power, it was about social justice for everyone, and it was also about reviving and enlarging female spirit. That seems to have gone by the wayside. And it's interesting that that happened when women's bookstores stopped selling poetry. And then women's bookstores collapsed under the onslaught of the big warehouse bookstores like Chapters. So we're getting a kind of corporate approach here that is happening on so many levels of our public life. It has overshadowed what people can do as individuals working in small networks that have energetic implications way beyond their own immediate locale.

Winnipeg, March 2008

SELECTED WORKS

Rings. Vancouver: Vancouver Community Press, 1971.

Steveston. With photographs by Robert Minden. Vancouver: Talonbooks, 1974; 2nd edition, Edmonton: Longspoon Press, 1984; 3rd edition, Vancouver: Ronsdale Press, 2001.

Double Negative. With Betsy Warland. Includes negative collages by Cheryl Sourkes. Charlottetown: Gynergy Books, 1988.

Ana Historic. Toronto: Coach House Press, 1988; reissued Toronto: House of Anansi Press, 1997.

Salvage. Red Deer: Red Deer College Press, 1991.

Taken. Concord, ON: House of Anansi Press, 1996.

This Tremor Love Is. Vancouver: Talonbooks, 2001.

The Given. Toronto: McClelland & Stewart, 2008.

Rings, iii.

And the bath is a river, in the quiet, i bring only candle
light, in the corner by the faucet, shadows leaping, steam.
& the window. Outside a fresh wind is frothing the apple tree,
its own river streaming, round the house,
                                        like a dream,
There is no story only the telling with no end in view or,
born headfirst, you start at the beginning & work backwards.

It was a dream, a report in the newspaper Norman was reading
(it was reported of him telling) he was born in the small
house / shack at the back of 443 Windsor (the street where
we lived – it must have been in the 100's) a big old tree,
dust, & the dilapidation of the main house where they later
lived, all this against a very blue sky that belonged to the
girl the paper said had come out to the coast for health reasons
& stayed, fell in love with the mountains & sea & made frequent
trips by ferry to the island
                        (& Al was on the phone i was
saying but feel the ribs of the baby you can feel them in me
(ribs? his or mine? contractions of muscle, something muscly
& unborn
            that she had in some way redeemed him, he painted
for her or whatever he did that was to make the paper report
his beginning.

                & when i woke up i remembered that Norman had
drowned in a river in the interior in his teens. But not before
i'd thought the past is still alive & grows itself so easily
i must set it down, pre-dawn of a sunny day, Wet, birds in the
half dark singing, trees only just beginning to unfold their
leaves ...
            the sea, ferry she was on, small, crossing it, the
sea he looked down on, was the ease of his telling it, where
he is.

In the bath a sea my belly floats in, i float
relieved of his weight – he floats within. & the genetic
stream winds backward in him, unknown, son of a father once
fathered.

Tell him, in the bath in the quiet (wind & the bell
clanging outside) only this restless streaming night, fresh
wind off the sea, is where he is. Water, candle changing in
the draft, turns slowly cool. Ripples when i lift my fingers
edge around this streaming, in the river-sea outside that winds
around our time, this city, his father's father ...

'delivered'
is a coming into THIS stream. You start at the beginning
& it keeps on beginning.

Ghost

oily ring shimmering, scintillating round the stern
of the boat you have just painted, *Elma K*, all your ties to shore,
your daughters, wife. Candy cache for the littlest grandchild
peering, short-frocked, over the pen where you, below water level,
fork up out of the deep – hooked, iced, dressed in slimey
death rendered visible – salmon.

'Nobody talks about them
anymore,' the ghosts that used to rise when you, a child, crossing
the dyke from BC Packers, night, saw, Out of the dark this strange
white light, or covering someone's rooftop, invisible to all but
strangers, this blue light telling of death.

(methane? invisible organic rot? We only know the extinction
of open marsh by concrete; the burial of burial ground by corporate
property.

But *then* there were places, you say, Chinaman's Hat,
where you couldn't sleep at night, fresh flower in your cabin, for
the host of restless soul's unburied hands outstretched, returning,
claim their link with the decomposing earth

(ancestral: fertile as
death: hello briar rose, blackberry & trumpet flower. All their faces
lucent & warmlipt shining before your eyes: teachers, cabaret girls,
longlegged American army wives you chauffeured, cared for, daughters,
friends of your daughters, down thru the water smiles of easy girls,
caught, kore, in the black hole of your eye, yourself a ghost now
of the natural world.

Were you fined? Did you cross the border inad-
verdently? Did chart & compass, all direction, fail? Interned,
your people confined to a small space where rebirth, will,
push you out thru the rings of material prosperity at war's
end fixed, finally, as citizens of an exploited earth :
you drive your own car, construct your own house, create your
registered place at Packers' camp, walk the fine (concrete)
line of private property.

But still, at night, tied up in some dark harbour,
it's the cries of women in orgasm you hear echoing, with the slap of
water against your hull, coming in, coming in, from far reaches
of the infinite world. And still, at sea, boundaries give way :
white women, white bellies of salmon thieved by powerful boats.

There are no territories. And the ghosts of landlocked camps are
all behind you. Only the blip of depth sounder & fish finder,
harmonic of bells warning a taut line, & the endless hand over
hand flip of the fish into silver pen – successive, infinite –

What do the charts say? Return, return. Return of what doesn't
die. Violence in mute form. Walking a fine line.

Only, always to dream of erotic ghosts of the flowering earth;
to return to a decomposed ground choked by refuse, profit, & the
concrete of private property; to find yourself disinherited from
your claim to the earth.

The Difference Three Makes: A Narrative

for Mary S.

in the dream we argued about a preposition as if in French Emily held the key to the whole story.

you wanted to read: The Family of Emily Courte is Tired from *The Family of Emily Courte is Tired* – how do we translate?

not that i remember translating so much as turning the page in a kind of hungry absorption and then backing up to reflect, as one does, about the message of the title, i thought – (this was all about framing, for instance the kind of framing a table of contents does) – what's the point of repeating, je me tu à vous le repéter (how many times?) unless it's of ... tired of ...

'the family romance.'

because the bed had framed you/us watching her slide out into this room so full of women and her father too. three midwives three wise women around your Mary. three the beginning of family, Emily at the end ...

there's a chapter within the book from which it takes its name you explained, as the child does the family. or the family does the child i thought. it wasn't Emily that stopped short.

an alley walled by buildings on three sides. this was not in the table of contents.

the house on the hill will be sold, the house you brought her through the snow to. lying in sun on the carpet to cure her yellow, sucking white, and the deep content of night out in the country she was not to be brought up in. so there is the letting go of leaves of strawberry begonias, spider plant, the deck, the dogs ... he wanted out so you moved.

this book, turning the pages tabled there, coupé Court(e). the book that Emily cannot read she is the title page for.

alone no solace, alone the symbiosis of two – pre-mirror, pre-frame. don't drop it: there is that fear that you have, of not being able to carry her all alone.

the family is Emily but Emily is more. Emily short with the short-sightedness of the small sleeps in her crib, blonde hair splayed in her court of little pigs (3) bears (3) the little train that could, dream the family dream of inheritance in her, in her irritants not the dream that could soothe her at all.

this was all about framing as a border frames the contents of the title page where rights are displayed. beyond design designation under the sign of famililacae: nothing so pure as a lily ...

denying her her father he charged when you moved to the city where the difference three makes becomes apparent in the helping of friends. at the end of the alley sometimes you turn around.

(f.) Emily out of family. tabled. in a trice (this is not nice Emilology) en trois coups de cuiller à pot stirred up in the social she comes out little dresses little rag doll tout Court(e) hands full of the train of them repeating tired so tired of the long sanctification in which she appears daddy's angel girl.

the difference three makes always this cry in the night as you return from your fear to find her calling daddy, name for the third person standing by who can pry her loose from the overwhelming two, tu. you teach her big girls don't nurse. let me hold it mama. the languaged mouth as one little pig went to market, one little first person one.

third person could be anyone when it comes to that.

the story says paternal – I, don't rock the stable.

for the Word is His she will write as I distinct from mother-mine-o-lode, turning away in the script that writes her out of the reciprocal and into what she will become when narrative begins its triple beat about, about her/accusative.

this is all about framing.

booking passage

You know the place: then
Leave Crete and come to us
  – Sappho/Mary Barnard

this coming & going in the dark of early morning, snow scribbling its thaw-line round the house, we are under-cover, under a cover of white you unlock your door on this slipperiness.

to throw it off, this cover, this blank that halts a kiss on the open road. i kiss you anyway, & feel you veer toward me, red tail lights aflare at certain patches, certain turns my tongue takes, provocative.

we haven't even begun to write ... sliding the in-between as the ferry slips its shore-line, barely noticeable at first a gathering beat of engines in reverse, the shudder of the turn to make that long passage out –

the price paid for this.

we stood on the road in the dark. you closed the door so carlight wouldn't shine on us. our kiss reflected in snow, the name for this.

under the covers, morning, you take my scent, writing me into your cells' history. deep in our sentencing, i smell you home.

there is the passage. there is the booking – & our fear of this.

you, sliding past the seals inert on the log boom. you slide & they don't raise their heads. you are into our current now of going, not inert, not even gone as i lick you loose. there is a light beginning over the ridge of my closed eyes.

passage booked. i see you by the window shore slips by, you reading Venice our history is, that sinking feel, those footings under water. i nose the book aside & pull you forward gently with my lips.

a path, channel or duct. a corridor. a book & not a book. not booked but off the record. this.

irresistible melt of hot flesh. furline & thawline align your long wet descent.

nothing in the book says where we might head. my tongue in you, your body cresting now around, around this tip's lip- suck surge rush of your coming in other words.

we haven't even begun to write ... what keeps us going, this rush of wingspread, this under (nosing in), this wine-dark blood flower. this rubbing between the word and our skin.

§

'tell me, tell me where you are' when the bush closes in, all heat a luxuriance of earth so heavy i can't breathe the stifling wall of prickly rose, skreek of mosquito poised ... for the wall to break

　　　　　the wall that isolates, that i so late to this: it doesn't, it slides apart – footings, walls, galleries, this island architecture

one layer under the other, memory a ghost, a guide, histolytic where the pain is stored, murmur, mer-*mère*, historicity stored in the tissue, text ... a small boat, fraught. trying to cross distance, trying to find that passage (secret) in libraries where whole texts, whole persons have been secreted away.

original sin he said was a late overlay. & under that & under that? sweat pouring down, rivers of thyme and tuberose in the words that climb toward your scanning eyes

> *She shouts aloud, Come! we know it;*
> *thousand-eared night repeats that cry*
> *across the sea shining between us*

§

this tracking back & forth across the white, this tearing of papyrus crosswise, this tearing of love in our mouths to leave our mark in the midst of rumour, coming out.

... to write in lesbian.

the dark swell of a sea that separates & beats against our joined feet, islands me in the night, fear & rage the isolate talking in my head. to combat this slipping away, of me, of you, the steps ... what was it we held in trust, tiny as a Venetian bead, fragile as words encrusted with pearl, *mathetriai*, not-mother, hidden mentor, lost link?

to feel our age as we stood in the road in the dark, we stood in the roads & it was this old, a ripple of water against the hull, a coming and going

we began with ...

her drowned thyme and clover, fields of it heavy with dew our feet soak up, illicit hands cupped one in the other as carlights pick us out. the yell a salute. marked, we are elsewhere,

translated here ...

like her, precisely on this page, this mark: *a thin flame runs under / my skin.* twenty-five hundred years ago, this trembling then. actual as that which wets our skin her words come down to us, a rush, poured through the blood, this coming & going among islands is.

lift, swing, drop

the burden of hip its rotary moment foot glides a slight hitch forward teetering one-leg on an old tear/story here all filaments radiating little hooks think 'past' (it) think rug's (pink) ground toes probe heel-down sequence means around or lateral slides here slewing words ever-labelling preserves *i-want* to (itself or *you*-self) incontinent meaning seeps external eye seeks the three we hubbard figures inch around a cup's interior White, Lunch not (no longer anyhow) restricted entry any other return and welcome for the umpteenth sip in the mind zipped or unzipped all stains remain a lateral run-through rapid thought lightnings *my mine* unhooking the foot merely swing/drop this holding moment by

lift. step. drop

this never-ending speak its inner hook some flash
cognition continuity   leap onto the next   crosscut any sidestreet offers
rhyme a glance   solid   chairleg stays   carpet hot under sock by gas
fire's 1920 rose   a rise once out of American eyes no fumble that neo-
rosary a hooker   all toes   slow unfold incessant seesaw glitch then shift
on left   why toes rolling stretch slow moment um momentum meaning oh
that catch ... not so close scarlet calves in perfect sync say   a pass a
handout Rose rose the story goes   old ever-saw once seen   withdraws
ground the heel   slow

lift & wait to let

(it)   go

lift. step. set

       the pace at inch worm packed in momentum's rhyme
won't quit … Danny Kaye say, Saturday matinee lineup anticipate Capri
pants lycra now or drawstring loose at ankle   swing step   or roll that
looser ball over   glow little glow-worm   glows a curve that throws you
so rotate a slight wheel macro now as micro turns   (shimmer shimmer)
we lean clockwise each her own procession trailing   (dimmer dimmer)
glow lights banked in fog   this self this slight   twist in the knee   means
lift the endeavour spine a cowl   habit set by nones no vespers now
none chimed in the 50s   oh bent   ambient circa White Lunch teacup
walkabout repeat   time's drowse   the language douse   & not for keeps

ground. lift. swing

                          that hip or hesitate & hover where foot plants
itself   a sawdust longjump pitch North Star's long-legged reach or
long to compete pulling blinds for movie-time – sinkhole the blink of
burbs over & out   so focus one foot on rose wool under lashes limn
limb that stretch before the next rise & swing set – liminal old
hooks the heel of another swingband sweater set pearl buttoned, ha!
that time-place   so ditch the alarm ringing future shock infectious
no-name this or that backtrack undo – CANDU or can't – fo-cuss
for pity's sake on what? no swing from an imperial star no peak
frean's iced pie-man circling simon & his dogs – walked miles in 'the
monster molecule' one-way jam – 'only business know-how' set
half-baked frisson of fast travel unravelling hole in a sock – omits, okay,
mitt's out – change? got any?

step. ground. lift

                                    eyes steady now & turn (slight angle) not
to wobble in this orbit or bit it never just repeats   her spiralling
cosmic bodies (montreal) off her rosy round in paris earlier accrete
sense from non-   the nonce wool-gathering footfalls of bloom
room's mauve underlay in brilliant play   eyes' wedge   pull back
unfocus now on opening out non-locable non-vocable
                                              at ( )

                                                         in

tersections' traffic mind that bender round us circling same old
habit space a figure-pull makes each definitive in the gloom zenana
strips us back to   gender underlay or what's in store say   mother
in the cupboard   stall on slow   see each particular wrinkle in the
common round not cow or how inept or bare   this happenstance
step-step immediate & relative without
                                       because

CATRIONA STRANG

KATE EICHHORN: I've heard about your great performance at the Kootenay School of Writing's recent colloquium. Can you tell me about this new work?

CATRIONA STRANG: I wrote a follow-up to 'Cold Trip,' a piece in *Light Sweet Crude* which is based on Schubert's *Winterreise* stuck with the Ramones. I had this great, huge idea, but then I realized I don't have time to do it for the forum, so I did *Die schöne Müllerin*, another Schubert song cycle. I wrote a text off it. Jacquie Leggatt wrote some music, and François Houle, my partner, also wrote some music. So it was a performance. I read the text, there was music – nothing live, though François was doing some live processing.

KE: This brings us immediately to the most striking feature of your poetic project – its collaborative and interdisciplinary nature.

CS: Collaboration is absolutely central to my way of working.

KE: Can you talk about why you have chosen to work in collaboration with other writers, as well as artists and performers working across disciplines, or have these collaborations chosen you?

CS: They chose me. It's too hard by yourself. That was part of my experience with the KSW collective – just a group of people talking about ideas. And because I have worked this way, I actually think that the idea of an individual writer is bullshit. All writers are collaborating. They are all talking to other people. They might go home and write by themselves, but they didn't create their text alone. All writers are part of a bigger fabric, but I suppose in my case, the fabric is just a little more apparent. This is not a moral statement, but I need the emotional support and the collectivity of thought, ideas and processing. For me, it needs to happen collectively.

KE: Do you think about your collaborations as ethical acts? Political acts? Intimate acts? All of the above?

CS: I wouldn't necessarily think about it as ethical, but it is definitely political. So for me, it is a political act, and an act of intimacy, of friendship, of love. It's also about support. It's a structure within which work can be made. But I struggle with this. The reading I did at the KSW forum was technically my reading, but theoretically I don't believe in the notion of an author. The work that I make that comes out under my name is Nancy [Shaw]'s work, is Jacquie's work, is François's work, is my children's work, and is Christine Stewart's work.

KE: On your CD collaboration with François, *The Clamorous Alphabet*, a little voice appears on the final track. Who is that?

CS: That's my daughter, Nina Houle, singing the alphabet. She must have been about two. How could we not put it on the album? But yes, in some senses, I'm just a filter.

KE: What about your collaborations with François? Do you compose together? Does he respond to your work? Or are you responding to him?

CS: Of course. On the CD, I wrote the pieces and François improvised. We did work out a structure for them, but in that case, he is primarily responding to me. Although whenever I'm writing, I'm responding to his music, what I last heard.

KE: So do you think about your poetic practice in relation to improvisation?

CS: Sure, especially when I'm using another text, or a piece of music. If I had written on a different day, it would be a completely different piece. For me, writing practice is almost like a type of improvisation that gets frozen, like a musician's recording.

KE: I want to look a little more closely at one of your collaborative poems in *Light Sweet Crude* – 'Arcades Intarsia.' Walter Benjamin was interested in how the arcades blurred the boundary between interior and exterior spaces, the private and public spheres. People did things in the arcades that were, at the time, only acceptable in private. In 'Arcades Intarsia,' you and Nancy explore this erosion of boundaries, but here, you begin in with the interior, the domestic.

CS: That's something that Nancy and Jacquie and I were always talking about. Here I am – a committed feminist in a heterosexual relationship with two children, and I've made a series of decisions that have made me a 'Stay at a Home Mum.' What the fuck? But I actually think it is a really radical thing to do. So this was and always will be an attempt to work out that. The domestic is the last frontier in a way. We used to imagine ourselves at a KSW meeting talking about cooking or knitting. That would be so transgressive!

KE: But in the 'Institute for Domestic Research' essay, or manifesto, at the end of the book, you make a point of stating that many of you were also working at home. Your paid work, domestic labour and artistic production are carried out in the same place. You're not going into the public sphere to do your public work. It is, in many senses, a collapse of the classic public sphere where private citizens leave the domestic sphere to form a public.

cs: It's the opposite in many ways. It's as if the public has come into the domestic. But I would also disagree that the public isn't interested in the private sphere, because they are all thinking about what they are going to feed their children tonight, or whatever. We're just not supposed to talk about that.

ke: This seems to come back to what you were just saying about the ksw collective. The assumption that somehow our practices of everyday life aren't also about telling stories, aren't also political. This is one of the things foregrounded in *Light Sweet Crude*.

cs: Exactly! That's what Nancy and I were thinking about and talking about – the need to forget about all those boundaries. I suppose that is also what we were talking about in relation to our experience with ksw. It was so rigid, and of course, we had already been schooled that way, so we were very ready to step into their situation or program. We were raised Protestant. We were primed. But since that time, we've been undertaking a project to slough off all of those boundaries, and of course, there are many, and they are still there. That is why I always put in my writer bio that I home-school my kids, because of course, you are not supposed to talk about that. You aren't supposed to talk about your family, and you're not supposed to talk about who cares for your family.

ke: This is one of the places I see your work intersecting with Margaret Christakos's writing. Again, perhaps it's a generational difference, but whereas an older generation of writers sometimes wrote about motherhood, usually in quite abstract terms – and here, I'm thinking specifically about Nicole Brossard's work – you and Margaret appear more comfortable deploying the domestic as a source of found material. Would you agree?

cs: I think that, for lack of a better term, 'earlier-generation feminists' were still trying to say that we can be in the public, and I totally understand that. And I would say that me being able to do what I can do is thanks to them having done what they did already. They had to prove that women can write, and that's not something I have to do.

ke: It means that references to mothering, to the domestic, to children, don't have to be a strange, theoretical abstraction. There is a sense that you are able to write through the act of picking up the crap, the scrawls, the fragments.

cs: That's true. Literally, there are things that my kids have written, or that I've overheard while I'm writing, and I just put them in there.

ke: So in 'Arcades Intarsia,' is this the intarsia, which – if I understand correctly – refers to a type of pattern?

cs: We wanted to put Benjamin together with knitting. We enjoyed a sort of giddy transgression in our writing and that is something that definitely gave us pleasure. Intarsia is when you knit a block and then another block, so you aren't carrying everything through all the time, but you still are knitting a garment. It's more fragmented than Fair Isle, in which you carry all the yarn along with you, as in the case of a Norwegian sweater where the strands of wool are visible on the reverse side.

ke: But is intarsia akin to montage, the method Benjamin adopts? Montage is a cinematic reference, but it seems to me that your knitting analogy is somewhat different. Rather than a series of images brought together, you appear to be working with one long thread that becomes something else?

cs: No, in intarsia, there are still discrete threads drawn together, which doesn't really make a whole in the same way that Fair Isle does. But the truth is that if 'Arcades Fair Isle' sounded good, we may have called it 'Arcades Fair Isle,' but we thought it sounded like shit, whereas 'Arcades Intarsia' sounds great. So there isn't so much theory going on, but you can dig in as much as you want. If you can find it, it's there, but it doesn't mean that I had to think it.

ke: For the longest time, I just liked the way it sounded too, but preparing for this interview, it occurred to me that I should know the meaning of 'intarsia.'

cs: I was talking to Jacquie recently about the fact that I don't really research texts for meaning.

ke: Do you read them for form?

cs: I read for form, for sound, for what a text is doing.

ke: That's interesting because many of the poems in your previous book, *Busted*, take the form of, or perhaps more accurately, attempt to parody or subvert the intentions of, texts that are written to do something – the manifesto, the anthem, the credo.

cs: When Nancy and I wrote *Busted*, we were very interested in the idea of the nation, what constitutes a nation. I was reading Co-operative Commonwealth Federation documents at the time.

ke: What else were you reading when you wrote *Busted*?

cs: Foundational documents – do you want to know which ones?

ke: Yes, if you are willing to reveal.

cs: The British North America Act. The *Vancouver Sun* gossip columns written by Malcolm Parry – I'm serious! The ccf foundational documents, including letters, meeting minutes, since at the time I had a job cataloguing these documents. We also used the Canadian constitution, a lot of stuff about hockey, and the War Measures Act, articles about the October Crisis and the flq Manifesto, Parti Québécois documents. Documents, all in some way connected to the question of the nation, but also just documents to plunder.

ke: You were writing this book on the west coast in the 1990s, so you would have had contact with many American experimental writers. How did they respond to this work, which is so focused on Canada?

cs: I remember people asking us, 'Why are you so aggressive? What are you so angry about?' Some of the pieces in *Busted* were written in response to a conference in Buffalo where we really realized that we are Canadians, that we had an awareness of the border, a certain sense of marginality, and a consciousness that when we got here, the land was already occupied – all of this stuff that we didn't necessarily see in the American writers. But prior to the conference, I hadn't realized that they didn't see it. It was really striking, I remember that. So we began to formulate for ourselves, at least in some provisional way, what it meant to be a Canadian writer.

ke: It's a very different book than *Light Sweet Crude*. But then, the domestic spaces explored in the newer work are still products of the ideologies examined in *Busted*. How do you compare the two books?

cs: *Busted* was written at a very different time. It's what I was talking about in relation to collaboration. For me, things just arise. This is what arose then, and *Light Sweet Crude* is what has arisen since then. It is pretty much by virtue of circumstance. By *Light Sweet Crude*, I had two kids and this was as much as I could do. It makes sense that we wrote them in the order that we did, but maybe Nancy would argue differently if she could be here.

KE: We've already talked about your collaborative work in general. Are you comfortable talking about the specifics of your collaborations with Nancy? I've always wondered whether you wrote separately and met to knit together the fragments, or responded to each other's work, or simply wrote together?

CS: Usually, I won't tell people who wrote what, but I will say that we wrote in all those ways. We did a lot over email. What we would do is talk, visit, have tea, knit, talk, watch movies, play with my children. Then stuff would happen over email. Sometimes Nancy would send me words or phrases. Sometimes I would send her really raw material. We would send this material back and forth. Those pieces we really wrote together. Sometimes I would say, hey, I'm looking at this and I'm writing a piece, and she would respond using the same material. Sometimes I would write something and she would write something and we'd decide they go together. So yes, we did all of the above, but always in the context that it was informed by our lives, what was going on in our lives.

KE: Would you say it emerged organically?

CS: Yes, but sometimes I would be too busy, and Nancy would get frustrated with me, and say, 'You're not writing!'

KE: When did you start collaborating?

CS: I'm not sure. We collaborated for at least ten years. I think it was in 1993 or 1994. Maybe earlier? The first thing we wrote together was a little chapbook called *The Institute Songbook*.

KE: What's up with the institutes?

CS: We like institutes, and at one point, we were also always writing manifestos. It's oppositional. But back to your question, it was probably 1993 or 1994, but that first collaboration was much more distant. We would write pieces and put them together. Then it became much more integrated, as we became closer. There were also times when Nancy would be away, so we wouldn't write for a while, or we would only write over email, or it was just Nancy telling me to read a certain book. That's something that I still haven't worked out now that she is gone. Since Nancy was in academia and I'm not, she often had more of a finger on what was interesting intellectually, and she would tell me to read this or not read that.

KE: You finished writing *Light Sweet Crude* alone. What was that like?

CS: It was horrible. It was unbelievably awful.

KE: How much was completed before Nancy died?

CS: Most of it. Where the inscription appears on page 102 is literally the point where she died. Although she had already written her part of 'Light. Sweet. Crude,' which comes directly after the inscription, I had to finish it. So there is not much. Nancy also wrote the 'IDR Manifesto' and 'Arcades Intarsia: For a Love of Knitting,' and the notes to 'Cold Trip.' Although they emerged from our talking, the appendices are all her.

KE: In our discussion, you've already alluded a few times to the fact that part of the work of 'Institute for Domestic Research,' however humorous, was to work out some of your experiences on the KSW collective. I know there have always been women involved with KSW. In this collection, there is you, Lisa Robertson and Dorothy Lusk, but there are many other women, unfortunately not included here, like Susan Clark, Deanna Ferguson and Christine Stewart. Although KSW was primarily founded by men, it appears to have always made a space for women, or is this a false perception?

CS: No, I'm sorry. I don't know if I want to be quoted on this, but in my experience, it seemed that women who didn't want to write just like men were writing had to push and create the space themselves.

KE: When were you first involved with KSW?

CS: I probably joined the collective in early 1991. I was invited to join at that time, but I had a sense that there were some things you just couldn't do. In my experience, there was a really firm ideology and you were to toe the line, and if you didn't, there was subtle disapproval.

KE: Are we talking about an ecclesiastical Marxism?

CS: Yes! But to get back to your original question about whether or not KSW has always created a space for women, certainly there were some women involved when KSW originally moved to Vancouver from David Thompson University. There were women on the collective when I joined. In fact, Lisa Robertson and I joined at the same time, but as I said, at times it was a battle. In lots of ways KSW could be a very supportive space, and I certainly don't regret the time I spent on the collective. But for me it was not without difficulties. Part of what Nancy Shaw and I did later on was spend a lot of time deprogramming. We talked about this a lot.

KE: KSW was established in 1985, within a year of the Tessera collective's formation. Despite everything, it seems to have fostered a certain kind of feminist poetic, albeit one that is distinct from other feminist poetic projects in Canada, such as the writing associated with *Tessera*. How do you think about the differences between these two projects?

CS: I don't know how I would distinguish between these two projects. At the time, when I joined KSW, I was interested in the politics of the writing. It's not that I wasn't a feminist, but somewhat innocently, naively, part of me thought that we were in a post-feminist moment. It was only out of my personal experience on the collective and elsewhere in my life that I realized there is still a lot of work to be done. So my initial project was not a feminist one, although I could see how this broader world of political activity had feminist implications, but that was not my primary focus. This, of course, was not the case with *Tessera*, which was always driven by feminism.

KE: Perhaps what is most difficult to articulate is how and where politics, gender and poetics meet. Yesterday, I was interviewing Dorothy Lusk, and she said something that I thought was great. To paraphrase her, 'Sometimes you are writing something and think, "That's exactly like something I would write," and you realize, I don't want to write like that!' Her observation made me think more about the necessity of breaking our own procedures – of using procedures, but not in the way Jeff Derksen or Christian Bök use procedures, which can appear to be about mastery. I hate to essentialize, but I wonder if this might be a difference between women's innovative writing and men's innovative writing.

CS: I think that that may be generally true, but there are exceptions. Colin Smith gave an absolutely incredible reading at the KSW colloquium, and I would say that Colin has little interest in mastery, but that is one of the things that sets him apart.

KE: I am interested in pursuing this question, because it is something I've been observing in relation to many of the writers in this collection. Most of you rely on some procedure, or set of procedures, but there is nearly always a slippage. I wonder about the necessity of these slippages.

CS: Again, I would say that it is generally very dangerous territory to talk about this at all, but I agree that women have a very different relationship to the whole concept of mastery than men, but you can't quote me on that!

KE: Then can I ask you about your own procedures?

CS: I know that I always rely on some kind of structure. I set up rules for myself, but I break them. I'm happy to break them, and I want to break them. Someone might say, 'You're breaking your own rules,' and what can I say, but 'Yes, I am!'

KE: Of course, sometimes, that's precisely where the play and the pleasure and the more subversive elements of a text are located.

CS: But I want to emphasize that I do pay attention to my materials. I'm not simply interested in randomly jamming stuff up together. For example, in 'Cold Trip,' we decided to put Schubert up against the Ramones, but there were all kinds of reasons for that, as Nancy expressed so well in one of the appendices to *Light Sweet Crude*. Here's part of what she wrote: 'In "Cold Trip," we probe the relationship between music and poetry, as well as romantic and contemporary conceptions of the lyric (Schubert meets the Ramones) ... Our conjunction of the Romantics' time with our own leads us to delve into the machinations of the free market and artistic expression.'

KE: We started by talking about your current work. What else are you working on now? It must be difficult to write without Nancy.

CS: The Schubert piece I performed at the KSW colloquium was a way to work without Nancy, which I knew I could do, but I'm not sure I know what comes next. My big idea, which I realized I couldn't do in time for the KSW event, was to have tea with people and record the conversations. That would be my raw material. Then I would read about tea. I still might do that.

KE: It's the opposite of Kenny Goldsmith just recording himself.

CS: That wouldn't be interesting to me. It would be boring.

KE: Of course, conversations have always already been your source material, so this makes perfect sense.

CS: That's true. But part of the reason I wanted to do this project was that I went on a trip with my kids to Fort Langley, which is a Hudson's Bay trading post museum. They had these boxes there that said, 'Extra Fine Imperial Twankay' and I thought, I've got to write something called 'Extra Fine Imperial Twankay'! I later found out that Extra Fine Imperial Twankay is a kind of tea, so this project would also be about imperialism. But this is where I need Nancy. I think of these massive projects, like writing about imperialism. How do I do that in the fifteen minutes a week I have to write? But Nancy would say, 'Just do it, just go ahead and start writing – just write ten more lines.' I suppose I will have to learn how to do that myself.

KE: What else is pressing for you now?

CS: What it means to be a feminist stay-at-home mother. The fact that people who generally speak for mothers are not speaking for me. That's what is pressing, and always, how to get rid of all those boundaries that people have, that I have, that are imposed on me and that I create myself.

KE: So do you think about writing as a spatial practice?

CS: Yes, when I write, I just want to create a space. The Zapatistas talk – and I found this so striking when I first read this – they talk about not being interested in dictating what the revolution would be. They just wanted to create the conditions under which the revolution would happen, and it would take whatever form the people wanted it to take, which is truly revolutionary when you think about how revolutions have happened historically. Usually, there are people at the top who have a very clear idea of how the revolution is going to happen, but this Zapatista notion is completely different. So I think of writing as a project of changing the conditions of language – or perhaps, not even changing the conditions of writing because change is a condition of language – but rather paying attention to what I understand to be language's conditions and writing accordingly.

Vancouver, September 2008

SELECTED WORKS

Low Fancy. Toronto: ECW Press, 1993.

The Institute Songbook. With Nancy Shaw and Monika Kin Gagnon. Vancouver: The Institute, 1995.

The Clamorous Alphabet (CD). With music by François Houle. Periplum, 1999.

Busted. With Nancy Shaw. Toronto: Coach House Books, 2001.

Cold Trip. With Nancy Shaw. Vancouver: Nomados, 2006.

Sinopie. Vancouver: Vancouver New Music, 2006.

Light Sweet Crude. With Nancy Shaw. Burnaby, B.C.: LINEbooks, 2007.

Hand

and ran along

these lines: so fettered labour's bargain

jobs a skilled round

(and is no bargain

but indigent

and On Sale)

Lobbed, or over

or slyly, or maybe *husbands*

terminal sleep stroke – how

the sharp pluck round any

eager little knack, always

yet now ever was

Bulletin 1: History

Who is able? And who gates the keys to our city of social redemption? The way is barred to all renovators, or barked. As for me, I have no peace and no independence. Such sultry fears. Only yesterday the way was deliberately paved over, so that we might always, always remember: there is no release. But should I say all that I think? Haunted – no, constituted – by a legacy of purges and upheavals, wracked with dissent and doubt which all felt and none revoked, our little party strove to inaugurate a climate of – of what? Of bloodless humanism? Of public intimacy? Of regulate, filial, agreeable love? Yet who might legislate our disparate happiness? Even disinterested, we can all clamour: 'Our present system is, and we are not.' But who remembers the dissolutions and withdrawals and all our private, secret battles? You, who have the alibi and use it to your own vigorous ends, use it maybe also to hide all shame.

Busted (with Nancy Shaw)

Gripe: A Social Column for the Republic

* Smirk trunk isn't
irony, I'm more
distant. Perpetuate
each posh
attack, or dubious
scam-free twinset,
but doubt about
his envelope, or
implicate, or
will (*who said it
twenty years ago?*) this
goes back to *completely trophy
            spotless heathen
            gregarious avatar
            pure goofer, hey*
we were never actually
getting there

Bulletin 3: Culture

What a messy, bloody, capricious business. Is lineage iced, or boarded, or unchecked? It's said once our frontiers were immutable, or at least once some fathered rhetoric could skate, smooth and slamming, all over our boxy little realm. But exactly when did the lucid rink around our discourse? And for which shift did all our plays lace up with capital? Ever more distant, ever more expansive. Was there ever a simple goal?

Busted (with Nancy Shaw)

Gripe: A Social Column for the Republic

* Luller, you were
marvellous, you can
always count on
me to waver
for a higher
cause (beyond blast-off
        beyond chronic device)
or: way too very giddy
        (a frail fucken flower)
I'd thank to spunk
your likers

Gripe: A Social Column for the Republic

* Pronominally how? This
important book-riff span
rucks all referentialityitis, *it's*
too early
to nail you

from Garble

11

'can goad of ants as eyes, as nuts as'

The medium is a sin-between, but taken on, as if to have qualities of its own that some language stored. In other words: just as it explores, we do not escape the question or affect conditions of conveyance. The medium and its 'pure' contents behold, inert. Nor is the north or our intention constituted, in all theriousness, as a radical moderate. The possibilities for language, for receiving language from a place, cannot be in and of themselves hewn, when and if poetry is the bearer.

Song for the Silenced

Unmarked by external (published) connections, I remain unsatisfied. How to debate information is a quiet moment, just as still is a relative odour. Gestures and symbols do not now renew me; nor are silent women and voiceless girls thus enabled. Ambient with noiseless skeins, what might not be revealed?

Touring at a comfortable distance from the present steely ones (no 'I' allowed in our calm carriage), thought is not speaking. Born of the inching gesture, in plain it declares 'bad transmission' and yet this is there, this remains unspoken. Not cagey, but contingent. They that charge us overbearing unveil a key role, emphasizing the tariff, the profit, under which entire populations labour: and yet the goal is to observe. Overbearing, that they load her; I think my dead ones will follow further. At present, harmonies will neither appear nor mobilize, nor approximate either.

'Vows to Carry On'

1 – Fragments of a General Layout

Question One: What is the historical object?

These can be messed with; the shawls were not documented. Here a defiant venture, a combat paid without approval, and an empire of a-certain shame-world poised to sprint from recapitulation to sell-off. And there our tasks are slightly easier? It was nothing more than rational convenience; that there is a larger connection may safely be doubted. As for my own personal terror – in order to decipher the contours of the collective dream, we must find space for provisions of all sorts, and coax a proliferating collectible context, i.e., envy-portfolio.

41 – Syndicates

  moreover, he is no buyer

*Three habits not to be shared:
        Life-style terrorism
        randomized home-off
        peer purchase, or: anti-largesse

Down-ante
        that is, thick with, and fringe
                                driven

To bid
                        (to give up)

            punctuated as

        she stepped aside
                        compare the following:

(nibble)   vocal
                brogue

while I regroup

In year two:

whoever postures
at a pageant (or avalanche)

in a dance hall
... skipping the line
disappearing on all sides

(distanced, or
gulfed)

the merit of volumes

a spring board
not
a
mire

wholesome and delicious

sprawls   (amalgamates)

upholds the recovery
as per a bad list

(its undue)

Question: ... is this the theatre ... of all my struggles and ideas
... or a formation we excavate ...

Are we:
– to observe
– to take a restricted promenade
– to secure, or know
(back the source)

rub, disseminate

or pirate

The records show one particular incident
... that we can cipher:

This is nothing more than elaborate furnishing
shrinking resident
official or alphabet
small islands align
(they sway)

we will probe
a heritage
gritty and bitter

a wrap

... if evident in house ...

(406)

these passages circumvent a dream

(396)

... and I shattered

steps forward and belts out sweetly

yesterday's eligibility

chiming,

the once loyal

riding cool

(405 and 395)

... when sudden upheaval is

looking down

not counting severance   nor massive tribulations

the thinnest laceration summons you

repeatedly

for an undefined period

hello, my name follows a litany

of proven speech

... drawing focus from the forgotten

Light Sweet Crude (with Nancy Shaw)

Notes for appearing compassionate

> *What good is talk of progress to a world sinking into rigor mortis?*
> — Walter Benjamin

Make it *seem* endurable
  i.e. cherry-rant or despicable
    loop-the-
      loop heaps inadmissible
        shifting: we had
          nothing going
by my decline, my cubicle, and my wardrobe malfunction

Oh inadmirable charity watch-dog!
Oh deficient dollarization!
Oh probe-less dissident!

and so we pin our hopes on the Auditor
                General

    [note: conceptual crisis]

    nor yet anywhere near
    asylum
    security
    risk
    analysis
    (citizen misnomer or
        droll emotion-management, my below-grade
            uses, endorse my now)

Train sets!
Tigers!
Clocks!

the joy of

DOROTHY TRUJILLO LUSK

DOROTHY TRUJILLO LUSK: So what do you need to know?

KATE EICHHORN: Let's begin with how your writing has been read. Jeff Derksen places your first book, *Redactive*, in a Marxist framework. Are you comfortable with this reading?

DL: At the time I wrote *Redactive* I was reading a lot of psychoanalytic semiotics and feminist film theory and Jeff chose not to include such sections that retooled terms from my readings, as he didn't see that they added anything very interesting to the rest of the writing. The Marxist thang I am comfortable with. My grounding is Althusser, Gramsci, Fanon – the usual sort of puzzling through one does. But I did more in conversation and writing as byproduct of misreading, rereading, bar-chat with university people who were given clear pathways through their reading. I'm happy, comfortable with, any reading of my work, really. I would only caution that as one reading – say that which foregrounds 'humorous' manifest 'content' over 'social relations' manifest content – can, by its very thoroughness, exclude other possible readings. My humble intent is that none be privileged to the radical exclusion of others.

KE: That's interesting, because later in an article on *Redactive*, Derksen uses a cinematic analogy, splicing, to describe what you are doing in *Redactive*, but you reject this comparison.

DL: In film editing, the sprockets must fit in a very particular way and so what you can go through is, of necessity, linear. Poetry editing, for me, can admit broader tolerances. It's open. You fit things in here and there but they can be scattered again. Also, the cuts can be words from different taxonomies parachuted right into the middle of something and then cut in another way. I don't think splicing is a good analogue. Just a deceptively similar term.

KE: Is there an analogy from another discipline that works? Would you choose something more ephemeral?

DL: Warren Tallman compares the work to jazz singing in his blurb on the back of *Redactive*. That's more how I see it too. Warren writes, 'To experience it in as hauntingly bitter sweet "ballads" as you are likely to encounter this side of the better jazz singers and instrumentalists.' Okay, I don't see the ballads. It's more like jazz improvisation, or extended vocal technique, but it's not just vocal, because it brings sounds in from diverse areas and material that exists more as linguistic traces of thought than as aural units as such.

KE: What kinds of sounds?

DL: Colloquial percussion, proscribed spelling, non-standard pronunciations, what have we here ...

KE: I wanted to ask you about how *Redactive* has been framed because although I entirely agree that we can theorize your work as being about questions of materiality and work, I also think you really work your readers.

DL: I do! I actually put that in one of the poems – something along the lines of 'do your homework and get back at me.' I'm not going to give you the references if you can find them. I actually have become kinder as I've gotten older. I may even offer a few footnotes and give some source materials, so readers don't have to be so mad at me. But yes, not 'get back to me' but 'get back at me.'

KE: The use of the footnote in poetry is a curious intervention. There are poets who appear to use such supplements as a display of knowledge, but there are also poets, like Susan Clark, who exploit notes as form. I think I know the answer, but why have you, at least until now, avoided pointing to any references? Why have you insisted on working us so hard?

DL: Simply so it won't be entirely monologic, and so it will be more polyvalent. And to lend more possibilities to that polyvalency. When you read anything, you're lending your particular brain hormones, your particular histories – your particular histories that are foregrounded that you aren't even quite conscious of at that moment. When you read anything, even the most straightforward mystery or genre novel, there are also going to be your own memories because your own memory lends images and sounds to the reading. What's going on out on the street – ambient sound – all of that is going to shift everything. That's what's foregrounded for me – the multiple possibilities, reading into whatever you find. Also, again, when you read things out loud, a different voice will often emerge. I never know what is coming up – that is not always good because sometimes it is really banal and flat. When I read at the University of Calgary years ago, I got into the modal groove reading from *Oral Tragedy*, and I was stuck in it, and my voice wouldn't move away from it.

KE: In an interview with Donato Mancini, you make a distinction between writing that is a political act and writing that is 'of a politic.' You tell him that your work is of a politic, but more importantly, it's about pleasure.

DL: I'm just not that deluded. I'm not on the barricades with this stuff. If I go too far, I sound too pessimistic, like I'm saying it's not really doing a lot.

KE: But you do maintain that it is 'of a politic.'

DL: I suppose it is about working through political material and more importantly, about being subject – subject to a politics that we live with every day.

KE: I want to talk about your use of the sentence. In *Redactive*, with the exception of 'Stumps,' you give us a book of sentences.

DL: 'Stumps' would actually be a good place to start talking about sentences. 'Stumps' started as things that were working too well as sentences. They were making too much sense. There was too much of an eloquent sentence construction. I was afraid that if people read them they would say, 'Ah, I see,' too quickly. So that's why they are stumps. Mina Totino did a series of paintings called *stumps*, and she did them when she didn't want to make things too pictorial. So these are chopped off, attenuated. This is how these poems work, but I also started to insert words in between. I actually saw them as being a sort of hippie spiral – then each thing could be picked up and scattered on the floor. I'm saying they were sentences, and perhaps they weren't all complete sentences. Perhaps they weren't traditional prose lines, but they sounded too precise, too eloquent – there was too much good writerliness in them, which I felt compelled to hamper.

KE: This is what is so striking about your work with the sentence. The reader experiences the comfort of the sentence and then it just stops – suddenly there is a comma or some other break where there shouldn't be one.

DL: I think about my sentences as club-footed iambs! Seriously. I don't mean that in a pejorative way. But in my work, instead of ta-dut, ta-dut, ta-dut, ta-dut, it's pa-jume! Lytle Shaw wrote a review of *Ogress Oblige* for *Publishers Weekly*, and he said something about tripping along and then I fall over my own feet, fall on my face, and some people thought that meant he didn't like the book, but I thought he really got what I was doing.

KE: Precisely! You're reading along and then you fall into the sentence, but it's not a fixed procedure that makes you trip. It keeps changing throughout the book, so it's always a surprise.

DL: I have been criticized for that. It was said that I should demonstrate exactly that same operation several times, very obviously, so the reader can see that I know what I am doing and so that they know what I am doing. To me that is one's first step into mannerism. Deanna Ferguson and I went through this years ago. We realized, quite separately, that sometimes you're writing and you read what you're working on and think, that is just the kind of thing I would write! You know, where you are reproducing the same act with the same kind of material. There's no sort of impulse. If you want to periodize it the way you would in art-historical terms – as in archaic, heroic, classical, mannerist and some kind of decay or dissolution – let's say that you have some sort of heroic impulse, like you are really working against or with certain kinds of material, but repeating that, reproducing that, you are just falling into a habit. It's like saying this is how we paint eyes now instead of really learning while you are doing it. One is expected to show that one knows one's stuff by continual reproduction. I am not compelled to demonstrate my competence for the professorial class. Does that make sense?

KE: Absolutely. And again, one of the things that makes your writing different from a lot of the other Kootenay School of Writing work is this deliberate inconsistency. You resist the repetitive motion that is such a marker of Jeff Derksen's work, which is an effective device for his project, but you're doing something different.

DL: Well, I was up and running before KSW existed and I had been writing and known other writers for years. KSW were people who had been students and teachers together at David Thompson University Centre, and I think their collectivity lent force and focus to each other's work as it was developing. As I pre-existed the KSW/DTUC configuration, I felt no obligation to write in any particular way, but I was delighted and energized by the convergence of their interests and practice with my own.

KE: You have this line in *Redactive* – in one of the poems that also appears in this anthology – where you say, 'from what level could I abstain from inventing.' I love that line, because it seems to me that it's a way to sum up your own poetics. There's no level from which you could abstain from inventing, because it seems that you get easily bored with your own voice.

DL: I agree. I think that's the closest I'm going to get to making a poetic statement.

KE: In *Redactive*, you also write, 'Shall I be able to read the menace of my intention?' That's really funny, but do you actually think about your intentionality as a sort of menace?

DL: Of course! Some people when they write do have very specific things they want to include. For example, some sort of truth they have absorbed, a theory, or a demonstration of a trait or skill they've mastered, whether it's an erased text or something with a line through it or everything bracketed and in parentheses. In my case, when I'm writing, it's the constant micro and macro interrogation of the position of address, self-regard, backward, forward – it's this really psychotic positionality.

KE: So let's talk about subjectivity. How do you think about the subject, the subversion of the subject? I don't think there is a classic evacuation of the subject in your work as there is in traditional Language poetry, but what's going on?

DL: Early on, many of us were reading much of the same theory as the Language writers, and at the same time, and this pre-existed our reading of the so-called Language writers so we weren't just mimicking what they did. We were reading the stuff that they read before we'd ever heard of them, so my interrogation or refusal of a unified subject is going to be very different than theirs. It is ethically important to me that the subject be not so much evacuated as such but that no subject position be valorized above another. I do not necessarily place my self within 'I' nor would I relegate readers to 'you' and send them off on spurious quests that 'I' would be reluctant to perform.

KE: So how have you thought about it?

DL: In some ways I never understood a refusal of subject because it still seemed to be an observing subject writing all this stuff down. It almost seems to be, and I'm not being specific to any geographic area or any specific writer, an adolescent naïvite akin to using a lower case 'i' as if that is supposed to do something. I'm probably still completely stuck on the subject these days, and the interrogation of the author's authority. I don't know what other people are on to these days. I kind of got out of the loop, and I'm still caught in the morass of subject interrogation. What are other people doing?

KE: In the context of innovative writing, I think they are still asking those questions too. How could they not be? But you also write about a 'social inter-subjective mirror.' It seems to me that there is this constant refraction enacted in your work, so your subject is also a refracted subject.

DL: I also came up with the term 'suprajective' at one point in the late '70s or early '80s. I thought, oh, so you don't have to choose! I remember being out drinking with idiots, and saying, 'Hey, have you heard of this word?' It was such a huge thing for me. As a person, in my own conscience, I have always had a really hard time with what is subject and object. I just didn't really get that binary. 'Supra' could mean above, but for me, it just meant that you didn't have to choose that either/or. This pre-existed the theory for me. It was always a problem for me. I wouldn't even remember the difference between object and subject. Then I would read the dictionary definitions and they didn't seem to exclude each other either. So I think there is something in my hard wiring that affects the way I deal with this issue.

KE: Of course, it also affects the way you work with the materials you choose to work with.

DL: True. I was also one of those children who believed that one need not be a carbon-based life form to have or be a soul or consciousness. So there is doubtless some nutty innate proclivity.

KE: I want to come back to something you said earlier – you used the term 'psychotic positionality.' Since it has come up, and because we've had other conversations about this, I want to ask you about the sort of psychosis or 'craziness' that many poets, especially poets who are really engaged in dismantling language, seem to experience. I know that we both agree that if you are smart and paying attention in the world, you naturally become a little unhinged. I'm not sure how to phrase this question, but on a very serious level, I want to ask you if you see a relation between dealing with anxiety and depression and innovative writing in general. I know, this is a difficult question ...

DL: To me, writing was one of the few ways that I could work with social anxieties. I mean work right in the midst of that. I was always someone who was desperately trying to get along with everyone when everyone hated everyone else. I would have friends who hated each other for political reasons – various types of stripes of Marxists and anarchists and they would be at loggerheads with each other – and somehow in my own mind, my own heart, I would be juggling all these ideas, possible truths, simultaneously. They would have all these arguments, and I would take them, the arguments, home after being out socially and write through them. Jeff once said my work was like big chunks of ideology bumping up against each other, and that's exactly what it was, because I would be trying to keep these ideological materials active, but somehow I would be trying to get everything to get along, but they can't get along. It's hard to explain. A definition of an ideologue is that you don't really know and you're just spouting off whatever has already been framed for you that you've internalized. Who knows what I'm up to? But that has to do with the anxiety stuff – anxiety, subjectivity, reading and listening – it would be almost harmful to my central nervous system and I would use that. I would work with that which was very, very irritating and diverse. What many would consider extraneous to the poem became the poem. Barry MacKinnon wrote a poem years back that's analogous to this situation. It was supposed to be an oyster, but he said 'clam,' a poem is like a pearl born of some clam's agony. It's what irritates and irritates and has to be worked out.

KE: So do you think about your books, your writing as an accumulation of the anxiety?

DL: An accumulation of my work through, my writing through the anxiety. So I wouldn't call it an accumulation of the anxiety, even if anxieties can definitely be traced there.

KE: It's mediated anxiety then?

DL: Exactly. I extend my fear amongst those I can't touch amongst resultant enemies. Trying to be a social person, a social self, you're always putting your foot it in by representing something they don't want.

KE: So *Redactive* is all that stuff swirling around in your head when you arrive home from a social event and think, 'Shit, I shouldn't have said that! I wish I could edit that out, but now it's too late.'

DL: Yeah, but I'm not that quick on the uptake. Sometimes it takes months before I realize I was deeply offended or how offensive I may have been. People come out and say the most preposterous things, and I just fold them in. So it's me, but I also wonder how these people can live with themselves.

KE: But then it becomes something else. I don't want to overgeneralize about your work, but your butting together of these ideological positions and social anxieties with classical works – canonical texts that you pilfer from here and there – are reflective of a broader anxiety. So it's not really your anxiety but a social anxiety that is the context in which we all navigate our lives.

DL: Perhaps, but really, how does anyone read or 'navigate' one's way through the 'chaos of mingled purpose'? I think I'm just being very conscious, micro-conscious of how anyone reads. I read this piece, 'Sentimental Intervention,' at the most recent KSW conference, and I realized that for once, I didn't introduce it. I didn't tell people what the material was. I don't put it in books, but I usually blab about the sources before I read. I'll even stop right in the middle! But in this one, I didn't say that this is based on Flaubert's *Sentimental Education* and Jeff Wall's essay on Dan Graham where he used the figure of the vampire. It was sort of odd that I just read the damn thing and gave it its own legs to run.

KE: What was that like?

DL: It was a bit weird. Jeff's wife, Sabine Bitter, who is an artist, came up afterwards and told me about this project they were doing. She liked the piece, but I realized afterwards that it is traces of language in there about different kinds of modernity that had piqued her interest. It's really just a thirty-year-old essay that Jeff Wall did. But I'm not doing that 'A-term' thing that everyone liked to talk about ... what is it?

KE: Appropriating?

DL: Yes, appropriating! Everyone was always talking about appropriating. I'm still just filching.

KE: I notice that you frequently make references to the visual arts when you're talking about your writing practice. You just mentioned Jeff Wall's work, and around the time that his essay on Graham appeared, you appeared in one of Wall's photographs in appropriate period dress. I'll assume you didn't necessarily choose the heels or the halter top or the scruffy guy on your arm, since this would all be part of Wall's conceptual practice. But I wonder how your writing has been influenced by the strong presence of visual artists in Vancouver, especially the conceptual photographers like Wall? Do you see any specific parallels between your writing, or the work of other Vancouver-based experimental poets, and these conceptual artists?

DL: I did help choose the heels and halter top. We went all over to second-hand shops seeking out what Jeff Wall called a 'buffalo bag,' a type of thick leather tooled shoulder bag that was very indicative of social position, education, lack thereof. The hooded cardigan we found had mouse poo in one of the pockets that he insisted stay as it lent verisimilitude to the piece,

my anxiety, I would suppose. I chose the scruffy guy on my arm, Pulp Press co-founder, writer/artist, Ontario College of Art alumnus Tom Osborne. Jeff had me help him cast some of his earlier pictures. Rod was an actor he found through an agency. Later on, I was the studio assistant for my former art-history teacher, Ian Wallace, another photoconceptualist, who had been Jeff Wall's thesis advisor. Although there were some overlaps in our reading, there were no parallels in practice – some in concerns, but it's pretty distant and there has never been any reciprocal interest from them to my work.

KE: Now you're working on this new book. How far along are you?

DL: Two new books. With *Decorum*, I really have enough material, but the editing process is always the longest part of the process. The other one, I'm going to call *Dazzle Camo*. I realize I'm going off on a tendency with that piece that is actually becoming a book. There is an overlap between *Decorum* and *Dazzle Camo*.

KE: In *Decorum*, you go outside the English language, as if it's not already problematic enough! You're working with Latin, Estonian and several other languages, I think. What motivated you, because you haven't really worked with other languages before?

DL: I've taken fragments of brochures and official documents that I found in Italy and Germany and Poland, so there are already traces of other languages in my writing. I've also always been interested in Latin. The most recent work involves Chinook and Estonian. Estonia and Finland are two countries that don't have any Latin incursion in their language, and I found it quite interesting to go in afterwards and kind of reverse imperialism in a way by deprestiging Latin and putting Latin in where it hadn't been before. With the Chinook, what I am doing is working in a language of contact, a pidgin language, which are mostly languages of trade but also languages of domination, of course. A pidgin is a language of forced contact, but here I'm the one who is actually forcing these languages, so there is a subject of forcing them myself in these writing spaces. I'm not really sure why I am doing that, but for some reason it's keeping me engaged.

KE: Is it part of a process of decolonizing language?

DL: Yes, but there is also a really sort of odd thing that I'm doing with it. When things are translated from original languages, Asian languages in particular, into English, the English readers think it's so funny. There is the whole genre of clothing that English readers love to wear. This goes back a really long way to the 1860s with José da Fonseca and Pedro Carolino's *English as She Is Spoke*. Everyone was just roaring with laughter at it, but how do we do without going into their languages? If by chance, someone who speaks or reads any of these languages, they can see me being the 'ignorant foreigner' as Mark Twain referred to these Portuguese guys. So, okay, I am the ignorant foreigner making a royal hash of this stuff. I can't figure out tenses to save my life. I was, at one point, fairly fluent in Italian, but I couldn't come up with tenses. I always ended up with these strange baroque constructions.

KE: Were you always in the present or some other tense?

DL: I think I was mostly in the present. Working now, I don't completely get it as I write. I make all this stuff up as I go along, and I'm not doing it as a scholarly project, obviously, but I really hope there can be some jokes at my expense, or at the authorial authority's expense for someone who reads a bit of Finnish or whatever. Years ago when I taught English as a second language in an elementary school, I had kids from Chile, Italy, kids from Fiji and many other countries. They really wanted to know the rules. I'd have to break it to them that their languages really are quite logical, but English has all these things that you can learn but then there are these things you just have to memorize, that are not born of logic, one explicable only with a greater historical context and forced standardization. This is what we have, this is what English is, and I realize that I'm so lucky that English is my first language because otherwise I wouldn't have been able to get it at all! My fascination outstrips my capacity to retrain.

Vancouver, September 2008

SELECTED WORKS

Oral Tragedy. Vancouver: Tsunami Editions, 1988.

Redactive. Vancouver: Talonbooks, 1990.

Ogresse Oblige. San Francisco: Krupskaya, 2001.

First

For Susan Lord

I've given attention to this impassivity yet previous commitments now allow some circumspect immunity, notwithstanding that I, am, (cautiously), the seat of responsibility – as if, here, I could pass from place to place; circulate, subscribed. As if I walk in circles, but with purpose.

I always place – surrounded, in fact. Some grand transitive doubt plays out & hardly bothers to specify particular sores, worries and really constant frets.

§

Sometimes I've attended more to silent, declamatory glands than actual live discharge. I am loathe to tell it, though others intervene on my behalf. I engender orphans.

Even at my fiercest, the basis is a misapprehension of the source's source – so where am I taken? I should be able to read the menace of my intention. But I am ideological historical & alive despite an horizontal and verbal agency and all screams that ensue.

But from what level could I abstain from inventing? From an innocent function to an accurate refrain from any response whatever or only adherence to specialized reduction acquainting my one familiar sophistication to another about to take place?

Whether the figurative body is 'already critical' or a simple way out of solipsistic nerve about to dissuade 'ME' from bungling another advantage on my behalf.

§

If I remember the scene of interpretation, I've given enough. I, though considerately impenetrable, must grant my friend this perpicacious moment, to include all that is hideous I would leach out for your sake.

I extend my fear to those I cannot touch among resultant enemies. Has seduction placated me so well? It is, if I wish to know, quiet need of extraordinal aim but framed by tiny voices.

Vulgar Marxism

All hail the crushed amber groin of Late Capital refines
within extant character

That nothing will please me
any more
or any less.

& That I am dimly informed by the wry suss of the well-irritated,
humbly chilled of presentient ironisms Swiftly contained as to be
neighbourhood insurgent mechanix.

Well mays't thou throttle the percipient louse, the bedstead
maintaining
the absence of the full-stop.

Completely addressing the territorial aspect
of purgatory AKA bowel dressage – a testicular device
whereby bummy
plants include stakeouts beyond sense declension
or shove under breath

GEO   PHIC   IONAL   Colum tailings

fortune incorporates factotum

                                        fetching ambient dread

in sheets, in sheets untied

GEO   PHIC   NAT

tinned Imperial measures and elbow room for archival vowel

Red Girls in sacristy – factor thus, shady spouse

face off in chains
garbed in perjoratrix enflatulalala easily
amiss of the swelter

in funny bums of bees ignite
in sinister missives, the breast of
the likely gnat on Jack the
Lad or seemingly harmless
midges

For awhile of time past, in a glandulate
small factory, in an elastic confinement
– excluding argument, containing aggro-inducement.

In a small landscape – pathetic larceny &/or estranged
that which is sultry and flics away at theft under $2.00

sheepish thoughtly shmoos in monaural diversifications incorporating
'BLANDISHMENT'
'VECTOR'
'DESIRE'
'BODY'
'YR'

Up floats salmonid enhancement as
a sprightly effect, gnomic in dispersal.

After past retrieval
Just apt shrinkage and drunkardliness
shoulder values
party lapses – animalian floral techtronics
sheet apropos goof
aspirate
PUNK SNOUT in LINSEY WOOLSIES
FINAGLIN' the DULL FINKDOWN MAN –
HOLE
SPECIES washing up coastal waters – each shivery aside binding
co-determinate froth management.

SPECIOUS ASIDE, FLUSH RIGHT

I personally enter
recalcitrant SANDOZ, putter about shifting shale, consider

Ogress Oblige

Cost-Benefit Analysis of Hominid Enhancement Project, retroactive
to the word GO.

Scheming little savours, collective glut
shove, Mighty River, shove

Folk art master comeuppance, quite rightly left
to narrate
an importunate cash cow or fuddled shirtwaist.

Shiny leaved myrtle
under extreme addiction
as when I was obuoy or mere slip of a deckhand,
I trod the undulant planks and lay anestle
in the drainy hold of this, my belovèd transience fidget, heft
awa barlwy, groats and unfinished fur.

I am convinced I have no father.

I am reduced to a generic being sniping at a hostile city-state.

LIBENS
VOLENS
POTENS

MULTO PLURIBUS VALE

Live in one. Put that mollusk on that throne. Onion share.
Stinky polystatic engorgement. In a preferred mode, the end rhyme
would best trick certitude. Could include cloth, may include
polyamides, wry bipeds.

Detractors of the designated hitter shirked retainer vengeance in the
shattered realm of Time's showroom *exegete. You are there.*

Sententious performance of Mighty word – I
want you all to give it up for Art!

Hoist allay avanticular horizon – go past astronomid outlet
camouflage FORTRAN, call off storm degradation

Million two Adirondacks encapsulated fustian DelPhonics
and thy potamus shall be my potamus
whereafter a generation of lubricious processors piss me off

puritan potty mouth

I'm not just making this up.

'I am convinced that I love her.'

I am poor and demonic and I've come to help!

omnifacet abattoir
misericorda

That which I have not

      misting stellate pinions and 'the Sydneys,' given
      to sulks in the cloakroom, have not wished
      to advance, advise nor
      articulate the buzzy notion
        of tidy water sprites
        in pliant unison.

Her Highness's gots pudgy hands, don't she
      but you must take her nicely to
        wash them e'er
she gets her tea.

            dishes of visceral pickerel, a victory
O'fisheral. Salient tendency, brackish tenacity.

Decorum
(Typical)

you loost certitiude, you youthless
louse
you

shield ensheltied terbonium
lice
ensnatchèd

youse titanium'rattum's amon
grelf
I bulationgs terbaccerrationgs

ditchmonde etude
demi-semi-clever
class'em

tababac a turnstim
maize merlottatoonal
continua

brava
pausa sanctos
cancrementitudenal

ownage
pushyface an
average glowbooty

spewtum, DDDDDD-Daddyum
logger robber
stalker

brother
incramentatonal

gladitorial saveyface

intragriftitatum
whither
thou

gladiatorix twine hic bugger
whyside
goonchix

hindsized poontix
& gastricidal excom
thesis seizure

not-de-menxian:

gopherottage
filched of
final diptych
tadon's owney
functum

poonisnaxion givena
chambered recourse

seema tonal filleta
sofasoil

Manque
(stɑve DECORUM)

FIN∂TU yapp
dehic
porqçque suter
sepht

crew
suprindicat sterol nuncios
astroil

th'nethr cheek 'o' Pomo
's
distaff (regiangst), wherein phantachron
s'mgrls?

Manque
früstedive
Them choice may
be to elongate a sleazy pun
to 'n epic disapportion

nor

has'm
y
colour e'er
factourèd such

Or

beer parlour   Yukonische

selfsameupyougoter

junct-

dudgeon, yclept

TRUJILLO

DECORUM
an Hystrical) Eye

WITHSTAND co-oz
pension
stuyvesant

I'm'llâbeauty'll
th'hindmost
grapplisch hakelnadeln, dispu
termicatugs

dinchñeé
duckemi-joqúe
instance der Latinate selbst-prong

lor'kine und
kinderlingum
road atluss fieldungsrue
dent
= ego brunt

ownage
peruse snatches
cachepot'ativixionelle

asperantaver
rage aglottal spectre

laparoscopaliangstraum

pelf apportion

naberoff

liet moncrief

aspectival sniderage seeping outward

t'wards
tad's downy
punctum

s'wards ycleptival

albejetsonaxion
bereftogivens chamfred scouse treffilte

belly

eau de

nultranixions,

as we cease
to become information

SINA QUEYRAS

HEATHER MILNE: How would you describe your most recent book, *Expressway?*

SINA QUEYRAS: It's a series of linked poems exploring the idea of mobility, the end of oil. One day I was looking out in Philadelphia over the sea of expressways and I thought, how dissimilar is this moment and my anxiety from what Wordsworth was feeling when he was looking around at these ghost trails becoming coach trails, and the things moving beyond the control of his imagination? I think in some ways that the tail started to wag at that point and we're at the other end of that tail wag now. But I think it's been one long unconscious swoon of mobility, not even thinking about the implications of physically moving around the world, the infrastructures that we've been laying out all over the planet that are now decaying and have led to decay around them.

HM: It is very interesting to me that your new work is taking that focus, because movement between places is a fairly important thematic in your work. I'm thinking about all the references to roads and bridges and tunnels in all of your books. It seems like you are now approaching the issue of mobility in a more overtly politicized way.

SQ: As a child I grew up, sometimes literally, in my mother's car, staring out the window. It's deeply part of how I look at the world.

HM: And that political angle is there in *Lemon Hound* as well, where you deal with issues like the environment, capitalism, globalization, the rise of the multinational corporation. Those concerns are very present in that text; you're raising rather postmodern concerns, yet there is also the strong presence of modernism through your engagement with Woolf and Stein. It's interesting to me how *Lemon Hound* brings those threads together.

SQ: Woolf and Stein both wrote to soothe. They both were dealing with a modern/ist world. Woolf's domestic situation was completely transformed in her lifetime. For her, movement was intellectually liberating. She took long walks and came home and composed. It's one way women can be public. Stein also took long walks and then came home and composed. There was this sense with both of them of moving through the city as a way of working things out. And that's what I tried to do with *Lemon Hound*, it was a kind of walking through all of the things I had been reading and trying to make sense of. One of the questions I had for myself was: are the lives of women today any different from the questions and concerns that Woolf and Stein would have been walking through Paris and London with in the '20s and '30s? I won't answer that, but that was one of the questions I had.

HM: In a sense they are and in a sense they aren't. The poems seem to suggest a kind of ambiguity in this respect.

SQ: They are and they aren't and I guess that's the great complication. I was thinking about this because I'm working on an essay about Lisa Robertson, and I love her notion of the erotics of doubt and the spectacular possibility of failure.

HM: *Lemon Hound* is a very open-ended book in many ways, yet it is also highly structured, especially in your engagement with Woolf and Stein. Do you see a tension between Woolf and Stein? How does that tension play out in *Lemon Hound?*

SQ: They exist in my head simultaneously, peering at each other with great disdain. I love their duelling sentences. Their writing projects are so dovetailed – it's really quite striking how similar their concerns were, very different approaches but similar projects. I imagine how irritated Stein would be by Woolf, who is ultimately a Romantic writer, very interested in beauty. I was talking to Vanessa Place recently and she was talking about writing as tatting, as lacemaking. That's something Woolf would like but Stein would be appalled at. I love these constant influences in my head going at each other.

HM: Where does the title *Lemon Hound* come from?

SQ: To me it's sort of feminist flâneur. It's somebody who is on the scent, somebody who's not afraid to sniff out, not just looking for the sweet but looking for the tart and for the not-pleasant.

HM: *Lemon Hound* is your blog name as well. Do you see yourself then as a kind of flâneur on your blog?

SQ: Yes. Writing *Lemon Hound* was very liberatory for me, so I sort of took on that persona because it just felt comfortable to speak publicly that way. I think of the blog as creating a public space because I really feel women struggling still with the creation of a public persona. I don't know a woman, actually, who doesn't struggle with it.

HM: Has it been a challenge?

SQ: Every post is a challenge. I always want to quit.

HM: You did quit it for a while.

SQ: I did. The reason I don't again is I haven't figured out the next incarnation yet.

HM: So when you do quit it will you redirect that energy to something else?

SQ: Yes. I really feel a lack of female public discussion, so it's a way of keeping a toehold in public discourse.

HM: Do you feel that lack is specific to Canadian feminist poetics or is it more general?

SQ: I think it's global. In many ways Canadian feminist poetics has been a model for feminist poets in the U.S., who look north to Canada as a promised land for all things left, and otherwise. Though, I don't know ...

HM: Are they looking to that past incarnation, though, and not to the present?

SQ: Yeah, I'm wondering what's going on now. How the baton, so to speak, will be passed – or what happened to the baton.

HM: I think the baton was dropped around 1990.

SQ: Yes, that was an important moment. Sad to think it's passed. In some ways it's still penetrating a lot of women's consciousness. The ripple effect from the first west-coast Women and Words conference and then that sort of energy from the *Raddle Moon* and *Tessera* moment. I was looking at some old issues of *Tessera* and I was completely blown away by the quality of the writing. I don't understand how that thinking did not penetrate outside of the circle of readership it had. I'm completely baffled on some level. On another level I see they weren't necessarily interested in breaking out.

HM: Margaret Christakos was saying in her interview that she feels that writers like Erín Moure, Daphne Marlatt and Nicole Brossard and others were profoundly influential but that that influence hasn't been adequately narrativized. She may be right.

SQ: I wonder how much it has to do with the mentorship, of role modeling a way of narrativizing? Daphne Marlatt had a community of men around her who were very powerful figures and supportive. Involved. You meet Fred Wah and within five minutes he's suggesting this or that project. There's a dynamic understanding of the need to get work out there. There are some women who get this. Barbara Godard has clearly been amazing for many women, but it's a skill one needs to have – creating a new conversation is difficult. Yes, there is the influence, but then what to do with that influence. I remember feeling that profoundly ...

HM: Did you have mentors?

SQ: No.

HM: Why is it difficult for women to mentor each other?

SQ: It's hard to be a mentor when you are unstable and unsatisfied with your own lot. And I think none of the women who have come in and out of my life, and none of the women you mention above, have had stable support, academic or otherwise. Or if they did, perhaps they were having so much trouble maintaining it – women are not professionalized in this country the way they are in other places. And fields.

HM: I think we often expect a lot more from our female mentors than our male mentors. We tend to invest more in those relationships and are more critical of other women.

SQ: I realized early on, when I started teaching, that the best thing I could do for my students and myself was privilege my own work. To be a working, engaged artist was much more effective than spending excessive amounts of energy on their work – it's mentoring by example, I suppose.

HM: Well, it does make you a better mentor in the end, and a stronger writer.

SQ: I think so, but not self-absorbed either. One must be connected to a larger infrastructure, a network that, quite frankly, people need to access. I didn't actually understand that until I moved to New York when I met people like Marilyn Hacker, who's a really great mentor. She's very engaged with her community. Jenny Factor writes about this in Arielle Greenberg and Rachel Zucker's *Women Poets on Mentorship: Efforts and Affections*, a new anthology of women and mentorship. Somebody else writes about Eileen Myles. All these women are very savvy about this problem and the question of how women professionalize – Anne Waldman, Carolyn Forché, I hear great things about these women as mentors. Annie Finch, the formal American poet, started her own listserv to try and resolve this.

HM: I've never lived in the U.S. and I don't know from personal experience what's happening there in terms of feminist poetics, but I get the impression that there are more interesting discussions happening there, and perhaps more exciting opportunities. Perhaps that's my own misperception, though. You can probably speak to this, having lived in New York. Is there something happening there that's not happening here? I'm thinking of things like the Belladonna Series which you were involved with and also some of the newer critical work on poetics coming out of the U.S.

SQ: I think that it's tougher to be a poet in the U.S. There's very little support and a lot of competition.

HM: In terms of funding?

SQ: Yes. Rachel Levitsky, founder and creator of Belladonna, pays for that series with her credit card. And she has, in six years, brought over a hundred of the most interesting feminist thinkers of our time to New York. Paying them a nominal fee, no travel, she has no money. She does what she can, she's very generous and she's in New York, which has its own draw. There's a kind of energy where people realize you can't wait to see if it's going to get funded, you have to do it. There's a sense of urgency that I don't see in Canada – that was the *Tessera* moment perhaps.

HM: Do you think the fact that poets have better funding opportunities in Canada paradoxically contributes to some kind of stasis?

SQ: I have a problematic relationship to the whole funding paradigm. I would argue for it, clearly, but I think anything uninvestigated is problematic.

HM: What do you mean uninvestigated?

SQ: Funding needs to evolve. The needs today aren't the same as the needs even five years ago. Funding bodies don't seem to know how to deal with online arts presence, for example. I say this ad nauseam, looking at Canada from outside its borders, it's just a blank, but there's all this great stuff going on inside our borders that isn't accessible, nor is that great stuff what's being funded, oddly enough.

HM: When you're thinking about an online arts presence, are you thinking of things like Penn Sound and other web-based poetry archives?

sq: Absolutely. These things are very valuable. We don't have that. We don't have a literary presence online – no serious online reviewing or publishing sources, no archives. We have all this great work that's not getting out.

HM: Coach House used to have an interesting website.

sq: They used to have a great website. And they have the bpNichol site. My main point is that women poets in the U.S. have developed more innovative and critical skills. With Belladonna I was interested in more critical introductions. It was a lot of work, but it seemed very important that women take the time to really get to know another woman's work. It gives the reader, the audience, a way into the work. I don't believe people aren't interested in innovative work, rather they don't always know how to read it. I think as women we need to do that critical work. That's a way we need to professionalize. That's something that American women know, it seems to me. Maybe they have a longer history, maybe there are just more women, or maybe they realize that much of this will be unpaid work.

HM: It seems that there is a larger body of critical work being produced in the U.S.; there seems to be more space to actually publish critical work on innovative poetry there.

sq: Right, but that's quite recent. I think, among other things, that Juliana Spahr's anthology in 2001 really solidified a moment outside of the avant-garde and Language communities. People realized, wow, there's something going on here and we need to be paying attention to it. But you're right, there are more places to publish. Or more serious conversations going on.

HM: There are also more presses there, so one or two presses can specialize in an area, whereas in Canada we have so few academic presses so there's not the space for that degree of specialization. Our market is much smaller.

sq: I think there is also a resistance to that model in Canada, which favours regionalism over intellectualism – it was important, but now we have paid a price for that. When I left Vancouver, KSW was still very Marxist, very grassroots and now you've got people like Jeff Derksen and Steven Collis at Simon Fraser University ... and you've got this whole strand of thinking evident in journals like *West Coast Line* that's much more theoretical, it's much more sophisticated, and playing at a much higher level.

HM: That is relatively new, though, and I would argue, somewhat specific to the west coast and to the KSW people, where there seems to be a very politicized academic discourse around poetics.

SQ: It's true. B.C. has always been a rogue state – and perhaps because there was nothing at stake, as Lisa Robertson says, people were willing to go way out on a limb. I would like to see the 'buy-in' to the table not be a book of poems but an essay on poetics. A coming to terms with one's time and cultural/literary history. You have to shift the emphasis from personal production to ...

HM: Reflection. I think. Because people don't read and they don't know what else is happening.

SQ: They're not reading. They don't know how to read. Nobody talks about how to read. Within a few months of writing they are learning self-promotion and grant writing.

HM: It seems that there's not a lot of value placed on being a good reader because when you're reading you're not producing anything. It's a system that's focused on production and not on reflection.

SQ: I know, and that's so problematic. As an undergraduate student I did my BFA at the University of British Columbia, and after class people were always, 'Where are you going to send that?' That was an exercise for a workshop – why would I send that out? People would make the one or two changes they thought were valid and send them out the next day. And I was just like, no. I see this as a sort of base and I'm going to develop a voice that is saying something beyond a basic workshop response. But there's no encouragement for that. When I was at Rutgers the first two years I taught Expository Writing 101, and it was the most beautiful experience, because you would get these incredible trajectories. The philosophy of the department was that in order to teach people to write you have to teach them how to think and read. The emphasis wasn't on the five-paragraph structure, or parts of a sentence, it was how to read connectively, how to engage with real issues in the world and attach those to theoretical models and expand your mind ... It was so much fun to see people really let loose and engage with texts and start to think for themselves. Sometimes we would literally read together line by line, and people were very empowered and excited. It's important work.

HM: Okay, I have to get back to your work, because we've cycled way off into something very fascinating, but I want to ask you more questions about your writing. I want to ask you about the 'Dizzy' poems because I find these very intriguing. They're so different from your other work. They are so pared down and sparse. I'm curious as to how they came about. The subtitle of these poems is 'My Mother's Life as Cindy Sherman.' Why Cindy Sherman?

SQ: Those poems came from a series I had written a long time ago, very narrative conventional poems about my mother. Perfect workshop poems, in fact, having achieved the stamp of 'Publishable, get them out.' But they weren't finished to me. Then I started to read Anne Carson and Lisa Robertson. I was thinking about Carson's fragments. I realized that one of the things that displeased me about my early poems was the false sense of wholeness, the sense of imagining that I could make a portrait that would represent a whole that I was remembering, or had overheard, or felt. If you want to talk 'realism,' I realized that telling story is more about trying to yell in a wind tunnel with turbines going at full blast. We only ever hear a few fragments of any given story that we're told. Even the most astute listener. I was thinking about Lisa Robertson's idea of the pastoral fragment, issues of self-representation. Women like Cindy Sherman are coming to terms with these iconic and limiting images of women. I mean, my mother is one of those women from Untitled Film Series, she's a dame, she's a broad, there's metal, or mettle, there. At least on the surface. But the way she looked created a lot of problems for her. I was thinking about that and while it's an impermeable kind of construction there are gaps. She doesn't see gaps in her presentation, or that it is a presentation. She's not interested in entertaining the idea of the gaps, although she does, she's able to, but it's terrifying to her. So I took a black marker to those old poems. I just started blacking out lines. And then I kind of reconstructed them from there. It felt like I was diving off a cliff, it was really fun.

HM: The poems create the impression of something being carved away and a new shape emerging, and again, there's the road imagery, roadside memories, it's that era of car culture, which is interesting given the subject matter of *Expressway*.

SQ: Yes. It's also nostalgic in a way my new work isn't nostalgic. It's actually not pretty, or not pretty in the ways we think. And that was the problem with 'Dizzy.' It's a challenge for me not to make pretty.

HM: Were the original poems pretty and is that part of the reason you rewrote them?

SQ: I hadn't even realized what I had done in the original poems, but yes, I glossed over, and yes, made pretty. But then to ungloss, sort of like a poetic ungloss, I can think of fictional unglossings like Dorothy Allison's *Bastard out of Carolina*, but I can't think of a poetic unglossing of that kind of childhood narrative.

HM: So much poetry is about aesthetics. It doesn't always lend itself to unglossing, although the possibility is very interesting.

SQ: Yeah, I mean, I guess Moure does that. I remember reading bits of *Furious* and thinking there's a part of this that's about molestation. There's something very dark at the core of this. And it's not pretty. It's also not direct, it's very slant.

HM: So the 'Dizzy' poems, you edited them ... were they initially more conventional lyric poems?

SQ: Very conventional lyric poems.

HM: Do you see yourself as a lyric poet?

SQ: In some ways, yes. I want to speak to people 'about life.' I think *Slip* is a very traditional book. It was a very sort of flat narrative until I read Marilyn Hacker's *Love, Death, and the Changing of the Seasons*, a book-length sonnet sequence about falling in love and the eventual break-up of a lesbian love affair set in New York and Paris. I read that, and I was like, Oh my god, I have never read metrically charged lesbian poetry, I didn't know it existed. I loved Donne, Hopkins, the Romantics, but didn't know I could use these devices today. I thought, I need to do this, I need to figure out how to make this relevant. So it became an exercise for me. There were three versions of *Slip*.

HM: So what do the other two versions of *Slip* look like?

SQ: The first series I wrote as a sonnet sequence. Each line measured, each syllable scanned. Another version is a prose poem, not a prose but a narrative poem sort of like Sharon Olds or Bronwen Wallace. But I found both of those very unsatisfying. To me a poem is not interesting unless there are at least three things going on in it. I thought that one of the three levels was changing, or working with form, sort of corseting or expanding or doing something. But now I realize, thanks to people like Moure, that those three levels, or lines of interrogation, can all be intellectual.

HM: Sometimes Moure's work seems to contain seven or eight lines of interrogation.

SQ: Yeah, but now that I've lived in Calgary I have a whole different reading of Erín's poetry.

HM: How has Calgary changed your reading of her work?

SQ: Well, you see, I have a lot of sympathy for people's difficulty with poets like Lisa Robertson, Erín Moure or Margaret Christakos because I had a lot of difficulty coming to those poets. I did not know how to read Erín Moure when I first encountered her. Nor Lisa Robertson. I remember throwing a book across the room. I hated it. I was angry with Moure for making things so difficult. So I really empathize with readers. I think that texts can be difficult. But I don't think that that's necessarily problematic. In fact, I think that it's part of what makes reading interesting and writing interesting. We should expect that. Or hope for that because otherwise we don't grow.

HM: The challenge of texts like that can be a pleasure.

SQ: Yes, once you realize you're not stupid – but rather the text requires a different approach. And then I learned that one poet can offer a way into another. In trying to understand Anne Carson, I had to read Stein, for example.

HM: Who did you read in order to understand Moure?

SQ: Well, I didn't really understand Moure until I went to Calgary.

HM: So Calgary was your other text.

SQ: Yes, but also maybe I had that whole experience of reading what she was reading – she offers a lot of clues. In fact she offers a whole reading list in each of the citizen/community books. So I knew that I had to read Jean-Luc Nancy and that she's really into Agamben. So, if you read all of those the poems open up ... I had a student in Calgary come to see me about her poems. She was doing this fragmented urban pastoral of Calgary. Very interesting. Not predictable at all. I suggested she read Moure and she was like, 'Moure? Why? What does she have to do with Calgary, nature or pastoral?' I pushed *West South West* across the desk and flipped it open and she was, wow ...

Moure seems so cerebral, but she's actually concerned with very basic, lyric human inquiries – and landscape, those books can be laid over the city of Calgary. I recently did a talk on Bronwen Wallace and Erin Moure and I realized that I could do a reading of *Common Magic* and *Furious*, which were written around the same time, and their concerns, line by line, their concerns and the language would be extremely similar.

HM: But they're such different poets in so many ways.

SQ: Yes, but similar concerns. It's just that Wallace is very invested in not having any gaps, right? She's wanting to make a little doily that, like the CBC, can be slipped under anybody's coffee cup in the kitchen. She feels very loyal to a certain set of readers she doesn't or didn't imagine would take that journey. Erin on the other hand is, 'Look, we're in a kitchen! What does that mean?' And then she proceeds to take it apart, expose the beams, seams, underbelly of the idea. Wallace wants to have coffee.

HM: It's sort of like that opposition between Woolf and Stein we were talking about earlier. Virginia Woolf's writing being like tatting. And again, your act of lining up Woolf and Stein, who are so different, and then lining up Moure and Wallace, who are also so different.

SQ: Well, I'm a working-class girl. Wallace and Moure are working-class girls.

HM: Whereas neither Woolf nor Stein were working class.

SQ: They were definitely not working class. They didn't give a damn about audience. Not as a political concern. But to touch on your earlier question, yes, I find difference expansive. I advocate for collaborative readings – letting texts speak to you through each other. Reading Marlatt with Woolf is good, reading Dickinson with Armantrout, Judith Butler and Margaret Christakos, try Susan Howe and Tim Lilburn – and so on.

And I worry about audience too. I think Moure does as much as Wallace did, but Moure loves her audience enough to say, 'Come to the text. I'm not going to dumb it down for you.' But as a working-class girl I understand that every book I read takes me further away from my roots. So I'm a bit torn. Which may be why I'm obsessed with form, obsessed with how the ideas come out because I can't have work that's going to take twenty years of preparation to enter into.

HM: Your work is complex, yet it's accessible. I read segments of *Lemon Hound* with my students, and it's a challenging text for them, but they don't need to have read Agamben or Jean-Luc Nancy to read it.

sq: Or Woolf.

HM: Or Woolf for that matter. Although many of them have read Woolf and they can pick up that thread of the work. I give my students the first passage from 'On the Scent.' 'Here she is in Banana Republic,' and the line about the Microsoft song. They know that Microsoft song and the familiarity draws them into the poem, yet the work takes them to a place that's new as well. They understand this, they engage with it. It makes them work, but it's not as alienating as giving them a piece of Moure's work.

sq: Maybe because on the page it looks more unified.

HM: Maybe that's part of it.

sq: Not that I think my work is as complex as Moure's, but familiar language and the prose-like line may be more gentle? I think that we have similar concerns. She's interested in making people aware of their cognitive assumptions, as I am. That's why I'm constantly pulling in things that people will connect with – what is the effect of that Microsoft song that we're all hearing? How does it affect our experience of the world? How did those things come together?

HM: And how that Microsoft song is changing us at a biological or even a spiritual level.

sq: Of our hearts and our minds and our looking. To me, it's amazing that we just embrace this stuff with so little critical discussion. I mean we allow a desktop operating system into our life with no thought whatsoever about the implications? We give much more thought to adopting a cat, or buying a car, than what happens to our brains every time we turn on those laptops. It's absolutely fascinating. We wire ourselves. We subscribe. We modify our behaviour for these technologies. I'm not resisting technology – I'm just asking why we are doing this so blindly?

HM: Exactly. And I think it does change the fundamental nature of our makeup. You have references in *Lemon Hound* to women storing toxins in their fat and folding the new into their ovaries. It's a very political book, and maybe it anticipates your new project in some of those respects. You also talk about the commodification of lifestyles, of feminism. Feminism has become marketed as a lifestyle choice.

SQ: That's what's going on in Number 2 of 'On the Scent.' All those ways in which what we believe has become just another bit of data to be marketed to. We're an unbelievably passive and captive audience. Very little resistance – except perhaps to 'difficult' feminist texts.

Toronto, July 2008

SELECTED WORKS

Slip: Poems. Toronto: ECW Press, 2001.

Teethmarks. Roberts Creek, BC: Nightwood Editions, 2004.

Lemon Hound. Toronto: Coach House Books, 2006.

Expressway. Toronto: Coach House Books, 2009.

from Scrabbling

6.

Got to remember who I am. Remember cabin, garden,
chickens, how I loved naked-walking to the bathhouse,

how even in winter I kept the door open, and from
the steaming tub hoped to catch a grazing doe.

I tell you of my pining, but it's more reminder than
I can admit. At least in this moment, the sun,

the Main, the calzone, the café – there's nowhere else.
But look at you. Not yet thirty, this is just a game.

Level-headed you'll return to the family way, marry
a doctor, lawyer, propagate, worship your career,

travel once a year someplace safe, and remember me
(fondly?) from your untamed student days.

7.

I've Scrabbled since the age of six, trusting, I'm willing
to spell words long before meaning. Tile by tile

I am betrayed, bead, seam, blouse, hand, skin; word
by word my undoing for anyone to read. We sit

in the window of the Euro-deli, marble table cool,
clowns on stilts, street performers, children screaming,

discordant harmonica gypsy music. The details insist
themselves: two dykes from L'Androgyne, tongues in each

other's mouths, Christoph with his green cap, the scent
of apples, maple leaves turning, and two dogs tied

to a meter outside do not stop whining.

8.

You invite me for dinner, a party to follow. Swollen-tongued,
I nod my acceptance, a waft of chlorine filling my nose, metal

rungs extremely slippery. No handrail, suddenly my brow,
my breast wet. Suddenly a belly flop of sky, and dizzy:

there's your hand again. Did anyone notice how close our
knees are? Did the light turn apricot to emphasize your eyes?

Are you a plot against my past, colour and curl designed
to entice me from my path? The questions logjam:

Is your hair heavy? How do you comb it? Were you born
with it like that? Do people touch it on the street? Does it

cushion your head at night? Does it shape your dreams? How
do you sleep? Or, more precisely, will you sleep with me?

9.

If I slip now
If my tongue is brash
If my thoughts betray
If my feet numb
If I fall
If my tongue
If the shell cracks
If our knees touch
If words fail
If our eyes meet
If my heart softens
If the sun
If tongue
If word
If numb
If heart skin tongue word embrace

Fall

I will deny it all

Untitled Film Still #35

Oh,
her hips,
        babies hang. For men
                a doorway
      arm
rift of
      flesh and
they move through her
        daily. She offers
bread, soup, lure
of open beaks.

Of course
        setting up house
               on an angle
        having babies
filling space, everything new
        one thing
maintaining another.

Where is the emotional budget
for stasis?

She polishes the floor
tugging
        babies

Roadside Memory #1

Five kids and
pee
construction. Cars crawling
     beetles on
sweltering
and muffled
      mops her breasts, tulip
and ochre shift, floral, sweat (her waist,
he can put his hands around her waist).

She points   neon
     a lighthouse, but he will not
never will do what she wants,
needs
     crying
she throws herself out
of the moving Valiant (black
red interior, red beaks) and walks:
it is Calgary. 1959. A man at a desk
lurid, puce but still, manners: May I?
    she feels the sweat
in her brassiere, imagines a swimming pool
the sound of slot machines, nickel and dime
(Oh God, the heat)
in the hall. Lack of air
(someone has leaned on the prairie,
elbow of shale, thumb of tree line)
    almost turning back, hoping
       at the side of the road,
          impatience. Angry. Controlling. Door
corrugated   small,   knob
    and foul. Shaving mirror   light bulb, window
(Who brought the f'ing cat? Who lost the house? Who could not
pay the bills?) and someone knocking.

This is private,
her dress. She hovers, trembling
      a lady never sits
(she is faint now) and suddenly banging
in here, she says again,   face seeping,
scurry of   in the sink
         here, she says, again,   harder, now
         she sways

pees on her shoes, reaching
to the sink for balance, pulls
now scrambles, yelling
pounding. She opens the window
as far as she can and cat-thin
         midsection of
hip bones bruised
she stands on the sink, snaps her
hips, hinges through
dirty laundry, head
first into
clatter of garbage

from A River by the Moment

THE RIVER IS ALL THUMBS

She is feeling brisk at the heel. She loves feeling brisk at the heel. She is feeling brisk at the heel and rivering her thumbs. She is at the edge of cool. She runs her thumbs along the hinge of river. She loves running her thumbs along the hinge of river. She feels river. She feels thumb. She is brisk and thumbing. She is numb and loving. She is feeling loving. She is feeling loving about feeling. She loves feeling about loving. She loves feeling about feeling. She loves feeling about feeling loving. Her loving feels. Her loving loves rivers. She is feeling loving about rivers. She loves feeling loving about rivers. She is feeling rivers about loving feeling. She rivers about loving. She rivers about feeling. She rivers about the hinges of rivers. Her feelings hinge. She hinges about feelings. She hinges about feeling the river of hinges. She is feeling thumbs. She loves feeling about her thumbs. She is feeling about her thumbs as she rivers her feelings. Her thumbs river. Her feelings cool. She feels cool rivering her thumbs. She feels her thumbs hinge the river and cooling she thumbs. She loves feeling that her thumbs hinge the river. She thumbs numb love.

NUMB IS MORE NATURAL

Who is more numb? Who feels more numb about love? Who thumbs love? Who is numb about thumbing love? Who is more brisk, more river than hinge? Who is under water? Who loves being under water? Who is feeling swift and hinging under water, thumbless and numb in love? Who has wings? Who is mourning? Who is exactly how small they must be? Who is loss of action? Who has walked the Brooklyn Bridge? Who is turning forty and hingeless? Who is turning fifty and numb? Who is willing to bear? Who sees themselves a river? Who floats? Who eddies? Whose back is scraped? Whose knees bleed? Whose breasts ache? Who has a mouthful of water? Who knows the shape of rocks? Who sees the sun as wavelength? Who smells like trout? Whose spine flexes waterfalls? Who hasbeen sixteen? Who is molten? Who is smoothed over? Who has not forgiven? Who has wet feet? Who has walked the river? Who has good drainage? Who has stubbed a toe on a rock? Who has felt granite on tooth? Who has seen the flash of red bellies? Who has eaten trout? Who has felt a bear paw? Who flirts with the snouts of wolves? Who is always fresh? Who is surface and depth? Who has walked the turnpike? Who is exactly how big they must be? Who has snagged the comma of mouth? Who understands trespassing? Who has not felt the earth under foot? Who knows the river bottom? Who of us is not hooked?

from On the Scent

1

Here she is inside. Walls and windows. Appendages and openings. Here she is sitting on a stack of books. Here she is digging out from under an avalanche of paper. Here she is swatting words with her coattails. Here she is wondering what to do with outdated memory. Here she is boxing and unboxing. Here she is moving stuff. Here she is deleting whole files, randomly. Here she is perplexed at the mounds of paper. Here, I tell you, here she is hiding under the Xerox machine. Here she is communing with resonators. Here she is clucking the MRI tune. Here she is earplugged and eyeshadowed. Here she is tall and long in the stride, here she is a force of circulation. Here she is sideways in a wind-storm. Here she is teal and persimmon. Here she is Italian plum. Here she is the palest interior of the pomegranate. Here she is. Here she is in Banana Republic. Here she is black and black. Here she is thinking of the colour blue. Here she is trying to see underwater. Here she is reading on the train to New York. Here she is wiping coffee from the seat. Here she is sitting next to seven young rappers, pants like circus tents, du-rags and ball caps piled on high. Here she is. Here she is in an office in Philadelphia thinking of the letter R. Where would we be without R, she asks? Where would we be without E? Where would we be without arms? Here she is with meringue and milquetoast. Here she is hiding behind a mapletree in October, the weather having changed too quickly and she without a sweater. Here she is walking down Bleecker thinking, how? How? How can she describe the windmill of her aorta? How tibia is her confusion? How like the Microsoft song her frustration flits and crescendos. How like the blue of the XP screen her mood flickers in the traffic-jam hour. How archaic the need to open a window and breathe.

6

Years crimsoned before her. Windows appeared and were washed. White, the laundry clung to her magnetic feet. She meditated on the iron, willed permanent press into existence. Sunday mornings the hallways hollow. Prayer books like paperweights. Cotton wool and cotton wool. Maternity ward as spa weekend. Moods flat as pancakes. Afternoons brief as half a Valium. Fish-tank calm. Years appearing like stains on the sheets. There was once a convertible and winding mountain roads. There was once a sapling waistline. There was talk of California. Padded and padded her life of Kotex corsets. Ankles exposed and pellet breasts. Years soft as spaniel ears. Swells and churning. The big book of prescription drugs. The doctors' bible. Bookends of days. *True Romance. True Confessions. True Stories.* Muffled and muffled. Curious: *Alfred Hitchcock Presents.* Her life between two fingers. Her life cracking on porcelain. Years arbouring opaque, crystalline. Asbestos and asbestos. Aperture closing. Underexposed, unmerited. Hours slippery as newborns. Days hard as nails. Years heavy as rain clouds. Her head an oven. Puppet mouth and marionette of limbs. Skin thin as foil. Drawbridge flimsy. Moat of heels. Lockless, braless, the patina of possibility. Gods shimmering in the altar of kitchen. The echo of her mind filled with pipe cleaners and devil's food. Years with the crusts cut off. Pink and bite sized. The footstool of her back, blue vinyl: easy to clean.

8

Yes there are coupons to clip. Yes I've been to Filene's. Yes I have stood in the shadow of the Eiffel Tower. Yes I've tried tempeh. Yes on a camel, on a horse and once while looking at an iguana. Yes I collect Air Miles. Yes I voted for Clinton. Yes with my cat, always after a busy day. Yes I've been to the Brooklyn Macy's. Yes in the CN Tower. Yes while listening to Tom Waits. Yes, yes, yes in the desert with a man in tasselled shoes. Yes I said tassels. Yes in the Tower of London. Yes I sometimes cook and do the dishes. Yes in the changing room at Lord & Taylor. Yes with a cousin in a photo booth in Vancouver. Yes on a 747. Yes in my grandmother's house. Yes in a car parked on the mountain. Yes in Snohomish. Yes in Summerland. Yes, yes, yes with Anaïs Nïn. Yes I've tried the Atkin's. Yes I've lost fifteen pounds. Yes I feel great about it. Yes I can feel my ribs. Yes when I bend over I imagine Johnny Depp's hands on my hips. Yes I have eaten raw meat. Yes I have hiked in the Laurentians. Yes, yes, yes I can find my way home. Yes with a zucchini. Yes with a water gun shaped like an eggplant. Yes there are good deals to be had. Yes I've thrown up. Yes I've considered suicide. Yes Todd Solondz gives me nightmares. Yes I've overdrawn my account. Yes, yes, yes I have a crush on Stockard Channing. Yes in a turret. Yes in a Chevy. Yes on the beach in La Jolla. Yes while reading Chekhov. Yes in a parking lot in Denny's. Yes on the turnpike. Yes in satin. Yes I think Cate Blanchett is hot. Yes in 501s. Yes women in wedding dresses turn me on. Yes with a bride. Yes with a groom. Yes with a brother and sister. Yes while watching porn. Yes with peaches. Yes in the blackout serenaded by sopranos. Yes insufferable in surf. Yes in the pantry while the poker game peaked. Yes in stilettos. Yes in flats. Yes in pink plastic. Yes you do. Yes I will. Yes while there's still time. Yes while I can. Yes whenever possible. Yes I'll be a top. Yes I'll be your bottom. Yes I'll whomp your ass. Yes after shopping. Yes with chocolate. Yes now. Yes here. Yes even alone.

from Viriginia, Vanessa, the Strands

AND IN THE DAYS I SPEAK OF, GOD, FAUN AND PIG WERE ... ALIVE,
ALL IN OPPOSITION, AND IN THEIR CONFLICTS PRODUCING THE
MOST ASTONISHING ERUPTIONS

White scuffing folding in white hands the light scissoring after yet another ball. Fragrant of slit-eyed something mewing. Nothing jagged in white and the dark interior of Virginia Creepers. What did you say Nessa? Where does the stamen fit? Walls of Watts and busts hushing unnatural gloom of a room. Here insulated, here spice buns and tea. Circle of a scene cut. Light gone out. Scuttling, scuttling. Make nothing of it. Making much of him golden as Hermes in a Kensington drawing room. And aren't women always in dim spaces with the lights off? Aren't women always holding out? Oh how they ripen like plums dangling overhead luscious and firm. After all there are diamonds and silk stockings. Everything is pleasant. Who needs to be copying out Greek letters? Who needs to know? The world is detail. The world is lighted candles and opera boxes. White scuffling how he advanced with his opera hat. Must break out of this sentence. Must lift off the asphyxia of words, words, each of them laden, each of them musty and clinging; each one a medal, gleaming on his chest. How they lull me. How there is a sense of going under. How they lay upon me like flattened wool. Muffle man, muffling. The cook serving up pig's feet. How he kneeled in front of women, adoring, imploring, how his layering goes on.

from The waves, an unmaking

TO FOLLOW THE CURVE OF THE SENTENCE, WHEREVER IT MIGHT
LEAD, INTO DESERTS, UNDER DRIFTS OF SAND, REGARDLESS OF
LURES, OF SEDUCTIONS

To be always becoming, always dangling; to be damp, inexact, always wanting to be closer, more precise; to want to explore *the exactitudes of language, and step firmly upon the well-laid sentences*; to live in a world that abandons the present moment and to want only that; to be in love with the world and have it turn its back; to be a poet of undetermined skill; to have given a piece of oneself and have it flung out; to understand the contemptible nature of self; *to be poor always and unkempt; to be ridiculous* in the Eaton Centre; to have written one whole poem and to have it spurned; to pour all of you into air; to know that all will come before us and none of it for me; to know that time presses in and no one comes closer; to have all desire roundly pummelled out of one's skin; to join the procession of the uncounted; to know that poetry exists even if we do not write it; to cling to one's *credentials, like a man clapping in an empty field;* to see the bottom but never touch it; to dream the top and not strive; to know that you have gone past choosing; to know that you let love die, to carry on anyhow, to embrace and wring every drop of time.

RITA WONG

HEATHER MILNE: Much of your work explores issues of justice and human rights. You write from an anti-racist standpoint, an anti-colonial standpoint, and a feminist standpoint. Why use poetry to address these issues?

RITA WONG: I don't necessarily think of poetry as addressing those issues so much as language being a way of thinking through those issues. I would say I came to poetry before I came to social justice in the sense that, as a reader or a writer at a very young age, language was a place where I could question and also reflect on what was going on in my life, things that I didn't necessarily have words for at the time. I might look back on something and say, 'Oh, that was a racist incident,' but as a child you don't necessarily have words for those things or even a way to analyze them, though you still write out of some sort of emotive reason or dissatisfaction with what is going on. Poetry's condensedness, its fragmentation, allows for me to move in and out of it in a fairly porous way. And I also think sometimes poetry has taken me into social justice rather than being the vehicle for social justice. Writing some of those poems in *monkeypuzzle*, the section in China for instance, there's a poem in there about the Yangtze River and the displacement of people there. When I wrote it, I didn't necessarily consider myself an activist per se. I was somebody who was teaching English in China, living there, trying to observe my environment and to question what was happening through language. You have to be responsible for what you write. You have to live by your words, and sometimes those words push me in a social justice direction after the fact. It's not that you're consciously thinking about language as an instrument for that, but it's more that it manifests what's going on in and around you so it's inevitably politicized. Maybe whether you choose to engage with it or not, or how you choose to engage with it, is the question. After I wrote that poem 'lips shape yangtze,' I found myself talking to the Chinese media about the Three Gorges Dam and talking about it at poetry readings, and it became a small platform to get people thinking about Canada's role because we do fund the Export Development Corporation that funds the Three Gorges Dam. So it's not like we're dissociated from it or somehow innocent of it. Through tax money and Canadian government actions we are related to what happens over there, so it's important to hold ourselves accountable as people who live in this country.

Chinese was the first language that I spoke in my family – Cantonese to be precise – but my best language is actually English – it's what I was schooled in. I'm a Chinese-school dropout. I don't speak or write Chinese at as high a level as I would like, but it remains my mother tongue and the language of childhood and familial comfort for me. I have a love-hate relationship with English. On the one hand, I have a love for most languages, but I don't like the way English has been used as a colonial force to limit perception or limit point of view because I feel language, syntax, diction, all of it, enables different ways of imagining the world or being in the world and that's one thing I love about language. I have it in a very fragmented way with Cantonese.

HM: When you write in English, how do you use the language against itself to expose how it works as a colonizing force? How does that work in your poetics?

RW: It works in different ways in different places. In *monkeypuzzle*, I was very conscious of how the mother tongue has been made to feel inferior by English as a domineering force, and how important it is to claim that tongue, even though it is fragmented, tentative, shy and awkward at times. What does it mean to own one's own life, to live it to the fullest extent possible? Whether we're talking about owning one's own history, language and labour, or one's own genetic inheritance, I'm interested in this question of power as it evolves from collaboration and communication, not as it is imposed by a hierarchical system. Language that excites me comes from a mindset of 'power with' or 'power to,' not 'power over,' which is the logic of colonization.

Some of what is going on in *forage* is a sense of the language itself being infected. It is spliced and respliced. I guess pushing around and questioning form as part of that process without necessarily knowing what's right or wrong but just trying to figure out how and why the language is working the way it does. So, for example, a poem like 'chaos feary' has a lot of anxiety and rage in it. I wrote it after reading a book by Vandana Shiva called *Biopiracy*. Some of what she does in that book is make that scientific jargon that is sometimes intimidating to laypeople more accessible.

HM: The language of genetic modification?

RW: Yes, and science. What does it mean to take that language apart and put it back together in unexpected ways? I feel like I've been put into this experiment through genetic engineering and the sale of foods and things that are not labelled. I've been put into an experiment that I didn't choose or give consent to but am still part of. So what does that mean in terms of how I work through my language? I think it disrupts syntax, and then you repiece things together as they are broken apart. It's not particularly pretty. It's painful at times but I think it's important to work through all of that rather than hiding from it or trying to make it prettier than it actually is. That said, I would like to write happier work. This past weekend I read at Gung Haggis Fat Choy, which is a Chinese New Year dinner. I was looking for a happy poem because I didn't feel like angrily reading about genetically modified food at this dinner. I have said at readings that photosynthesis gives me hope. Mushrooms give me hope. It's not that there isn't hope, but I have to work through some unhappy places before I can get to that space.

HM: It's interesting to me the way you work with the idea of modification at the level of language. Language is something that can endlessly mutate, or be 'infected' with different poetic procedures and techniques, and it's actually a really rich terrain upon which to explore these issues.

RW: Yes. And I'm particularly interested in collaborative or multivoiced work. In *forage* there are lots of fragments of other texts circling around in the pages and in the margins. I feel like there's poetry all around us if we pay attention. A kind of commingling or pushing up against different discourses is going on all the time. How can form manifest that rather than having the singular poetic voice?

HM: Is that what foraging means to you as a practice?

RW: Yes, as a reader, I'm trying to read my way through this world to make sense of it. Foraging in terms of looking for things that can help me imagine a better place for language, for myself, for the future. Also, the word 'forage' breaks down 'for age.' What would it mean to have slowness, or length of time? I don't know how to do it, but I really think slowing down is important. I work too much, too hard. It's not healthy. Can poetry ask that question of how to slow down, how to take the moment as it is to just be in it without having to rush off to the next thing so quickly. So yes, 'forage' in terms of the verb, but also in terms of 'for ... for what?'

HM: I'm struck by what you say about slowing down, particularly in relation to *forage* because it's a busy text. You work with a lot of found texts in *forage*. Given the fact that appropriation of voice has been such an important issue within the feminist writing community, is the issue of appropriation something you ever wrestle with when you are using those other voices in your work?

RW: I think so. I think about it in terms of citation. I try to document where those things come from, and there's a works cited at the end. It is a fine line for sure, what you decide to quote, or what you decide to reference. It can be very playful sometimes. When Larissa Lai and I were writing *sybil unrest*, we were constantly rehashing or repeating pop culture songs, slightly twisted but still recognizable. I think with certain texts I feel I can be less respectful because they have been so mass-circulated and have their own power. Thinking about the power differentials between different writers and texts, I guess in terms of appropriation, one has to draw a line between what is appropriation and what is quoting. I also think acknowledging one's sources in really important. Jeannette Armstrong has a really good essay called 'Land Speaking' that made me wonder what it would feel like to try to crack English open and have Halkomelem words or indigenous words come in ... language that is indigenous to the land wherever you happen to be living. That feels very fraught in the sense that you don't want to be stealing the language when so much else has been stolen. At the same time you don't want that language to die out either, and languages die out if they are not used or learned. It feels like a very hard place to be because my only access to Halkomelem is through websites and it feels to me very inadequate. Yet if one doesn't begin to ask those questions ... if not now, when? The poem I read at the Gung Haggis Fat Choy dinner was an English poem but it had these Halkomelem words or indigenous words cracked into it or sprouting into it. I prefaced it by saying, 'I'm not sure about this poem,' but I felt like I wanted to at least try that. One has to think about one's intention. Is it respectful? What are the possible outcomes of it? As Joy Asham Fedorick asked in the book *Give Back: First Nations Perspectives on Cultural Practice*, does it create space, or does it take away space? I hope that if I venture into this experiment, it will generate a giving back to the languages and cultures invoked. You can't always control or predict that, but you still have to think about it.

Coming back to your question about English and how to work with it, a lot of writers have talked about how it can be shaped or moved. I mentioned Jeannette Armstrong. Marlene NourbeSe Philip has a good essay about place in poetry. I guess it's by trying to shift the syntax, trying to break it open, trying to make space for other ways of perceiving or structuring or organizing. I think also when I reference other texts in *forage* it's partly with the hope that other people will go and read them. I want people to go and read Rachel Carson or Richard Van Camp. It's like leaving clues to say, 'You might want to check out some of these thinkers and writers.'

HM: In *monkeypuzzle*, you write about the history of immigration and about historical figures like China Annie and policies like the Head Tax.

forage seems to be more engaged with a contemporary moment. When you write about history do you feel a certain ethical responsibility, and is it different from the ethical responsibility you feel when documenting the present in poems like 'canola queasy'?

RW: That's interesting ... I haven't really thought about the difference time-wise because I don't necessarily think of time in a linear way.

HM: Perhaps there's a continuity between something like the Head Tax as a destructive form of governmentality and the forces that have allowed a company like Monsanto to operate in the way that it does. These things are removed from one another in terms of time and history, but maybe not so removed from one another in other ways.

RW: What comes to mind for me is the government apology for the residential schools. On the one hand, it is important that that apology happened. On the other hand, there continue to be all these First Nations struggles: against development of the Sun Peaks ski resort in B.C., and up north in Ontario the K.I. – Kitchenuhmaykoosib Inninuwug – not wanting platinum mining, and the Tahltan people in northern B.C. trying to stop Shell from coming in. There are ongoing struggles against mining, against development, etc., and it seems to me that the apology deflects attention from the present by focusing on the past. The past is important to acknowledge, but if it's disconnected from the present then that's a problem. The continuity you are talking about makes sense in terms of analyzing what's going on, politically but also linguistically and rhetorically. It's a deflection. At what point can you even catch up with what's going on in the present moment when it feels like it's happening so quickly and out of one's control? I don't necessarily have the power to change much but I do have at the very least the power to respond to it, to think about it, to say it's worth paying attention to. I don't know that it's enough. I went on this retreat for burnt-out activists a few years ago organized by Maggie Ziegler and Jackie Larkin. They propose that we need three concerted actions that are coordinated together rather than isolated. One of those actions being just the protections of the gains that previous generations have made, things that are front-line work but also high burnout. You're always in a reactive or defensive position trying to combat something else. And that needs to be done in combination with analysis of the system. If you don't have a systemic analysis, you'll get stuck in one spot without seeing the bigger picture. The third thing is just making what it is that you want, having the ability to imagine what it is that you want. It seems to me that poetry has partly that role to play, hopefully. I'm not convinced that it does, but I offer it hopefully. All three of these things need to be working together. And one person might find herself located at different parts of that triangle at different times.

HM: What do you see as the relationship between your poetry and your activism? Do you see them as part of the same impulse, or is it difficult to reconcile the two?

RW: I think there is never enough time in the world. The difficult thing is trying to figure out where to put your energy and when. I'm not always sure I make the right decisions, but I do what I can. One of my supervisors in university was Roy Miki and I could see with Roy that his political work fed the analysis in his academic practice. I learned from him that there's a way in which there can be a synergy or working together of those things rather than a compartmentalization, but it means thinking about it differently. I try for that. I don't know if I'm successful at it, but ideally I'd like to see those things feed one another. In terms of the poetry and activism, I do see them as complementary rather than as totally separate things. I think the process that you do activism by is very different from the process of writing, but the analysis or experience that causes you to do those things is what is shared.

HM: You were talking earlier about the fact that Cantonese was the first language that you learned but English is the language you speak most fluently. You talk a bit about that space in between languages in 'write around the absence' where there's a line that reads: 'pictograms get flattened out by the steamroller of the English language.' There are pictograms in the poem, and I'm not sure what they say ...

RW: They correspond with the Romanized Cantonese and mean 'Are you hungry?' – reversioning the common Chinese greeting 'Have you eaten yet?'

HM: It's such a different language from English in terms of how it operates at the level of semiotics. I'm curious about the poetic potential of pictograms.

RW: You might take a pictogram like the character 'good' and if you break down the character it's a woman and a child and that signifies 'good,' whereas in English it's just letters that are random and arbitrary in a certain sense.

HM: That's really interesting because that pictogram carries a gendered meaning around the maternal which is very rich and interesting from a feminist standpoint.

RW: Yes, and if you're using it in everyday life you might not think about it, but if you look at the character and unpack its story it's pretty amazing. All these characters have histories and stories. The character for 'big' is a person holding her arms out to show how big something is. You don't always have access to that meaning unless you study it. I don't write as much Chinese as I would like, but I find that when I am taking notes, Chinese can be just as compact or a faster way of notating or recording what it is you're trying to say as English. But it's such a hard language to learn because there are so many characters. I learned some in Chinese school, before dropping out, and university. I also lived in China for a year. But to really get into the language, it's a lifetime study. The other thing about the language is it takes me back to my family, not just in terms of the writing but the sound. It's very reassuring or guttural. It taught me that there are things you can't convey in English.

HM: Those poems in *monkeypuzzle* about travelling in China are really interesting, particularly the way you write about not wanting to exoticize China, and about wanting to remember that it's not foreign to the people that live there.

RW: There is a pressure on Asian-Canadian and Asian-American writers to self-Orientalize. I really don't like that, but at the same time you can't not talk about things that are part of your culture or history. The challenge becomes how you talk about them knowing that there's this long history of imperialism and western colonization. I think sometimes you have to not think about that stuff as you're writing but once you've written it and you want to put it out in the world, that's when you have to think about how it's going to be seen.

HM: How did your collaboration with Larissa Lai, *sibyl unrest*, come about?

RW: Larissa and I were reading at the Hong Kong literary festival and that's how the beginning of *sibyl unrest* happened. We were there in Hong Kong when SARS hit and Iraq was invaded by the United States and we felt very depressed. We tried to write our way through it but we couldn't really write in that moment. I can't remember what we wrote ... I think we threw it away. A few months later we started up again in Vancouver. It just had its own momentum.

HM: Have you worked collaboratively with other people?

RW: I've also worked with Cindy Mochizuki, who is a visual artist. We did a collaboration in Banff a few years ago. It was a performance along Banff's main strip. We called ourselves 'FeastFamine' and we were thinking about what it would mean to decolonize the space. We had decolonization wish boxes that were hand-screened and we were giving them out to strangers on the street, trying to engage with them about the history of Banff, and handing out a document that we had done based on archival research on indigenous histories of this place.

HM: How did people react to that?

RW: Some people were appreciative. Others thought we were selling something and they didn't want to buy it. There's this layer of commodification that exists before you even open your mouth. There was a range of weird responses. It was quite funny actually.

HM: You've lived in Calgary, Vancouver and Miami. How do you think about your relationship to place?

RW: It is really important to me. I think one of the things I'm still in the process of trying to learn to do is to see things through a less human-centric lens. That's certainly the lens I'm most familiar with and the lens I have been inculcated in, but when Jeannette Armstrong says language comes from the land, I really want to think about what that means and try to take that very seriously.

HM: So by seeing things from a less human-centred viewpoint, you're thinking about trying to see things from the perspective of the land?

RW: Yes. What does it sound like? What does it look like? I don't necessarily know. It's just more of a question.

HM: I wonder if some languages come from the land more than others. English probably doesn't come from the land as much as some other languages.

RW: Yes, or it's been displaced or unrooted. In NourbeSe Philip's essay about place in poetry she talks about a British writer and how his words were all about dreariness, gloominess and rain, and it makes sense in the context of England, in contrast to a Caribbean landscape which is burning-hot sun and the sense of never being able to hide from that ever-pervasive heat. Land makes a big difference in terms of one's experience of daily energy and life. I feel increasingly like the language that interests me is one that grapples with the effects of the land rather than ignoring it or artificially shutting it out.

HM: There's a history of nature poetry in the English tradition that goes right back to the Romantic era, but it is so human-centred. The sublime is ultimately about the human subject rather than the mountain or water-fall that is being described in the poem. To try to write about the land from outside of that framework is quite radical in its opposition to how nature has been written about from within a western tradition.

RW: That's where I really want to acknowledge and say that writers like Jeannette Armstrong and Kateri Akiwenzie-Damm – who have written about these things – are making me think through them more. As I said, I'm interested in the question of what decolonizing means. How does one decolonize respectfully and not in a way that's just reappropriating indige-nous culture? The video artist Mike MacDonald writes in one of his artist statements that the crime wasn't just that indigenous languages were taken away and cultures were stolen but also that the people who took this land didn't learn the language or culture of the land, so what does it mean to do that in a respectful way? I think that's crucial to changing our own patterns of consumption and patterns of behaviour. The idea that you can even buy or own property is a cultural paradigm or delusion. What would it mean to have a point of view where you belong to the land rather than the land belonging to you? I don't begin to know how to answer that ques-tion, but it is a question that I'm going to spend my whole life asking.

HM: And certainly writers like Jeannette Armstrong are very instructive in helping develop ways of doing that.

RW: And Lee Maracle. When I was fairly young, in the 1990s, she came to Calgary and did a workshop with the Woman of Colour Collective. Just to think of oneself in terms of physical, spiritual, emotional and intellec-tual aspects was really helpful. I feel like there's a lot that needs to be learned from and listened to in terms of what indigenous writers have to say. Any way forward has to deal with what is applicable or relevant knowl-edge from the land and its original cultures. What people hold in terms of their cultural heritage can help us see and live differently. I think decolo-nization is a project that's not only for indigenous people but for anybody who lives on this land.

HM: In terms of writers whom you turn to or who inspire you, you mentioned Jeannette Armstrong and Lee Maracle. Do you find this kind of inspiration mostly from aboriginal writers?

RW: I wrote my dissertation on representations of labour in Asian North American writing, but I'm interested in all kinds of writing. I do think in terms of this particular place, this particular landscape, this particular history, respecting indigenous perspectives is crucial. I've been influenced by a lot of different writers ... Dionne Brand, Jam Ismail who used to live in Vancouver and is now based in Hong Kong. Jam has a very playful and peripatetic sense of language that I really enjoy. Sky Lee, Frances Chung, Cecilia Vicuña, Hiromi Goto, Larissa Lai, Lydia Kwa, Fred Wah, Roy Miki, Sesshu Foster, Walter K. Lew, Wayde Compton, Olga Broumas – I could go on and on. It's dangerous to start listing because you inevitably leave out important influences ...

HM: I feel that your work is quite spiritual, not in the sense of organized religion, but it's there in your attentiveness to land and place. I don't know if you have any thoughts on the place of the spiritual in your work ...

RW: It's quietly present. I don't want it to be loudly proclaiming itself so I don't know if I have much to say about it. Where it maybe pops up a little bit is in the dedication in *forage*. I was really struggling with the dedication and that term 'interbeing' comes from Thich Nhat Hanh, who has a wish that people would begin using that word more. I was just responding to his wish. Yoga and meditation are really important to me. I don't necessarily have a name for my spiritual practice but I feel like there is one.

HM: What writing communities do you feel that you are a part of?

RW: My closest friends are writers. One big marker for me would be the Writing Thru Race conference in 1994.

HM: What was that experience like for you?

RW: It was amazing. Really empowering. I know the media was all over it and attacking it, but my experience of it was just great. It was a moment that made me realize that I had something to offer. I think it was Dionne Brand who said we have an opportunity now to just write. We have to grab it and run with it.

Vancouver, February 2009

SELECTED WORKS

monkeypuzzle. Vancouver: Press Gang Publishers, 1998.

forage. Madeira Park, B.C.: Nightwood Editions, 2007.

sybil unrest. With Larissa Lai. Vancouver, LINEBooks, 2008.

write around the absence

write around the absence, she said, show
its existence
demonstrate
its contours
how it
tastes
where
its edges
fall hard
on my stuttering tongue, how its tones &
    pictograms get flattened out by the
        steamroller of the english language,
live   its etymology of
half-submerged   assimilation
in the salty home of   tramples budding
my mother tongue,   memory into sawdusty
shallows   stereotypes, regimented capitals,
            arrogant nouns & more nouns, punctuated
        by subservient descriptors. grammar is the dust on the streets
waiting to be washed off by immigrant cleaners or blown into your eyes
by the wind. grammar is the invisible net in the air, holding your
words in place. grammar, like wealth, belongs in the hands of
the people who produce it.

this is
the sound of
my chinese tongue
whispering: nei tou
gnaw ma? *no*
tones can
survive this
alphabet

: meeting implies purpose
             – Erin Mouré

in san francisco county
four times as many asian women as asian men
married whites

where does the river of one race end
& the sea of another begin?

children leap oceans in their births
raised in new lands, carry silt in their genes
river offspring, shift deltas
tangential shades merge in twilight's blood

spontaneous burn & simmer
glow & kiss as candles tip together
before water & after it:
when a woman blossoms you into her
whose seed will history record?

because it is possible to decolonize
to recognize the aperture within opening
to feel change in your bones
i can carry the day forward once more

:I speak to you without election because the cells know nothing of
democracy.
They think not of the good of the whole, but of themselves.
They think of their thin unguarded border.

because the cells know hope
know the spiralling word's structure
know the touch of a stray cat
they can replenish in the night

---

*Italicized lines are from Erin Mouré, Furious.

when i squeeze the orange, pull it off the tree,
do the roots cry out? will the tree forget its pain?

:*It must have to do with love, at its root.*
No matter how it is obliterated after that

the relevance of salt water: our bodies
an ocean of immigrants' tears

my digestive stomach gurgle relevant
because it is the sound of the orange after the tree
& the sound of one pen writing
visible skin
furiously

furl of a rhubarb leaf
its red, red stem
the colour of the triangulation
in my chest: mothers,
daughters, holy ghosts

politics. with its trail of bodies.
seaslip. saltslick.
blood sticks.

"In April 1997 Monsanto pulled two varieties of genetically engineered canola seeds from the Canadian market after testing revealed that at least one of the patented herbicide-tolerant transgenic varieties contained an 'unexpected' gene. This was after 60,000 bags of the seeds had already been sold throughout Western Canada." - Mae-Wan Ho

canola queasy

vulture capital hovers over dinner tables, covers hospitals a
sorrowful shade of canola, what gradient decline in the stuck
market, what terminal severity in that twenty-year monopoly
culled the patent regime, its refrain of greed, false prophets
hawk oily platitudes in rapacity as they engineer despair in
those brilliant but foolish yellow genetically stacked prairie
crops. how to converse with the wilfully profitable stuck in their
monetary monologue? head-on collisions create more energy
but who gets obliterated? despire misgivings i blurt, don't
shoot the messy angels with your cell-arranging blasts, don't
document their properties in order to pimp them. the time for
business-as-usual died with the first colonial casuality. reclaim
the long now. hey bloated monstrosity: transcribe your ethics
first or your protein mass shall turn protean mess and be
auctioned off in the stacked market and so you can reap
endless cussed stunts.

*Dedicated to Percy Schmeiser, the Saskatchewan farmer harassed and sued by
Monsanto because genetically engineered canola blew into his fields.*

the girl who ate rice
almost every day

riceworld was sold out of brown rice so she went to the sundown mall on the street of no return. strolled past low maintenance, high risk properties in search of plump grains. distracted by gloss and air-conditioned spectacle, she said to the manager in the supermarket, what big beets you have,

all the better to tempt you with my dear, he replied. that most ungenerous of storekeepers frowned, for she had fingered his goods without purchasing them. try one, he urged, it's a free sample. the red silver stained her lips, a cosmetic wound.

slow, for that was the girl's name, paused as she was wont to do. had these beets been crossed with cabbages to make them so huge? not cabbages but cows, replied the manager, with a drosophilic glint in his melanophore eyes.

the land of extinct animals was expanding exponentially, and she would be added to it too if she ate those beets, she realized too late. dangerous allergies and surprising properties made each object that crossed her lips an epiphany.

oryza sativa inter alia

go to the U.S. patent database, http:// www.uspto.gov/patft, and do the following search:
search term: monsanto
field: assignee name
a search of records from 1976 to january 2007 yields 3,894 records. if you add a second term, soybean, in the search field, title, you will find 210 patents.

if you change the second search term to rice, in the search field, title, and keep monsanto in the assignee name field, you will find 4 patents.
tomato yields 2 patents.
potato yields 2 patents.
wheat yields 5 patents.
cauliflower yields 1 patent.

dear reader, please note that these numbers are current as of January 2007; there is a high probability that the numbers will be greater by the time you access the database yourself.

U.S. Patent 6,153,812: Rapid and efficient regeneration of transgenic wehat plants. Nov 28, 2000. Inventors: Fry, Joyce Ellen (St. Louis, MO); Zhou, Hua-Ping (Ballwin, MO). Assignee: Monsanto Company, St. Louis, MO).

why, just yesterday, the oysters in the chiu chow congee yielded a small, imperfect pearl on her tongue. magic was all around her, had she the eyes to see it. corporate magic, crossing goats and spiders who had no desire to become one creature, pigs crossed with people until they collapse under their own immense weight.

elm and larch trees offered her some comfort. their roots and the roots of their bach-flower sisters reached deep into the earth that would outlast her.

ah, but this was a story about rice. fluffy rice, hard, undercooked rice, white rice full of glucose waiting to enter the bloodstream, wild rice that turned the water purple with resistance, the rice that could be harvested three times a year in some parts of the world, and the brown rice that was her daily staple.

slow realized that she had been eating imported rice from china (white) and the united states of amnesia (brown) for most of her life. now that she had eaten the beets of no return, and did not have long to live on this earth, she wanted to know what a grain of rice grown on the land where she lived, the land of salish, musqueam, halkomelem speakers, would taste like? how could it grow?

'A rapid transformation regeneration system is disclosed. This system takes two-three months to obtain transgenic plants. Transformation efficiencies are very high. This system also has been demonstrated with several different selecting systems and is particularly useful for transforming wheat.'

U.S. Patent 5,663,484: Basmati rice lines and grains. Sept. 2, 1997. Assignee: RiceTec, Inc. The invention relates to novel rice lines and to plants and grains of these lines and to a method for breeding these lines. ... Specifically, one aspect of the invention relates to novel rice lines whose plants are semi-dwarf in stature, substantially photoperiod insensitive and high yielding, and produce rice grains having characteristics similar or superior to those of good-quality basmati rice. Another aspect of the invention relates to novel rice grains produced from novel rice lines. The invention provides a method for breeding these novel lines. A third aspect of the invention relates to the finding that the 'starch index' (SI) of a rice grain can predict the grain's cooking and starch properties, to a method based thereon for identifying grains that can be cooked to the firmness of traditional basmati rice preparations, and to the use of this method in selecting desirable segregants in rice breeding programs.'

she determined to try to grow a small crop hydroponically.

she turned onto the avenue of final warnings and noticed a manhole cover that was ajar. peeking beneath, she saw a steel ladder that would provide entry into the sewers of her city. wet and warm, with occasional spots of light provided through the stained-glass sidewalks, the sewer had promise as a potential bed for her rice. she enlisted the sewer rats to help her guard and cultivate this crop, by promising them half the yield, if it grew. her time was short, so she quickly tracked down some organic brown rice through ebay, which she used to see the bed.

the beets had infused her excrement with a permanent red glow, but she still used it as fertilizer. the rice that grew from this experiment was rouged by the fertilizer, and became a sweet, rosy coloured grain that spread like a weed through the urban catacombs.

long after the last beet eaters disappeared from this spinning planet, the slow-cooking rice continued to make its way through the sewers and alleys of many a struggling city.

U.S. Patent 6,229,072: Cytoplasmic male sterility system production canola hybrids. May 8, 2001. Assignee: Adventa Technology Ltd. (Sleaford, GB). 'Our invention comprises a gene restorer line of Brassica napus which contains a Raphanus sativus restorer gene but is essentially free of Raphanus sativus genes which produce high glucosinolate. In particular, we provide a gene restorer line, and progeny derived therefrom, seed of which is low in glucosinolates...'

U.S. Patent 6,498,285: Methods for producing transgenic pigs by microinjecting a blastomere. Dec. 24, 2002. Inventors: Ebert; Karl M. (Millbury, MA). Assignee: Alexion Pharmaceuticals, Inc. (Cheshire, CT). 'A transgenic large mammal is produced by a method including the steps of obtaining one or more early embryos, selectively preparing an embryo having at least three cells, and preferably at a stage in development corresponding in time to the onset of transcription of the embryo's paternal genome, and introducing isolated nucleic acid molecules into a blastomere of the selected embryo. The introduction of isolated nucleic acid molecules into such embryo's results in the generation of transgenic large mammals at a significantly increased frequency...'

ricochet

when the ship leaves the harbour, she hears the vomiting below. circling the ship, huge lanterns hanging from choppers. the ocean is angry. no, she is angry & blames the ocean. i can't bear the weight of history & i can't not bear it. when her clothes are burned, the stench sounds like canaries trapped in her throat. she knows she must make home up, tallying words & numbers into skeletons off which to hang her coat. the ship has left the harbour. it's not coming back. if i never see another ship again, it'll be too soon. when she yawns, the canaries flutter their smallest feathers. her breath smells of worms. until the melancholy becomes cholera, i do not know the name of this language. the shadow in the periphery would like to enter this room. why turn away? she only wants to rub her face against your faithless arm. tremble. ache. her name is slow. you have waited for her for a long time. why don't you look at her face? her gentle grimace. an anchor cold inside your belly. you don't know what she calls for because your ears are plugged against uterine howls of pain. when the dried clams became bloody soup, i smelled the harbour.

in for a penny, pound of flesh. crush the ginger. palm against the knife. smash the root wide open. her nostrils accept ginger. the air is in the kitchen. always carry a backup plan. garlic. flashlights. codes in case the cops are invading your privacy. until the root was smashed, i didn't know the sound of breakage. broken further than you knew you could. then break it again. the language that turns your verbs into nouns. messy accidents. argue incessantly if you have nothing better to do. noise levels are rising. be still my scared heart.

when the door opened, it was round. a moon. a woman in a moon. her gates wide open. just like that. the thresholds more vomiting the smells she refuses to name as if forgetting were its own solution. not a door today but a window. what are you saving the door for? don't you know that intruders are welcome? until the handcuffs appeared, she thought this place was benign if deluded. when the ship left the harbour something inside broke. there is no fixing this. the oceans will swell with prayers, flotsam landing in places you'll never see. you have more trust than you know what to do with. blessings & curses are cousins. her palm wide open. knife reverberates, tremor of her adamant tendons. when she looked up, the canaries had fluttered off to other homes. she was still piling up words like they

were cages she could turn into nests. couldn't she learn from the birds?
fractured like your entry into the language. why don't you pull weeds out
of your garden for the slugs to feed on? why does your grandmother keep
sticking her hands in the crumbling earth? wary of her bony frame. some-
times you have to approximate before you go precise. all intentions are
dangerous. you know yet you still proceed. sharp objects cause bleeding.
until i ate the sharp object, i didn't know it would slice the inside like so
many question marks. hooks into syntax force of abortion. mammoth
prints in the rumbling earth.

from sybil unrest, part 2
co-authored with Larissa Lai

gestures towards absence
allure of failure fills
heart's almost stopped watch
ticks countdown to
yesterday's launch
picnic all the theatres
of all our wars
sized small medium
culprit at large in
hope's extra vacuum
we wash our hands
antiseptic wringing
unaware toxin's already
entered bloodstream
doting aunties birth
what can't be borne
clipped wings contemplate
hollow bones regrowth
say 'aye' to re-subject
all in favour

§

'i' resurrect 'oui'
because the heart
won't stop
tackling
how plenitude
could shatter habit
how germinate
could smash
inhospitable lurch
to failed utopias

sibyl unrest (with Larissa Lai)

i-topia books our digital
revolutions six weeks in advance
slick surface informs
highways mapped on wireless connection
i'm fido
mobility's dear faith
love me
love my cog

§

ignition flickers contagious contiguous
sex weakens diatribe
that's why
giant vulvas venture
through patriarchal corridors
their ragged magma
turns convention to convection
from diode to subduction zone
girlfriend might moan
for the long night's
crone performs
catholic money slandering
tricks in lieu of
subservience

weekly menu feeds babely
tribe our beloved amazon
gushes effusive
i'm lovin' it
explaining her beef
as die cast
on probability of profitability
we clock our overdraft
in times new roman
loose mysteries
twist forked laughter
as goddesses sign in triplicate
'the pleasures of being multiple'

§

hailed wonder of being several:
while she goes on dispensing
business-as-usual
another she sits
in silent mourning
another she
actively seeks distraction
but the barbed dolls
stiff with artifice
leak plastic trauma
choke on
missing addresses

rendered inoperative by viral horses
our trojan interface seeks
indiscriminate revenge against those who sleep
on-line regardless of dreams
my distracted double
dolls herself up
sweetened by sham
our vulnerable firewalls bird ashes
to rise as electronic copy
do you read me?
emotion registers
cash on the nail
sorrow sells charity to 1-800
irritation buys convenient packages
anger markets management to white collars while
laughter irons redux in fresh paint
retro palettes and en route magazine declares
the death of cool

§

going through the notions
economists pantomime
the pollution of oceans
the razing of old growth
on spreadsheets
foolish eyes burn, water,
no safe specs
under the drum of the monitor
unreliable hoards
no protection against
the bellicose lair of the bush

LISA ROBERTSON

KATE EICHHORN: Over the past few years, you've lived in France and now here in the United States. Has this cultural displacement informed your writing, and if so, how? And what do you see as the major differences between innovative writing in Canada and the U.S.?

LISA ROBERTSON: I don't consider my movements as displacements – they've felt more like distributions. But I think it would be easier to answer your second question first. I see a huge difference between innovative writing here in the U.S.A. and in Canada. For one, generally speaking, the established innovative writers here are privileged. The fact that there is no functional granting program means that there is a self-selecting process. Typically, people who have what they call here 'personal resources' are able to persist with this work. There are definite exceptions – Eileen Myles, for example, Dodie Bellamy, and I could name others. Connected to this class hegemony is the fact that here innovative writing is fuelled by the MFA culture, which is not so profoundly rooted in Canada, where it's a much more recent phenomenon. In the U.S. these programs are mostly private, and are very expensive. $30,000-a-year tuition is quite typical, I was shocked to learn. I currently teach in part in such an MFA program. What I'm seeing is a normalization of innovation into a kind of style – what Foucault would call a regularity. I'm seeing young writers being told to 'fragment more,' for example. There seems to be a series of institutional agreements as to what experimentation or innovation consists of and how one goes about it. This has never been my experience in Canada, where experimental practice has been a much more contested terrain – there are people coming at it from an extremely Marxist perspective or from a feminist perspective or combinations of those. Other people come at it from a postcolonial perspective. When I think of the variations of what gets termed innovative writing in Canada – if you think of the span from Rita Wong to Nathalie Stephens to Gail Scott to Dionne Brand – that's very, very broad. What each of these people is doing is bringing their politics into writing directly. They're investigating ways to innovate in language that reflects and analyzes their own political experience. I don't see that happening here very much, especially not institutionally. Our Canadian writing cultures are much more discursive.

KE: I agree that there is not as much invention in innovative American writing. It seems that from early on they are trained to invent and schooled in what tradition to follow or slightly modify. Many of the selections in this anthology are striking in part for their visuality, but I can't imagine these visually inventive texts, including the selections from *Debbie*, coming out of this context. Always, there are exceptions, but it seems that in the U.S., there is generally a much clearer division between what gets categorized as experimental writing versus what gets categorized as text-based art, with the latter often falling into the book arts rather than writing.

LR: I do think that in part it is again because most writing is going on in an academic context here. So the departmental tradition and structure, which remains very profoundly inscribed in institutions, has also structured creative and aesthetic practice. People have to stream very early on, and what they are streaming toward is an academic job. Writing then becomes an expression of disciplinarity.

KE: Like many of the writers in this book, you have never been in that stream. For much of the 1990s, you were running Proprioception Books in Vancouver, but this was a bookstore for serious readers, so you were interacting with many academics throughout this period. How has your place on the edges of the academy informed your work?

LR: Although I don't have any degrees, I certainly wouldn't say that I've been entirely outside of academy. But I have never had the motivation to end up in an academic career. I did study at Simon Fraser University with Roy Miki and with George Bowering and Donna Zapf. They were really connected to what was happening in the city. So once I quit doing my BA to take over the bookstore, I continued to have those ties with those individuals. I've always felt that I've been a bit of a fence-sitter when it comes to the academy. I've been neither in nor out, and as a bookseller, I was always deeply connected to academics in the humanities. I was their supplier – one of their intellectual nodes – and I was attending every conference in the humanities held in Vancouver for six years, whether it was postcolonial studies or art history or literary studies. These were conferences that Stephen Greenblatt, Homi Bhabha, Gayatri Spivak were speaking at, and I wasn't just sitting docilely behind the book table, I was attending the whole conference. So I had an interesting way of being present in academic culture from a different perspective, and it supplied me with a bibliography and endless conversations and relationships I'm still involved in.

KE: So you were engaged at the level of knowledge but not being trained as a writer, which are two very different things.

LR: When I was studying at SFU, I don't think there were any creative writing courses. Writing was something I did with people I met at SFU, but it's something we invented for ourselves outside the university.

KE: I have a series of questions about your involvement in Vancouver's various creative communities in the late 1980s and into the 1990s. The first, and most obvious, question is about your involvement in the Kootenay School of Writing. It was never a feminist project –

LR: It was a feminist project briefly.

KE: Certainly, it has supported the development of many feminist writers. Can you talk about when it was a feminist project?

LR: In the early 1990s. Nancy Shaw was on the collective. Catriona Strang was on the collective, as were Kathryn McLeod and Susan Clark and Julia Steele. I was on the collective. Deanna Ferguson and Dorothy Lusk were not on the collective at that point, but they were around. One of the great things about the Kootenay School is that it just keeps reinventing itself. There are these three-to-four-year intensities. For a few years, I think that Vancouver was known as a centre for feminist innovative writing because of the stuff that we were doing – who we were inviting, what we were producing, what was being edited.

KE: But this was a very different project from the one happening in Montreal during the same period.

LR: It was a different project, but we were explicitly feminist identified. Our discourse was explicitly feminist discourse. It was not the same as the feminist discourse in Montreal, but it was inflected by that discourse. We were all readers of Nicole Brossard and Gail Scott. *Raddle Moon*, Susan Clark's magazine, was very international. We looked beyond Canada too, to the U.S., France, and later, England.

KE: One of the striking differences, I think, between the kinds of dialogues happening in Vancouver and those happening in Montreal or Toronto at that time, was that many of the dialogues you were having were with American Language writers.

LR: That's true. Something else that I think is a little less recognized about the poetry coming out of Vancouver in the late 1980s and into the 1990s was the strong involvement with feminist visual arts practice. In the late 1980s, Mary Kelly, the British feminist artist, was teaching in Vancouver. It was a hotbed of feminist visual conceptualism. Nancy Shaw was a curator and an art critic and an artist as well as a poet. We had all these friends who were visual artists – Kelly Wood, Lorna Brown, Margot Leigh Butler, and I could go naming people, but the discourse that was circulating in that art community was huge for feminist poets. There were, and still are, amazing feminist curators: Cate Rimmer, Helga Pakasaar, Karen Love, Karen Henry. We were reading feminist film theory – Constance Penley, Laura Mulvey, Teresa de Lauretis. *Visual Pleasure and Narrative Cinema* was a very important text, for example, since it brought the discourse of pleasure into the innovative writing community from a feminist perspective. I would say that it was these critical and visual art and film discourses that strongly differentiated feminist practice in Vancouver from feminist practice elsewhere. I'm not saying that feminist writers in Montreal did not have access to this discourse, but this was a specific exchange going on in Vancouver. When I started to publish critical writing it was as a feminist art critic. I was not publishing literary criticism. To this day, almost every piece of critical writing I have produced has been for the feminist visual arts world. I'm not unusual. Many others experienced something similar.

KE: And this is part of a very long tradition in Vancouver. Rita Wong is currently collaborating with sculptor Linda Sormin, but looking to an earlier generation, there are Daphne Marlatt's collaborations with photographers and other visual artists. Multidisciplinary dialogues and collaboration seem to be an integral part of the Vancouver writing community.

LR: I don't see this anywhere else. It's a particular texture of feminism, as well as cross-disciplinary practice. Perhaps the horizontal politics of feminism make cross-disciplinary practice more normal or possible.

KE: The overlap between the visual arts and writing community in Vancouver in the late 1980s to early 1990s wasn't simply happening in the context of the feminist community. I've been wondering how those conversations and collaborations affected the writing. At the level of poetics, what were those conversations with photographers doing?

LR: I was working on a minor in fine and performing arts, so I took several art history courses from Donna Zapf. I heard lectures from all sorts of smart people. Jeff Wall gave a couple of guest lectures in some art courses I took. But I mostly worked with women. There was much more of a presence of psychoanalytic discourse in the feminist conceptual-art community, and I think that all of the questions around the problematics of identification and narrative, for example, were influenced by those dialogues. Identification, corporeality, the gaze, pleasure as problematic nodes, not just things to be rejected or accepted but things that needed to be investigated because of their problematic nature – concepts that needed to be opened up critically – it was an involvement in that discourse, which carried into the development of a different approach to writing poetry as a practice. If as feminists we were free to reconsider the place of pleasure as a critical axis in our work, rather than simply just an example of false consciousness, that gave a different kind of access to a much wider range of language. In the late 1980s and early 1990s, the people I talked to most intensely about writing were Christine Stewart and Catriona Strang. Then, we got to know Nancy and Susan through the Kootenay School. We were reading all sorts of things – 17th- and 18th-century literature, classical texts. This was not true previously in the Kootenay School, which had held to pretty much a straight-ahead contemporary, post-1950s literary reading practice. This different critical discourse around identification, pleasure and narrative, which came from the way artists handled psychoanalytic discourse, gave us access to the entire history of literature. Although I think extremely highly of and have been influenced by Kevin Davies's work, Jeff Derksen's work, Gerald Creed's work, there wasn't such a synchronic involvement in the history of literature with them. We felt that all literature was equivalently accessible. At that point, we could be reading Susan Howe and Lady Mary Wortley Montagu next to each other and that was considered a good thing.

KE: In her interview for this anthology, Catriona talked about this reading practice being one of the tensions between the women and men in the Kootenay School, because at the time, there was still a deep suspicion of anything historical.

LR: When Catriona and I entered that community, since we were not part of it when it formed, there was a lot of doubting going on. We were having so much fun with what we were already doing that I don't think it ever occurred to us to change our minds. Our impulse was to do more, to intensify.

KE: Did you ever run up against any of the hardline Marxist dogma that was prevalent on the collective at the time?

LR: I don't think that Peter Culley's work could ever be located in a hardline Marxist avant-gardism. It was Peter Culley who recommended that I should read William Cobbett, Gilbert White, 18th-century naturalism. We were not the only ones who had these special tastes. But yes, it did cause conflict. I feel that that conflict helped me to gather my wits and learn to defend and develop what I was doing.

KE: All this, of course, is happening in a collective. Again, this seems unique to Vancouver's writing community. From writers of the Tish generation to much younger writers today, collaboration appears to be integral rather than peripheral or tangential to how people work in that community. I'm not just referring to collaborations with visual artists in this case but to an entire approach to making art and sustaining artistic communities. Do you have any sense of the conditions that have sustained this way of working? What has made collaboration the norm?

LR: Almost all my projects at the moment are collaborative projects. There's the video with Allyson Clay and Nathalie Stephens. I'm also currently translating a text by Henri Meschonnic, a French linguist and translator who is working on political theories of prosody, rhythm and ethics. I'm translating his work with one of my graduate students. I'm doing digital sound work with Stacy Doris. All of my projects now are collaborations, so that's constant. There have been periods when I have lived in a more isolated way, but it's never been a desire to leave collaboration. Sometimes it's simply harder to work that way for geographic reasons.

But why has it been like that in Vancouver? I don't know for certain. It's too bad we can't just write the recipe, because a lot of people are curious! But if you think back to the 1960s, to the work coming out of the Western Front and to artists like Carole Itter, Roy Kiyooka, Gerry Gilbert, Judith Copithorne, Maxine Gadd, Jam Ismail, Rhoda Rosenfeld, Trudi Rubenfeld – they were all coming out of the Intermedia culture of the 1960s where cross-disciplinarity was the regularity. One thing that occurs to me is that architectural culture in Vancouver has developed differently from architectural culture in other Canadian cities. The kind of modernism that developed in Vancouver is really different from Montreal-style international modernism, for example. It was connected to California and Japan. Artists on the west coast have developed different trajectories of aesthetic affiliation and conversation. There weren't even direct flights from Vancouver to Toronto until 1962. It seems like a long time ago now, but within the cultural development of a city, that's like yesterday. So Vancouver has been geographically isolated enough that it has been forced to fall back on itself, to create its own culture. It's very far from centrally defined Canadian culture in many ways. We all seem to fly very often now, but there was a time when I didn't get to Toronto for ten years even though my family was there.

At the Kootenay School, we were also poor. A lot of people involved in the Kootenay School were on welfare, and those who weren't were just barely scraping by. We were really just inventing culture without a dime. I think that you have to invent things differently when you're in that situation. We were poor but young and full of energy. I think there has been a different history in Vancouver, more of a sense of immediacy and perhaps necessity. Also, the culture that was happening in the 1960s was very international. We know about Tish and their connection to the Black Mountain Poets, and Warren Tallman's presence at UBC, and the Vancouver Conference and Phyllis Webb's participation in those events, Robin Blaser and the San Francisco renaissance at SFU, and we're aware of those connections. But the academic experimental poetry was going on at the same time as the Western Front and Intermedia culture was going on downtown. There was the connection with Fluxus. There were some people moving across those communities. I believe that Roy Kiyooka would have been a real bond between those communities. Kootenay School emerged in the middle of all those scenes. It was not Tish, it was not Warren Tallman's scene at UBC, it was not specifically linked to SFU, although some of us studied there. It was downtown in the traditional stomping ground of the artist-run-centre movement that emerged around the Western Front, so our access to how to speak together and what to do and how to organize came out of the artist-run-centre movement, which I think has been much, much more open minded and ideologically critical about how practices and politics are formed than literary culture in Canada has been.

KE: This wasn't just happening in the traditional stomping ground of the artist-run-centre movement. With the exception of a brief period when the Kootenay School was based in Nelson, it has tended to take up various spaces in buildings in and around the Downtown Eastside of Vancouver. Anyone who has lived and worked in this community knows –

LR: It's the poorest postal code in the city.

KE: Yes, and one of the poorest postal codes in the country. This is a community where, statistically speaking, the average life expectancy reflects figures for parts of the developing world. So the Kootenay School is meeting and staging events in a community where you have to think about poverty, you have to think about the strain of everyday life, you have to think about the effects of colonialism. And this community is there, in direct and indirect ways, in your work, Catriona's work, Dorothy's work and the work of many other writers too.

LR: None of us have been isolated from those politics and contingencies. Sometimes I feel that here, speaking of the Bay Area's innovative poetry community, that politics is something that you inject as content into writing. There is a sense that you can say the words – use the word 'Marxist' and chastise privilege – but I really feel that what was happening in Vancouver was different. Politics in Vancouver are always immediate and not buried. When you talk about how real-estate politics affects everyday life, or how racism is institutionalized, you see the immediate effects on the Downtown Eastside. When you go there now, you see that it is so much worse than it was ten or fifteen years ago. It's the barometer of what is going on in the political economy – what you see in that community is the direct result of globalized economies. Writers here seem much more isolated from that. Though no one agrees with it. In the intellectual communities that I've had any contact with in the U.S., people do have profoundly engaged critical positions on the effects of political economy on daily life. So it's hard for me to understand how it developed differently in Vancouver, but I feel it has in part to do with the fact that in the Kootenay School, the collective structure is completely non-hierarchical and everyone has equivalent say. I don't know exactly how they run things now, but we had grant-writing bees and everyone would sit around writing grants together. Everyone did everything from washing the floors to writing the press releases to writing the grants to hosting the visiting writers. That's a politics. Our writing was coming out of that very, very directly. It's hard for me to say exactly how that affects poetry because I think that I am still too much in it to have a clear perspective. But now that I'm in academic life, I can see that the academy is basically modelled on the medieval Catholic Church! One is profoundly aware of one's rank and one knows or quickly learns what one can and cannot say to whom, and it is an utterly and profoundly and deeply hierarchical structure that everyone pretends is not so because we're a 'community.' Coming into writing within – I don't know if it is more church or military ... perhaps more church, since the chair of the department is named after some sort of Catholic seat – the difference between coming into writing within that fundamentally hierarchical structure and entering at the level of collective labour has got to be doing something to your attitude toward language.

KE: Despite the fact that most innovative writers would say that they are interested in undermining the primacy of the author, I rarely see this enacted. Coming to writing through collective labour suggests a set of conditions where this might be possible at the level of theory and practice.

LR: The very first time I went to a conference as a writer rather than a bookseller – I think in Buffalo – someone asked me if I was faculty or administration! This was a regular person, just another writer who was studying there. It felt like a surreal question to me at the time, but now I understand where it came from. I can't remember how I responded. I think I said that I'm the one who lays down the roach chalk, but that was a very important job!

KE: You've been talking about conditions of production – how the writing that came out of the Kootenay School was informed by collaborations with other writers and artists, by cross-disciplinary dialogues with visual artists and by collective labour. Those conditions were part of a particular politic, of course, but I want to press further on how these politics inform poetics. It produces a different attitude or approach to language, but how? On what levels?

LR: I think that it is happening on a few different levels that are always coming at one another. In certain ways, the kinds of conversations you have as a writer – the way you deal with students, with editors, the way you manage or don't manage to deal with email – that's all politics is. It's the construction of relations between people. That's how I think about politics. We make relationships between people by speaking and listening and responding. We make relations with language that we are giving to and taking from one another, so in that sense to write a poem, publish a book, give a poetry reading, is just part of a continuum of discursive practices happening in many ways all at once. I try to keep these conversations as open as I can. I try to notice how we are being positioned and positioning ourselves in a language vis-à-vis one another.

KE: As a poet, what's your role in this chain?

LR: I'm just one of the people who is noticing and positioning and being positioned. It's less a chain than a web. I have no particular role. All of those relationships with language as a material rhythmics among people is what writing works with. When I was writing *XEclogue*, a long time ago now, the sections beginning 'Dear Nancy' were all given to Nancy Shaw as gifts first. The first one was a surprise. I read it at a reading knowing she would be there. The second was a birthday present to her. That is a very simple explanation of what I am trying to say because obviously not every piece of writing has been a gift framed in that way, but the fact is that every word that I've written has arisen out of a specific matrix of relationships.

KE: What about the place of feminism in experimental poetics? Where is this discussion now?

LR: I don't think that the negative structuring of a gendered subjectivity is finished. One of the great things about teaching is working directly with young people. A lot of my conversations now are with women, men too, in their early twenties. I see gendered politics shaping in an active and insidious way the potentials of young women's access to language. I see young women being told by figures of authority how to conduct themselves. I sit in rooms and hear the sentences being said to them. I feel like it is one place where I can actually be useful, and basically just put my experience to work. What young women are experiencing now is not better than what I experienced twenty-five years ago. They may not all call themselves feminist, but they want to have real access to agency, and they want to be constructing the terms of their own agency. As a teacher, I explicitly position myself to enable that in whatever way seems most pragmatic.

KE: You're enabling that as an educator, but what about as a poet at the level of the writing?

LR: But I'm educating as a poet. My entire access to language is shaped by my history of writing and my history in communities of writing. I learned how to write in many different ways at different points in my life, but I was able to write in ways that excited me intellectually once I had access to a feminist discourse. So for me, writing and feminism are completely entwined in my life. It's not just a matter of choosing one's mentors, although that's important, it's also an analysis of how power circulates and articulates itself on bodies. How I've learned to conduct myself – as a listener, as a speaker, as a writer – enters equally into my writing and my teaching. So I teach as a poet. I say that in the same way that I say I write as a feminist. But this is not necessarily a matter of content, or, god forbid, accessibility, but rather an ethics of conduct.

KE: So it is a performative act.

LR: True, because a performative ethics is what is happening in both writing and teaching.

KE: This discussion of performativity makes me leap ahead to some of the questions I want to ask you about genre. One of the early iterations of *Soft Architecture* was presented as a manifesto. In your essay, 'The Weather: A Report on Sincerity,' which appeared in the *Chicago Review*, you say that the best part of manifestos is their lapses and practical failures. But most people write manifestos because they have an illocutionary force, because they at least promise to do something –

LR: Or to form something, but they certainly aren't utilitarian!

KE: But you seem to be attracted to manifestos because of their performative potential and at the same time, you claim that what you love about them is that they often fail to fulfill this promise. What to make of this contradiction?

LR: Well, I have a double relationship to manifestos because I write them and I read them. That comment about failure was made specifically in relation to Wordsworth's 'Preface to *The Lyrical Ballads*,' which was a manifesto for the collaborative avant-garde that Coleridge and Wordsworth were envisioning. Coleridge later pointed out in *Biographia Literaria* that Wordsworth didn't come through on many of the claims he was making for the new writing of that revolutionary period. We know in fact that he didn't. But in a way, that leaves a lot of work for us to do. I think that these astoundingly ambitious – ambitious in their openness, their desire to actually create new politics – these ambitious manifestos have made space for us to work in. So it's hard for me to say where my work in that form is failing, but I'm sure it must be, and I hope that whatever problems people are having with what I am saying in my manifesto work is giving them something to do too, something to kick against!

KE: Any manifestos in progress?

LR: The translation work I am doing right now with Avra Spector is a manifesto. It's Meschonnic's *Manifesto for the Party of Rhythm*.

KE: Do the manifesto and poetry overlap?

LR: Manifestos are faster. I tend to be a very careful writer of poems. I've never been a 'first thought, best thought' writer. Never.

KE: If you're never inspired, don't worry – inspiration is not a prerequisite for inclusion in this anthology! But is urgency the only difference between the manifesto and poetry?

LR: It's also that with a manifesto you're writing into a specific situation, often with others. Catriona and Christine and I were writing in that mode for a while. *The Office for Soft Architecture* wasn't strictly speaking collaborative, but I felt the urgency of urban politics around me at the time. I felt that all at once I had this flash of insight about how I wanted to represent what globalism was doing to urban politics. Writing that Soft Architecture manifesto was a way to get it out there. In poetry there is a slower research that circles back on itself to ask questions about form. For me, a manifesto is a rhythmic propulsion, a direct agent. A poem recursively investigates kinds of shapeliness and duration in thinking.

KE: You write manifestos and poetry but also essays. What about your attraction to the essay? In many ways, your essays capture much of the original energy of the essay exhibited by Montaigne, although your essays are not nearly as narcissistic or self-indulgent!

LR: I came at writing essays via Montaigne. It's an experimental form – perhaps *the* experimental form. Much of what gets called innovative poetics now – citational poetics, fragmentation, open form – all of these aesthetic moves are already happening in Montaigne's *Essais*.

KE: Montaigne's essays appear with and are arguably integral to the rise of the subject in the late 16th century, but experimental poetics has been, in varying degrees, committed to the subject's evacuation, or at least its interrogation.

LR: I've never been committed to the evacuation of the subject – not at all. I think there is no politics of language without the subject.

KE: And this is different than being committed to the subject's stability.

LR: No, I haven't been at all committed to its stability. To be interested in subjectivity as experimental form is also to be interested in politics. But I don't think that Montaigne was necessarily interested in the subject's stability either. I reread those essays from time to time and I find that they are very open in terms of subject position.

KE: Perhaps because the subject is only beginning to take form at that time.

LR: The various modern institutions that shape the subject as a stable, governable entity were just beginning to consolidate themselves in Montaigne's times. I think we can tend to conflate the subject with identity, and I am definitely not interested in the subject as identity. The fixity of identity just completely disinterests me. But once you separate the subject from identity, it opens the subject to collective dynamics. I think many of the institutions that have shaped our current conceptions of the subject – the family, understood as an institution; the Church; the education system; the banking system – what all of those institutions shape is the subject as identity, as seamless, as a fixed point that can be maintained on a taxonomic grid. Our institutions are interested in insisting that the subject is in need of identity, but if you look at the subject from the point of view of mobility, and the point of view of discourse, and the point of view of ethics, the subject opens as being one of the most exciting political terrains. There is no language without the subject, but thankfully, there is language without identity.

KE: I want to ask you another series of questions, which are about another apparatus with which you are deeply engaged – the archive. In Foucault, the archive is first and foremost the law of what can be said, the conditions of enunciation. I know that for a book like *The Weather*, you went into the archive and deployed textual fragments culled from the archive. But what I am interested in discussing here is not simply what you have taken from archive, your use of the archive as repository of raw materials, but rather how your writing has been structured by the archive. You have, elsewhere, talked about creating indices and finding aids – for example, while writing *Rousseau's Boat*.

LR: For me the archive has almost an Oulipolian status, or perhaps Cagean. It's a tight frame – a bounded frame – in which unimaginable and anarchic variability appears. One of the interesting things about physically working in the archive is the wonderful and bizarre rituals you have to go through. At the British Library, you have to put all your possessions in a clear plastic bag. Other archives have pencil-only rules. Other archives have white cotton gloves. Special book-cushions. Little lamps. You are going through something that is almost like a religious set of rituals, so you are in a space, once you've entered, that is not the world. This, of course, is one thing that distinguishes the archive from the library. Its authority is differently enacted.

KE: The archive is, on every level, constraint-based.

LR: True, but I love that about it! Most of my work has been constraint-based in some sense, so in a way, to choose to work in an archive is just a multi-dimensional projection of that constraint. There is no language that is not framed by law, or what you call the conditions of enunciation. In the archive, these conditions are visible, palpable, so perhaps for a time manipulable, available for transformation. Foucault said in an essay on

Flaubert – *The Temptation of St. Anthony* – he said that in Flaubert, you see for the first time a dislocation of the unconscious and the imagination. In Flaubert, for the first time, the imaginary situated itself between the book and the lamp. Here the imagination is not private. It activates critical perspectives. I love that all the variability and strangeness and opacity that has been in many ways attributed to a certain concept of the subject, in the archive, is blatantly exterior. In the archive, you are working with a material cultural unconscious.

KE: So how do you break that? When you enter the archive as a poet, you don't want to simply reproduce the order.

LR: But often there is no order. You often go and they can't find what you ask for, or the document or book you ask for has been damaged in a flood, or what you expect to find does not exist. The order of the archive is a falsity, but that's always very interesting given all the insistence on order. It's almost the most disordered space you could imagine. The order of the archive is a function of disciplinarity. It's projected, not actual.

KE: Since that's the case, do you see yourself bringing order to the archive then?

LR: You have to bring some sort of question or problem to the archive. You don't necessarily have to bring a system of order. It's like Tarot. You don't lay out your cards without having a question. When I go to an archive, it is always because I have something I want to know. The question will always be answered but usually in the way I least expect. That is such an enormous pleasure.

KE: Are you in the archive now?

LR: Well, this may simply prove that like Montaigne I am a complete solipsist, but I am currently editing a book that is a series of indices of my own archival material. My archive is now housed in the Contemporary Literature Collection at Simon Fraser University. That was a very weird decision to reach. They asked me at a time when I was moving internationally and broke, so I sold my garbage for the same reason that most writers sell their garbage. But I felt very self-conscious about it, so I thought the only way I could deal with this was to also turn it into a project. While I was organizing my papers and after they were there, I would systematically make my own indices of this garbage. Two of those poems appear in *Rousseau's Boat*. I've written three or four more of those poems. I was going periodically to the archive, although not often, since I lived in France at that time and my location posed another constraint. But each time I visited, I was asking a different question. Later I would find ways to sequence the material I had gathered.

KE: What questions were you asking?

LR: The first one was 'Face.' In that case, I decided I would find every first-person statement and copy that out and later figure out what to do with it. The second was 'Utopia,' and my objective was to find every statement that had something to do with place or site, so that is why it became 'Utopia.' There is another where I went to find every statement that seemed to relate to the concept of interiority. There was another simply composed of last lines of notebook pages. And another comprised just of negative statements – a negative index. These fragments were culled from my notebooks – sixty-nine of them. The questions guided my transcriptions. I wanted to see if I could construct an autobiographical text which was indexical but not self-referential in a narrative sense. I wanted to see what linguistic subjectivity could become in relation to the pure exteriority of the archive.

KE: Did you find yourself in your archive?

LR: Absolutely not! But I wasn't trying to. It was the opposite. It was a way to leave my archive. It was a way to let those papers no longer have anything to do with me. Once anyone's papers are in the archive they come to be seen as one group, as a body. If anything, this was my way of taking that body apart, of distributing it across a surface.

Oakland, February 2009

SELECTED WORKS

XEclogue. Vancouver: Tsunami Editions, 1993. Reissued Vancouver: New Star Books, 1999

Debbie: An Epic. Vancouver: New Star, 1997.

Soft Architecture: A Manifesto. Vancouver: Artspeak Gallery, 1999.

Occasional Work and Seven Walks from the Office for Soft Architecture. Astoria, OR: Clear Cut Press, 2003; Toronto: Coach House Books, 2006.

The Weather. Vancouver: New Star Books, 2001.

Rousseau's Boat. Vancouver: Nomados, 2004.

Liberty

What follows is the interminable journal of culture. This neutral and
emotive little word seems, in the operatic dark green woods, so harmless
and legal but it's liberty totalized, an incommensurable crime against the
girls. To question privilege I'm going to shame this word. I will begin by
gathering around my body all the facts, for they affect my person. Consider
my feelings of resentment. I could have used it to fortify my courage. But
everything was happening very fast and I thought it would be a waste to
use it then. Violence and deceit, contempt and envy changed their colour,
enclosed our labour. The phantom body now buttresses the vilest swindles
with sub-Garbo hauteur. Violence and contempt, deceit and envy, sabotage
my method and I learn to love it. I am aware that I bring horror – I embody
the problem of the free-rider, inconveniencing the leaf-built, the simple-
hearted, the phobic, with the unctous display of my grief:

Enormous grief as if outside 'our culture' a sense of peace floated or
languished with no historical precedent. As if we could *invent* liberty, as
if peace and liberty had no place in that slow starvation. As if, subject only
to 'the laws of nature,' a gendered life were worth three years or nothing.
As if, allowed to believe and to own and to publish, newly hurled from the
impartial sun, a person's coy reticence meant fraternity. As if nervous yet
flung yet decorative – someone a noun discarded – this sweetie went down
on a khaki blanket glittering.

Superlative mistress who hurts! My grief is no accident. I am hovering
between plunder and awe. I am howling though the thick accretions of
liberty, not harmonious, not patterned, but inconceivably voluptuous as
thick rope. The enchanted world of harmonies has disappeared! The
martyred world has disappeared! And I am not sorry for I tingle with the
exquisite cadence of boredom – that flower's prodigious purple! If you
slowly gilded flowers (or didn't), fact: this slow bloom holds the buttery
promise of a meaning.

I want to remember how, couched in a tone like a windy cotton sleeve,
the parenthetical real girls shuck the empire of convenience. The aristoc-
racy of irony has never been their riskiest hope. They loll in the incom-
mensurability of embarrassment, the semi-honesty of their slick
membranes. Felicity is their glamour, the key. I have chosen for my fate
their verdant garment, and also the particular verdures of Libertie. For the
image does not need me: rather I feel it is my calling to annotate the
sheathed cadence of life beside power. Yet I don't mean to seem fantastic

in the old sense. When I say 'life beside power' I mean destruct the formal destinies, destruct the phantom body, destruct defunct ritual, unlock that paradise I mentioned earlier and give them back a renovated flower. (For whose utopia, peopled with sorrow, will annul such mollifying tokens?) Before turning I need to repeat that pornographic verb 'to mollify.'

What is this thought that refuses to reverse itself, that in the cool shade of fantasy creates an institution? that, shot-silk at the turn of a fold, not constructed but pursued, satisfies my kilted wit? Beardless boys stripped to the waist might illustrate my ability to think, but, like any experts in hope, they'd just deflate my perfect barbarity. If you took this prudish ornament, exuding moody sex as his own ornament, with his woozy shimmer, his bobbing glamour, fondler of the long-sleeved and lobed, he'd poach. Which means I must invent my own. So, by stepping from that house, I celebrate the death of method: the flirting woods call it, the glittering rocks call it – utopia is dead. High Loveliness was born *here* to cut back prim sublimity. She's a member of the lily tribe whose materials follow themselves. She's a bitch of the inauthenic; her ego's in drag. I flaunt her on my pink finger flipping backwards for Libertie into the saline crux of a lily. She's lying in the pagan flowers, sweet-faced in her pompous velvet, swathed in the crude luxury of my rhetoric, strewn with the pearls of aptly faded hope.

She Has Smoothed Her Pants to No End

This is the light Debbie steps into. Her
toffeed flanks roll with greatness and sustenance   110
in their sockets and her hearty hands bear
the bruised sea. Mighty amazing beauty
moves her and all the whirling majorettes
are her marvelous squadron: their bare throats
spill analysis.[†] Dactylic   115
eastern desks pom-pom
from puddles of yellow
mud. For rhetors bathed
in scent of chrome and split hide her senses
coin dictions: 120

If Luck's nameless girls love me
I'm happy. My city
minting history

[†] Toast!

Whence! giddy swish so skin-like
as a dress
trailing theft
as a spill

Riddled, cloaks
this pink text:
for her we could
be female

and so on
I Debbie with spurred ankles and purple knee-skin   125
stand free to forget
species anxiety. What happened to the century?
the ship's planks sing
a lithe keel twins
ears of Catriona, hair   130
of Kathy, Dan's fine nape, Christine's corded
hips, Susan's sea-scarf
moving with me as philosophes
into felicity and in the midst of elation
the thrones of Erin's vowels   135
a liberal dose
or I have not hauled this waxen heart
from the gnarled bole of a great tree
nor fleshed it with portents

To burnish
would thus shuck
with conundrum's
beak – but

Abstruse and dulcet
tongues
of paint
tease carnal wit

In demotic kiss
well – I digress

and new sports   140
Swimmers! Your sweet strokes beat so fast
I must dare all!
... I will do lovely things in taxis
and count myself among the lucky, I will
comb the pale hair of boys with muttering   145
hands wanting only the satiate fact
of that silk, I will discuss perfidy
with scholars as if spurning kisses, I
will sip the marble marrow of empire.
I want sugar   150
but I shall never wear shame
and if you call that sophistry
then what is Love

_____

(who love
with tripled

Pronouns know
pomposities
in gender

(Debt))

We toast her armies from our beds.

In My Heart as Drooping Pith

I have often had to seek in events   280
the significance of complicity
– for instance, this morning ontology
puts 'my hand' into 'the body' – proving
the vicarious truancy of self
is vernacular. I should want to be   285
intelligible and indifferent
so announce to my internal splice: I
am kissing – in order to nourish the
foreign part. I believe I am never free of
those beautiful woods – they excite   290
me powerfully as does the ultra
clear manufacture of girlhood. If I
broke a branch from the interpretation
what difference would that make? Whereas the
nakedness in the words 'break a voice from   295
this tree' amends chronology. I quote: each
nation flowers with fear. What has
occasioned us? Pride dilated
and idle? Far limits purchased by loss?
Father! Founder! I cry inasmuch as   300
narrative requires it. The archive
of the green hills fold eagerly in
to neglect

For Girls, Grapes and Snow

Pardon me if I throw myself
absolutely outside of my sex   510
for I was between the wall and love, a
dreaming drevity in dazzled font
diverted. If my sense of body
can include both dog and owning state's daft
glamour, I'll graft soft logics to myself   515
and shall send for either. Please Frank, up
towards the grapes and fleece, quote something kind
about a decent use for the passions
and speak to me of weariness Frank in soft iambic
since on torn apart sleeve of my thrifty   520
freedom dress, the tethered part twists from
servility to dreck – ah terrific
girls idiolects avenues proofs the
ramps and the glimpses, even the elevator
and the morbidity of sex say some   525
thing sort of nice about opulence and
majesty. Like my Nurses always said –
No Bees no Honey. No Ambition no
Money. No Master no Metre. No Soul
no Rigour. No Adage no Axis. So   530
I am going behind the arena
to get some pleasure – and all the civic
ornaments of my clever flesh: Borrowed
from rivals. Roman I, I father my
subservience the sententious   535
thrill the organ public
in magnificence I will have borrowed
what animal and dire rumour outwore
Ponderous Ponderous Charismatics!
I shall continue preening for how long?   540
– alas I'll bite into complicity's
proper structural pinkness the rolling
lank and blue languor of her wither, stroke
the sexual face with gorgeous
meaning as a good shield embraces   545

ineluctably so
by the demotic pads of the fingers
I shall open an item, by supple
lucite turn on embroglioed pivot
with fatal garland decorate public   550
catalogues which I won't repudiate
since by such precise ambition some have
tumbled into candour and human wit
at cool shore in happiness less con
trite than economic – or practised   555
doubt – a dainty thorn had I not posed
kisses against frugal will o stiffened
spine of snow, sure, I thought (softly) scaffold
in erudite bucolic – if by that tracing
more sweetness could be possible. Sometimes   560
reddened, I would try to feel palatial
or some such quasi-horror. Yes perhaps
I stack these auguries, expedient
as speculative heart in cry: I
am the middle one. I was present at   565
nothing. I maintained certain memories.
I was both a man. I was fated. I
did not relax. I stay where I always
stay. I am the last to take part. I was
its absentee. I should not know. I am   570
afraid. I get thankful for sleep. I was
made responsible. I feel certain.
I stayed where I sleep. I was no small
part. I will begin. I fear I have no
place. I fulfill its proper duty. I   575
I begin. I fear I have no place. I
call your names. I get it to witness. I
both ascend. I will even to forget.
I have made no wall. 'Human!' How shall
it call out so that you will pity me?   580
Good Evening Modernism.

from Tuesday

Days heap upon us. All plain. All clouds except a narrow opening at the top of the sky. All cloudy except a narrow opening at the bottom of the sky with others smaller. All cloudy except a narrow opening at the bottom of the sky. All cloudy except a narrow opening at the top of the sky. All cloudy. All cloudy. All cloudy. Except one large opening with others smaller. And once in the clouds. Days heap upon us. Where is our anger. And the shades darker than the plain part and darker at the top than the bottom. But darker at bottom than top. Days heap upon us. Where is Ti-Grace. But darker at the bottom than the top. Days heap upon us. Where is Christine. Broken on the word culture. But darker at the bottom than the top. Days heap upon us. Where is Valerie. Pulling the hard air into her lung. The life crumbles open. But darker at the bottom than the top. Days heap upon us. Where is Patty. Unlearning each thing. Red sky crumbles open. This is the only way to expand the heart. But darker at the top than the bottom. Days heap upon us. Where is Shulamith. Abolishing the word love. The radical wing crumbles open. The scorn is not anticipated. We have given our surface. Darker at the top than the bottom. Except one large opening with others smaller. Except one large opening with others smaller. Gradually. Days heap upon us. Where is Patricia. In the dream of obedience and authority. The genitalia crumble open. It is only ever a flickering. We never worshipped grief. It has been stuccoed over. Half cloud half plain. Half cloud half plain. Half plain. One in the plain part and one in the clouds. Days heap upon us. Where is Jane. Looking for food. Hunger crumbles open. All this is built on her loveliness. We have fallen nto a category. Love subsidized our descent. Streaky clouds at the bottom of the sky. Days heap upon us. Where is Mary. In the extreme brevity of the history of parity. Rage crumbles open. It felt like dense fog. What is fact is not necessarily human. Memory anticipitates. Authority flows into us like a gel. We cross the border to confront the ideal. Streaky cloudy at the top of the sky. Days heap upon us. Where is Grace. Spent in sadness. The underground crumbles open. There is no trangression possible. We publicly mobilize the horror of our emotion. It is a phalanx. The clouds darker than the plain or blue part and darker at the top than the bottom. Days heap upon us. Where is Gloria. Pushing down laughter. Utopia crumbles open. It is an emotion similar to animals sporting. We don't plagiarize shame. Like this we solve herself. The clouds darker than the plain part and darker at the top than the bottom. The clouds darker than the plain part and darker at the top than the bottom. The clouds lighter than the plain part and darker at the top than the bottom. The clouds lighter than the plain part and darker at the bottom than top. The clouds lighter than the plain part and darker at the top than the bottom. The lights of the clouds lighter and darks darker than the plain part and darker at the top than the bottom. The same as the last but darker at the bottom than the top. The same as the last but darker at the bottom than the top. Days heap upon us. Where is Violette. Walking without flinching. Doubt crumbles open. It is not a value but a disappearnace. We come upon the city in our body. The same as the last. The same as the last. The same as the last. The tint once over in the plain part, and twice in the clouds. Days heap upon us. Where is Emily. Out in all weather. Dignity crumbles open. There is not even a utopia. We would have to mention all the possible causes of her death. The tint once over the openings and twice in the clouds. Days heap upon us. Where is Olympe. Going without rest. The polis crumbles open. This is no different than slow war. The tint twice in the openings and once in the clouds. Days heap upon us. Where is Michelle. Homesick for anger. Midnight crumbles open. The tint twice in the openings. The tint twice over. Days heap upon us. Where is Bernadine. At description. The tint twice over. Days heap upon us. Where is Kathleen. The tint twice. The clouds darker than the plain part and darker at the top than the bottom. The clouds lighter than the plain part and darker at the top than the bottom. The lights of the clouds lighter. The others smaller. The same as the last. The same as the last. The tint twice in the openings and once in the clouds. Days heap upon us. The tint twice over. Days heap upon us. With others smaller. With others smaller.

A Hotel

(after Oscar Niemeyer)

I will take my suitcase into a hotel and
Become a voice
By studying stillness and curtains

I will take my stillness into a hotel
Careening, not flowing, through
Cities become his voice

Into a hotel I will take my city
And roads
And the entire moving skin of history

§

Utopia is so emotional.
I'm speaking of the pure sexual curves
Of utopia, the rotation
Of its shadows against the blundering
In civitas. History does not respond
To this project – History, who has disappeared into
Architecture and into the
Generosity of the dead. This states
The big problem of poetry. Who could
Speak for the buildings, for the future of the dead
The dead who are implicated in all
I can say? On this very beautiful surface
Where I want to live
I play with my friends
Like they do down there.
I don't understand what I adore.
I think of my body in the night
And remember my grandparents. With
Blood running through my wrists I represent
This. I believe my critique of devastation

Began with delight. Now what surprises me
Are the folds in political desire
Their fragile nobility, Sundays of
Rain. Listening to music, things pass.
I cry softly thinking of friendships then
Begin again to invent the line of
My life amidst utopia. Probably
This is the centre – the worn-out house, walls
Humming the repose of systems, the
Modest light, but I wanted an urgent
Line to begin the future, something like you,
What will you do with your legs and your heart?
Some think only of pleasure in their projects.
I am one of those people
Or so desire. I needed to make a living
So provoked astonishment. What I said
Is already gone, locked in
Migration. Sometimes we make things that seem
To have will – yet the beautiful life of
The house is each day more fragile. We suffer
And laugh and swim. We go
Daily to the botanical gardens to witness
Complication. Each plant becomes what we
Love in its other language as we rest
Near the privacy of women. I wait patiently with this voice
At this late hour, in our rudimentary
Lodgings, in our migrations, and the future
Is terrible and is a play
Of liberty. Work that ignores the night
Is not my work. I'll solicit nothing
But ornament, that spacious edifice –
Kinds of ornament are change
Because it will change anyway
Beside the privacy of women
When I'm with them I forget
The simplest fact
Of loneliness which is not regret
I will take my privacy
Into its hotel.

About the Authors

NICOLE BROSSARD was born in Montreal in 1943. Since 1965, she has published more than thirty books, including *Museum of Bone and Water* (House of Anansi, 2003), *The Aerial Letter* (The Women's Press, 1988) and *Mauve Desert* (Coach House, 1990, 2006). Her contribution and influence to Quebec and francophone poetry is major. Brossard has twice been awarded the Governor General's Award for Poetry, first in 1974 and again ten years later. In 1965, she co-founded the literary periodical *La barre du jour* and, in 1976, the feminist journal *Les têtes de pioche*. That same year, she co-directed the movie *Some American Feminists*. She was also awarded the Prix Athanase-David, Quebec's highest literary distinction. In 2006, she won the Canada Council's prestigious Molson Prize for lifetime achievement. Most of her books have been translated into English and Spanish and many others in different languages. Her collection *Notebook of Roses and Civilization* (translated by Robert Majzels and Erín Moure, Coach House, 2007) was shortlisted for the 2008 Griffin Poetry Prize. Her most recent book is the novel *Fences in Breathing* (translated by Susanne de Lotbinière-Harwood, Coach House, 2009). Nicole Brossard lives in Montreal.

MARGARET CHRISTAKOS is a poet and fiction writer living in Toronto whose work has shown consistent interest in feminist and recombinant poetics, process writing and seriality. She has published seven collections of poetry and one novel, *Charisma* (Pedlar, 2000), and has given readings and seminars from her work for two decades. Her poetry books are *Not Egypt* (Coach House, 1989), *Other Words for Grace* (The Mercury Press, 1996), *The Moment Coming* (ECW Press, 1998), *Wipe Under A Love* (The Mansfield Press, 2000), *Excessive Love Prostheses* (Coach House, 2002), *Sooner* (Coach House, 2005) and *What Stirs* (Coach House, 2008). Recent chapbooks are *Adult Video* (Nomados, 2006) and *My Girlish Feast* (Belladonna, 2006). A new collection, *Purple*, is forthcoming in 2010 from Your Scrivener Press. She has a BFA in Visual Arts (York, 1985) and an MA in History and Philosophy of Education (OISE, 1994). She has worked as a creative writing instructor, editor and production coordinator, and has three children. She runs 'Influency: A Toronto Poetry Salon' twice annually, through the University of Toronto School of Continuing Studies.

SUSAN HOLBROOK's poetry books are *misled* (Red Deer, 1999), *Good Egg Bad Seed* (Nomados, 2004) and *Joy Is So Exhausting* (Coach House, 2009). She teaches North American literatures and Creative Writing at the University of Windsor. She is particularly interested in feminist experimental writing, publishing on Nicole Brossard and Gertrude Stein in journals such as *American Literature, Differences* and *Tessera*. She has just co-edited *The Letters of Gertrude Stein and Virgil Thomson: Composition as Conversation* (Oxford University Press, 2009).

DOROTHY TRUJILLO LUSK is a Vancouver student who was born and raised in the Ottawa Valley of Quebec and Ontario. Her books include *Oral Tragedy* (Tsunami,

1988), *Redactive* (Talonbooks, 1990), *Volume Delays* (Sprang Texts, 1995), *Sleek Vinyl Drill* (Thuja Books, 2000), *Ogress Oblige* (Krupskaya, 2001) and the forthcoming *Decorum*. She is a longtime audience member and sometime collective member of the Kootenay School of Writing. Her concerns in writing include displacement agronomy, psychopathologies of colonization and the effects of forced contact within language groups.

Born in Luanshya, Zambia, KAREN MAC CORMACK is the author of more than a dozen books of poetry and, most recently, a polybiography, *Implexures (Complete Edition)*, published in 2008 by Chax Press and West House Books. Titles include *Nothing by Mouth* (Underwhich Editions, 1984), *Quill Driver* (Nightwood Editions, 1989), *At Issue* (Coach House, 2001) and *Vanity Release* (Zasterle Press, 2003). Her poetry appears in a number of anthologies, among them *Another Language: Poetic Experiments in Britain and North America* (LIT Verlag, 2008), *Out of Everywhere: Linguistically Innovative Poetry by Women in North America and the UK* (Reality Street, 1996), *Moving Borders (Three Decades of Innovative Writing by Women)* (Talisman House, 1998), *The Art of Practice* (Potes & Poets Press, 1994) and *Antiphonies: Essays on Women's Experimental Poetries in Canada* (Toronto: The Gig, 2008), and has been translated into French, Portugese, Swedish and Norwegian. Of dual Canadian/British citizenship, she currently lives in the U.S.A. and teaches at the State University of New York at Buffalo.

Vancouver writer DAPHNE MARLATT has written over twenty books of poetry, fiction and essays, notably *Steveston* (Talonbooks, 1974), *Touch to my Tongue* (Longspoon, 1984), *This Tremor Love Is* (Talonbooks, 2001), the essay collection *Readings from the Labyrinth* (NeWest, 1998) and two novels, *Ana Historic* (Coach House, 1988) and *Taken* (House of Anansi, 1996). She has co-edited several little magazines including the feminist journal *Tessera*. In 2006 Pangaea Arts (Vancouver) staged a bicultural, bilingual production of *The Gull*, her contemporary Noh play about Steveston's Japanese-Canadian fishing community, winning the international Uchimura Theatre Prize. Talonbooks will be publishing *The Gull* in the fall of 2009. *The Given* (McClelland & Stewart, 2008), a long poem in prose fragments, has been shortlisted for both the Pat Lowther Memorial Award and the Dorothy Livesay Poetry Award. 2008 also saw the release of *Between Brush Strokes* (JackPine Press, 2009), a limited-edition poetry chapbook designed by Frances Hunter about the life and work of the painter-poet Sveva Caetani, and a CD, *Like Light Off Water* (Otter Bay, 2008), a collaboration with composer-musicians Robert Minden and Carla Hallett. Marlatt is currently working in collaboration with Aerlyn Weissman on a short filmscript for the Queer History Project in Vancouver.

ERÍN MOURE is a Montreal poet and translator. Since her first book in 1979, she has published a dozen books of poetry in English, which have received several prizes including the Governor General's Award. She has translated, among others, the poetry of Nicole Brossard (with Robert Majzels) from French, Chus Pato from

Galician, Fernando Pessoa from Portuguese and Andrés Ajens from Spanish. She has published poetry, reviews, essays in Argentina, Australia, Canada, Chile, England, France, Germany, Norway, Portugal, Serbia, Slovenia, Spain, U.S.A. and Wales since 1973 and has given hundreds of readings in Canada, England, Wales, U.S.A., France, Portugal, Spain, Japan, Germany, Slovenia. Her poems have been translated into French, Spanish, Portuguese, Serbian, Japanese, Galician, German and Slovenian, and she has published translations of poetry from French, Galician, Spanish and Portuguese in Canada, U.S.A., England and Spain. In 2008, she received an honorary doctorate from Brandon University in recognition of her contributions to poetry. Her own most recent works are *O Cadoiro* (House of Anansi, 2007), a book of poems inspired by the medieval Iberian cantigas, and *Little Theatres* (House of Anansi, 2005). Moure's translation of Chus Pato's famed *m-Talá* appeared in March 2009 from Shearsman (UK) and BuschekBooks (Canada). Her essays on writing practice, *My Beloved Wager*, will appear from NeWest Press in fall 2009, as will a collaborative work with Oana Avasilichioaei that playfully questions the limits of translation and authorship, *Expeditions of a Chimæra* (BookThug, 2009). Her next book of poetry, *O Resplandor*, will appear in 2010 from House of Anansi in Toronto.

SINA QUEYRAS is the author most recently of the poetry collections *Lemon Hound* (2006) and *Expressway* (2009), both from Coach House Books. She edited *Open Field: 30 Contemporary Canadian Poets*, for Persea Books (2005), and continues to serve as contributing editor for *Drunken Boat*, where she most recently edited a folio on conceptual fiction with Vanessa Place, and a folio on visual poetry with derek beaulieu. *Lemon Hound* won the Pat Lowther and a Lambda Literary award, and an excerpt from *Expressway* recently received Gold in the National Magazine Awards. Her work has been published internationally in journals and anthologies. She has lived across Canada, in New Jersey, Brooklyn, Philadelphia and Montreal, where she currently teaches. She keeps a blog, Lemon Hound, from which BookThug will publish a selection of writing in fall 2009.

M. NOURBESE PHILIP is a poet, essayist, novelist and playwright who lives in the space-time of the City of Toronto. She practiced law in the City of Toronto for seven years before leaving to write full-time. She has published four books of poetry, one novel and three collections of essays. She was awarded a Pushcart Prize in 1981, the Casa de las Americas Prize (Cuba) in 1988, the Tradewinds Collective Prize in 1988 and was made a Guggenheim Fellow in Poetry in 1990. In 1994 she was awarded the Lawrence Foundation Prize for short fiction and her work was recognized in 1995 by the Arts Foundation of Toronto by its Writing and Publishing Award. In 1999, her play *Coups and Calypsos* was a Dora Award finalist. She recently completed a residency at the Rockefeller Foundation, Bellagio, Italy.

LISA ROBERTSON was born in Toronto and lived for many years in Vancouver, where she worked with several artist-run organizations, including Kootenay School of Writing and Artspeak Gallery. Her first book, *XEclogue*, was published in 1993 by Tsunami Editions; *Debbie: An Epic* and *The Weather* followed, from New Star (co-published by Reality Street in the UK); then *The Men* (Bookthug, 2006) and *Lisa Robertson's Magenta Soul Whip* (Coach House, 2009). A book of essays, *Occasional Works and Seven Walks from the Office for Soft Architecture*, was published by Clearcut (2003) and Coach House (2006). *R's Boat* will be out with University of California Press in 2010. She has been the recipient of the Relit Award and the bpNichol Chapbook Award, and was nominated for a Governor General's Award for Poetry in 1998. She has worked as an editor of poetry, a freelance arts and architecture critic and a teacher, since leaving the bookselling business in 1995, and has taught and held residencies at California College of the Arts, University of Cambridge, Capilano College, University of California Berkeley, University of California San Diego, American University of Paris and the Naropa Institute. She is currently working collaboratively on sound and video-based projects.

GAIL SCOTT is completing a new novel, *The Obituary*, and a radio play, *Werther Lives*. She has written seven other books, including the anthology *Biting The Error*, edited with Bob Glück, Mary Burger and Camille Roy (Coach House, 2004), shortlisted for a Lambda Award; her novel, *My Paris*, about a sad diarist in conversation with Gertrude Stein and Walter Benjamin in contemporary Paris (Dalkey Archive, 2003); the story collection *Spare Parts Plus Two* (Coach House, 2002). The novels *Main Brides* (Coach House, 1993) and *Heroine* (Coach House, 1987), and the essay collections *Spaces Like Stairs* (The Women's Press, 1989) and *la théorie, un dimanche* (Éditions du Remue-ménage, 1988) with Nicole Brossard et al. Her work has been translated into French, German and Spanish. Her translation of Michael Delisle's *Le Désarroi du matelot* was shortlisted for the Governor General's Award in translation in 2001. She was named one of the ten best Canadian novelists of the year 1999 by the trade magazine *Quill & Quire*. She is co-founder of the critical journal *Spirale* (Montreal) and *Tessera* (new writing by women). She teaches Creative Writing at Université de Montréal.

NATHALIE STEPHENS (NATHANAËL) writes l'entre-genre in English and French. She is the author of several books, including *Carnet de désaccords* (Le Quartanier, 2009), *The Sorrow and the Fast of It* (Nightboat Books, 2007), *L'injure* (2004), *Paper City* (Coach House, 2003) and the essay of correspondence *Absence Where As (Claude Cahun and the Unopened Book)* (Nightboat Books, 2009). Her book, *...s'arrête? Je* (l'Hexagone, 2007) was recently awarded the Prix Alain-Grandbois. *Je Nathanaël* (2003) exists in English self-translation with BookThug (2006). There is also a book of talks, *At Alberta* (BookThug, 2008). Other work exists in Basque and Slovene, with book-length translations in Bulgarian (2007). In addition to translating herself, Stephens has translated Catherine Mavrikakis, Gail Scott, Bhanu Kapil and Édouard Glissant. She is, she thinks, in Chicago.

CATRIONA STRANG's latest book, co-written with the late Nancy Shaw, is *Light Sweet Crude* (LINEbooks, 2007). Other works include *Cold Trip* (Nomados, 2006) and *Busted* (Coach House, 2001), both co-written with Nancy Shaw, and *Low Fancy*

(ECW, 1993). She is a founding member of the Institute for Domestic Research, and frequently collaborates with fellow institute member composer Jacqueline Leggatt and clarinetist François Houle, with whom she recorded *The Clamourous Alphabet* (Periplum). She lives in Vancouver, where she and her two kids are active in the home-learning community. She is currently working on *Extrafine Imperial Twankay*, a long work based on the history of tea.

RITA WONG is the author of three books of poetry: *sybil unrest*, co-written with Larissa Lai (LINEbooks, 2008), *forage* (Nightwood, 2007) and *monkeypuzzle* (Press Gang, 1998). Wong received the Asian Canadian Writers Workshop Emerging Writer Award in 1997, and the Dorothy Livesay Poetry Prize in 2008. An Assistant Professor in Critical and Cultural Studies at the Emily Carr University of Art and Design, she is currently researching the poetics of water.

RACHEL ZOLF is a poet and editor born in Toronto and presently living in New York. Her most recent book, *Human Resources* (Coach House, 2007), won the 2008 Trillium Book Award for Poetry. Previous collections are *Masque* (The Mercury Press, 2004), *Her absence, this wanderer* (BuschekBooks, 1999) and the chapbooks *Shoot and Weep* (Nomados, 2008), *from Human Resources* (Belladonna, 2005) and *the naked & the nude* (above/ground, 2004). She has given readings across Canada and the U.S., and her poetry and essays have appeared in journals such as *Xcp: Cross-Cultural Poetics*, *West Coast Line*, *Capilano Review* and *Open Letter*, as well as in the anthology *Shift & Switch: New Canadian Poetry*. She was the founding poetry editor of *The Walrus* magazine and has edited several books by other poets. Her next poetry collection, *The Neighbour Procedure*, will appear in 2010 from Coach House.

KATE EICHHORN is the author of *Fond*, shortlisted for the 2009 Gerald Lampert Award. Her essays and reviews on Canadian literature have appeared in journals such as *Open Letter*, *West Coast Line*, *Mosaic* and *How2*. She is an assistant professor of Culture and Media Studies at the New School in New York City.

HEATHER MILNE is an assistant professor in the English Department at the University of Winnipeg. Her essays on women's writing have appeared in journals such as *Canadian Poetry*, *Canadian Literature*, *a/b: Auto/biography Studies* and *Open Letter*. She is currently working on a book-length study of 21st-century innovative North American feminist poetics.

Acknowledgements

We wish to thank Coach House Books for supporting this project and for their ongoing commitment to promoting Canadian innovative women's writing. A special thanks to Alana Wilcox and Christina Palassio for their enthusiasm and advice throughout the making of this book.

We are grateful to the Faculty of Arts at Ryerson University for two grants supporting this project in its early stages; this enabled us to interview most of the writers in person and to work with two interns. For preliminary design, we thank Chrystina McNeil, and for assisting with research, transcription and permissions, we thank Anna Candido. We also acknowledge the support of the Department of English at the University of Winnipeg.

Although we are unable to list all of the people who generously shared their thoughts and opinions on this anthology, we are indebted to everyone consulted. We are especially grateful for ongoing dialogues with Elena Basile, Margaret Christakos, Roewan Crowe, Jennifer Firestone, Barbara Godard, Luanne Karn, Rachel Levitsky, Gail Scott and Rachel Zolf. For her insights and the cover photograph, we thank Cheryl Sourkes.

An anthology of this nature would not be possible without the generosity of the participating writers and their publishers – we thank them most of all.

Permissions

The following authors and publishers have kindly given permission for the texts to be reproduced here.

NICOLE BROSSARD

'Igneous Woman, Integral Woman' from *Lovhers*, trans. Barbara Godard (Guernica Editions, 1986).

Pages 34–35 are from *Après les mots*, trans. Robert Majzels and Erín Moure (Trois-Rivières: Ecrits des Forges, 2007).

Pages 36–37 are from *Vertiges de l'avant-scène*, trans. Robert Majzels and Erín Moure (Trois-Rivières: Écrits des Forges, 1997).

Pages 38–40 are from *Notebook of Roses and Civilization*, trans. Robert Majzels and Erín Moure (Coach House Books, 2007).

MARGARET CHRISTAKOS

'May 20,' from *Not Egypt*. Reprinted by permission of the author.

'Mother's Journal Notes,' 'M1,' 'M2,' 'M3' from *Excessive Love Prostheses* (Coach House Books, 2002).

'Grounds 20A,' from *Wipe Under A Love* (© The Mansfield Press, 2000).

'An Open Erotics of Gzowski,' from *Sooner* (Coach House Books, 2005).

'My Attaché Case,' from *What Stirs* (Coach House Books, 2008).

SUSAN HOLBROOK

'misling the laureate,' from *misled* (Red Deer Press, 1999).

'Insert,' 'News Sudoku #19, Level: Lowest' and 'Nursery' from *Joy Is So Exhausting* (Coach House Books, 2009).

DOROTHY TRUJILLO LUSK

'First,' from *Redactive* (Talon Books, 1988). Courtesy of the author.

'Vulgar Marxism,' from *Ogress Oblige* (Krupskaya, 2001), courtesy of the author.

'Decorum (Typical),' 'Manque (stave Decorum),' 'Decorum: an Hystrical) Eye' from *Decorum*, unpublished, courtesy of the author.

KAREN MAC CORMACK

'Approach' from *Quill Driver* (Nightwood Editions, 1989).

Pages 175–176 from *Quirks & Quillets*. Courtesy of Chax Press and Karen Mac Cormack.

'At Issue IX: Diminish,' from *At Issue* (Coach House Books, 2001).

'Otherwise,' from *Vanity Release*. (La Laguna, Tenerife: Zasterle Press, 2003). Reprinted by permission of the author.

'One' and 'Three' from *Implexures*. Courtesy of Chax Press and Karen Mac Cormack.

DAPHNE MARLATT

'Rings, iii,' by permission of the author. Rings was originally published in 1971 by the York Street Commune, Vancouver, as *Georgia Straight Writing Supplement: Vancouver Series #3.*

'Ghost,' from *Steveston* © 1974 Daphne Marlatt, Talon Books Ltd., Vancouver, B.C. Reprinted with permission of the publisher.

'The Difference Three Makes: A Narrative,' from *Salvage* (Red Deer Press, 1991).

'Booking Passage,' from *This Tremor Love Is,* © 2001 Daphne Marlatt, Talon Books Ltd., Vancouver, B.C. Reprinted with permission of the publisher.

'Short Circuits,' unpublished. By permission of the author. Some of these poems appeared in the *Capilano Review,* Vol. 3, no. 102, Winter/Spring 2007.

ERÍN MOURE

'Memory Pentitence/Contamination Eglise,' from *Search Procedures* (House of Anansi Press, 1996).

'Calor' is from *The Frame of a Book* (House of Anansi Press, 1999).

'vigo papers' is from *O Cidadán* (House of Anansi Press, 2002).

Erín Moure's poems are reproduced with permission from the author and House of Anansi Press.

M. NOURBESE PHILIP

'Discourse on the Logic of Language' from *She Tries Her Tongue, Her Silence Softly Breaks* (Ragweed Press, 1989). Courtesy of the author.

Pages 153–154 from *Looking for Livingstone* (The Mercury Press, 1991).

'Zong! #1,' 'Zong! #2,' 'Zong! #15,' 'Zong! #25,' 'Zong! #26,' 'Ratio' from *Zong!,* © 2008 M. NourbeSe Philip and reprinted by permission of Wesleyan University Press (originating publisher) and The Mercury Press (first Canadian edition).

SINA QUEYRAS

'Scrabbling,' from *Slip* (ECW Press, 2001). Printed with permission of ECW Press.

From 'Untitled Film Still # 35,' 'Roadside Memory #1' from *Teethmarks* (Nightwood Editions, 2004).

'A River by the Moment,' 'On the Scent,' 'Virginia, Vanessa, the Strands,' 'The Waves, An Unmaking' from *Lemon Hound* (Coach House Books, 2005).

LISA ROBERTSON

'Liberty,' from *XEclogue* (New Star Books, 1999).

'She Has Smoothed her Pants to No End,' 'In My Heart as Drooping Pith,' 'For Girls, Grapes and Snow,' from *Debbie: An Epic* (New Star Books, 1997).

'Tuesday' from *The Weather* (New Star Books, 2001).

'A Hotel,' from *Lisa Robertson's Magenta Soul Whip* (Coach House Books, 2009).

GAIL SCOTT

'Everyday Grammar' contains excerpts from:

The Obituary, a novel in progress, courtesy of the author.

'The Sutured Subject,' an essay in progress, courtesy of the author.

My Paris (The Mercury Press, 1999).

Main Brides (Coach House Press, 1993), courtesy of the author.

Heroine © Gail Scott, Talon Books Ltd., Vancouver, B.C. Reprinted with permission of the publisher.

'Paragraphs Blowing on a Line' from *Spaces Like Stairs* (The Women's Press, 1989), courtesy of the author.

'GS + GS,' an unpublished talk, courtesy of the author.

'Bottoms Up' from *Spare Parts Plus Two* (Coach House Books, 2002).

NATHALIE STEPHENS

'Paper City' from *Paper City* (Coach House Books, 2003).

'Scatalogue' and 'A Fuckable Text' from *Je Nathanaël* (Bookthug, 2006).

Pages 79–81 from *The Sorrow and the Fast of It* © 2007 by Nathalie Stephens. Reprinted by permission of the author and Nightboat Books.

Pages 82–84 from *Absence Where As* © 2009 by Nathalie Stephens. Reprinted by permission of the author and Nightboat Books.

CATRIONA STRANG

'Hand' from *Steep: A Performance Document*. Courtesy of the author.

Pages 279–284 are from *Busted*, with Nancy Shaw (Coach House Books, 2001).

'Song for the Silenced,' from *Sinopie*. Courtesy of the author.

'Vows to Carry On' and 'Notes for Appearing Compassionate' from *Light Sweet Crude*, with Nancy Shaw (Burnaby, B.C.: LINEbooks, 2007). www.linebooks.ca

RITA WONG

'write around the absence' and ':meaning implies purpose,' from *monkeypuzzle* (press gang, 1998). Courtesy of the author.

'canola queasy,' 'the girl who ate rice almost every day' and 'ricochet,' from *forage* (Nightwood Editions, 2007).

Pages 363–366 from *sybil unrest*, with Larissa Lai (Burnaby, B.C.: LINEbooks, 2008). www.linebooks.ca

RACHEL ZOLF

Pages 197–198 from *Masque* (The Mercury Press, 2004).

Pages 199–205 from *Human Resources* (Coach House Books, 2006).

Pages 206–211 from *The Neighbour Procedure*. (Coach House Books, 2010). 'A failure of hospitality' and 'Loss has made a tenuous we' were published in *Shoot and Weep* (Nomados Literary Publishers, 2008). Courtesy of the author. Some poems have been revised.

Index

Typeset in Scala and Scala Sans
Printed and bound at the Coach House on bpNichol Lane, 2009

Edited by Kate Eichhorn and Heather Milne
Designed by Alana Wilcox
Cover photograph, *Audience*, by Cheryl Sourkes, courtesy of the artist

Coach House Books
401 Huron Street on bpNichol Lane
Toronto ON   M5S 2G5

416 979 2217
800 367 6360

mail@chbooks.com
www.chbooks.com